THE MONEY MOTIVE

THE MONEY MOTIVE

THOMAS WISEMAN

RANDOM HOUSE NEW YORK

Originally published in Great Britain by Hutchinson Publishing Group

Library of Congress Cataloging in Publication Data

Wiseman, Thomas.
    The money motive.

    Bibliography: p.
    1. Money—Psychological aspects. I. Title.
HG221.3.W58   332.4   74-8033
ISBN 0-394-47965-3

Manufactured in the United States of America
9 8 7 6 5 4 3 2
First American Edition

FOR MY FAMILY:
my mother; my wife, Malou; my son, Boris

Contents

Introduction, xi

Part One: T H E F O R T U N E

1. The Dream, 3
2. The Quest, 17
3. Origins and Consequences, 45
4. Uses, 67

Part Two: M O N E Y T Y P E S

5. The Romantic, 81
6. The Company Man, 95
7. The Collector, 107
8. The Hustler, 120
9. The Double-Dealer, 145

10. The Criminal, 170
11. The Gambler and the Loser, 182
12. The Non-Player, 202

Part Three: M O N E Y   R E L A T I O N S H I P S

13. Money and Sex, 211
14. Money and the Family, 246
15. Money and Society, 281

Notes, 315
Bibliography, 325
Index, 331

Introduction

In preparing this book, I talked at length to many people, questioning them about their money practices, their money attitudes, their money dreams, their money apprehensions, their money foibles.

Some found these matters too private to talk about and closed up, or asked that their names not be used. Others were remarkably revealing: a respected businessman talked of how he used to go in for handbag snatching; a happily married woman spoke of how she had been seduced by a Casanova flashing his money about; a multimillionaire related how, at a time when he had nothing, he made £1,000,000 out of a single deal; a man from Brooklyn spoke of his ambitions to be the Lord of the girlie magazines, out of which he had already made $75,000,000; a gangster told me that he beats up people for a fee; a former Madam spoke of the role of money in the slave scene rituals of her New York bordello; a go-getter told how he had sacrificed his marriage to get ahead.

These and many others provided me with the material on

which this study is based, and I wish to thank them all for
allowing me to question them about matters that are still
"not talked about" in some circles.

Trying to understand the varied and often irrational forms
of money behavior that I was discovering and documenting, I
reexamined the classic psychological theories.

It was in 1908 that Freud first postulated a connection
between "anal eroticism" and the hoarding of money. As can
be imagined, this theory was highly offensive to the spirit of
the day, which was one of deep respect for money and everything it stood for. At the same time the equation of "the most
valuable stuff" with the least valuable had a paradoxical
appositeness. And eventually the excremental nature of
money became a tenet of popular psychology.

When I came to examine its applicability to the material
that my initial research had produced, I found that while
some money types did seem to fit the pattern of "the anal
character," others very clearly didn't. The thrusting acquisitors, the makers of overnight fortunes, the adventurers and
high-flyers, the hustlers and wheeler-dealers did not have the
characteristics of parsimony, pedantry, obstinacy and orderliness that were said to be definitive of "the anal character."

Attempting to go beyond the "anal theory," I found that
Melanie Klein's explanation of primal greed, as she observed
and analyzed it in young children, revealed a whole spectrum
of meanings behind the acquisitiveness and possessiveness expressed in moneymaking.

Melanie Klein has been a highly controversial and profoundly influential figure in the psychoanalytical movement.
I believe that her particular understanding of envy, greed,
gratitude, reparation, idealization, and her postulation of the
"depressive position"* as the highest and healthiest form of

* The term "depressive position" is easily misunderstood; it is to be distinguished from depressive illness. What is meant by the term is a state in which

maturity attainable by human beings—equivalent to Dante's Paradiso—will in the years ahead drastically reshape the conventional wisdom and give people a more accurate understanding of themselves. But as yet her far-reaching ideas have been little applied outside the analytic session. This is beginning to change. Dr. Elliott Jaques has been applying Kleinian psychology to management-labor conflicts in industry, with positive results. He is at present engaged in a government-sponsored psychoanalytical study of relationships in hospitals. Jaques believes that the application of the understanding of deep human motivation to our social institutions can be of crucial importance in changing the defective structures of our society. I agree with this view, and it is on this basis that I have attempted the present study of money, an institution whose "sickness" is daily evident.

The sources that I have used in this book are, then, of two main kinds. My factual evidence comes from people I have interviewed, and from documents, newspaper stories, research projects, psychiatric case histories, statistics, company reports, biographies, novels. It will be seen that certain names, or incognitos, recur in the course of the book. These people were my principal witnesses, and what they had to say was for me representative of a particular money type or money relationship.

For my interpretation of the evidence, I have drawn extensively on the ideas of Freud and Melanie Klein, and it will be quickly apparent to the reader how much I owe to their discoveries and insights. But it is not only the written word that has influenced me; on a personal level, I have been much affected and enlightened by Dr. Donald Meltzer; and also in different ways by two other psychoanalysts, Dr. Albert Mason and Dr. Eric Brenman. To the latter I must express special

there is tolerance of the inevitability of loss, and joyousness is possible without recourse to a manic denial of life's realities.

thanks for having read this book in manuscript and for advising me on matters of psychological theory. In acknowledging my indebtedness to these individuals, I must however add that final responsibility for anything said here is mine, and that nobody else can be blamed for anything I may have got wrong.

The author wishes to express his gratitude to the publishers for permission to quote extracts from the following: *Collected Papers*, vols. II, IV, V, by Sigmund Freud, *Beyond the Pleasure Principle* by Sigmund Freud, *The Ego and the Id* by Sigmund Freud and *Civilization and its Discontents* by Sigmund Freud (all Hogarth Press); *Contributions to Psycho-Analysis* by Melanie Klein (Hogarth); *Collected Papers on Psycho-Analysis* by Karl Abraham and *Selected Papers on Psycho-Analysis* by Karl Abraham (both Hogarth); *Papers on Psycho-Analysis* by Ernest Jones (Hogarth); *The Collected Works of C. G. Jung* (Routledge and Kegan Paul); *Work, Creativity and Social Justice* by Elliott Jacques (Heinemann Educational Books Ltd., London); *The Empty Canvas* by Alberto Moravia and *Down and Out in Paris and London* by George Orwell (both published by Secker and Warburg); Aristotle's *The Politics*, translated by T. A. Sinclair (Penguin Classics); *Thalidomide and the Power of the Drug Companies* by Henning Sjöström and Robert Nilsson (Penguin Special); *Advertisements for Myself* by Norman Mailer and *An American Dream* by Norman Mailer (both André Deutsch); *Play Power* by Richard Neville (Jonathan Cape); *The Rich and the Super Rich* by Ferdinand Lundberg (Lyle Stuart Inc., Secaucus, New Jersey); *A Harlot High and Low* by Balzac, translated by Rayner Heppenstall (c/o David Higham Associates Ltd.).

PART ONE
The Fortune

1

The Dream

There is nothing in biological necessity to account for the drive to get rich, nor is there any equivalent for it in animal life. It is something that serves no fundamental purpose, and it does not fulfill any basic need; indeed, by definition to "get rich" is to get more than one needs. And yet this seemingly purposeless drive is one of the most powerful known to man, and it is probable that people have done more injuries to each other in the name of money than for any other reason.

Money, it is said, is a measure of value, a medium of exchange, and a store of wealth. But this ignores its other nature, its intoxicating, maddening, inflaming aspect. It denies that aspect of money the love of which John Maynard Keynes described as "a somewhat disgusting morbidity, one of those semi-criminal, semi-pathological propensities which one hands over with a shudder to the specialists in mental disease."[1] Karl Marx sensed something of this other side of money when he spoke of it as "the alienated power of humanity."[2]

There is blood money and bride money, conscience money

and stolen money, easy money and money that has been earned by the sweat of the brow, money to burn and money as the prize of merit; there is money that is a king's ransom and money that is a whore's pay; there is money to squander and so much money as will make it difficult for its possessor to get into heaven; there is the mistress's allowance and the wife's due; pocket money, spending money, hush money, and money in the bank; there are the wages of sin and the bequests of rich uncles; there is the price that every man has, and the pricelessness of objects, and the price on the outlaw's head; there are the thirty pieces of silver and also the double indemnity on one's own life.

Behind its apparent sameness lie the many meanings of money. Blood money does not buy the same thing as bride money and a king's ransom is not the same kind of fortune as a lottery prize. The great exchangeability of money is deceptive; it enables us to buy the appearance of things, their physical form, as in the case of a "bought woman," while what we thought we had bought eludes us.

It is characteristic of money that, in the words of Isaiah, "it satisfieth not," or as one of the newest of the rich, Mick Jagger, put it in song: "I can't get no satisfaction." And yet the pursuit and amassing of this unsatisfying stuff is probably the strongest motive-force in our culture, although this will often be strenuously denied by the very people who are most deeply committed to the money-goal. An aspect of the passion is that for a particular type of person it remains rather dubious, the last of our shameful secrets. Perhaps because of this, the subject, in its personal ramifications, has been very little explored. We have more information about people's intimate sexual behavior than about their money-motivated behavior. Certainly nothing comparable to the Kinsey Report exists, and I know of no institute that is systematically studying the way people act with money. Of course, economics and economic problems receive enormous and deeply erudite attention, but this is really the equivalent of the Victorian novel about marriage that left out all mention of sex. What the studies of our economic dilemmas leave out is *money lust*, the underlying impulse, craving, obsession, whatever it is, out of which our present economizing/accumulating culture has arisen.

Though the evidence around us is that this passion is now approaching its apotheosis in the United States and the other technologically advanced societies of the West, there is no reason to believe that there is anything specifically Western in the love of money. The one god to whom the ancient Chinese never failed to offer up sacrifices was Ts'ai-shen, the god of Wealth, who headed a Ministry of Wealth, with departments such as the Celestial and Venerable Discoverer of Treasures. We know of the Hebrews' worship of the golden calf. Hermes, the indefatigable runner, was also god of profit. The Egyptians filled the tombs of their kings with great riches so that they would be well supplied for their journey into darkness. Among the primitive tribes of Samoa a man could be a millionaire in *diwarra*, seashells. In fairy tales, whether European or from the Arabian Nights, living happily ever after has nearly always meant *richly*. The indications are that there has always existed in people a desire to get rich, even if there was no real possibility of doing so. It was a dream, a fairy tale, and for many that is what it still is, though nowadays it has a certain realistic basis, since it can be made to come true.

But still, it is as a dream that the desire to get rich is first encountered. If we examine the features of the dream, several leitmotifs emerge. First, there is a *longing for security*. Women marry for it, sometimes; astute young men plan for it, putting their savings into pension schemes and into long-term growth stocks so that one day, even if only in old age, they will be able to live off their investments. A top property dealer and financier says that when he had no money his goal was "to establish a position of security" for himself and his family, so that he would not have to worry where their next meal was coming from. In the dream it seemed to him that if he could establish "a capital position of £50,000" they'd be all right, and wouldn't have to worry about money any more; that was really all he wanted, and this objective became a tremendous driving force in his life as a young man. In the event, he exceeded his aim somewhat, going on to make over £50,000,000, which may be taken as an indication of how powerful the longing for security is, and how the sum of money required to achieve it keeps rising.[3]

A version of this dream is contained in the Grimms' fairy tale of a magical table that on being told "Table, cover thyself" at once does so with a fine cloth, plates, knives and forks, and dishes of roast and baked meat, and red wine. "Our young fellow thought to himself: 'Now you have enough for your lifetime' and hereafter he need never trouble himself whether an inn was good or bad, or whether it contained anything or nothing."

The wish for a private income or to be able to live off investments clearly has the same source as the story of the tailor's son who wanted to be set up for life. It is really a dream of retirement, of being able to live on what one has accumulated without having to do any more, and although this would seem to be a rather negative aspiration, it is commonplace, and not by any means confined to those who have become wearied by struggle and endeavor. J. Paul Getty did actually retire at the age of twenty-four, after having made his first million, and spent two years in idleness.[4] A person who has done well will use the phrase "I could retire," which is really an odd way of putting it. Usually such people do not for a moment intend to retire, but they entertain themselves with the notion that they could if they wished. If this fantasy of retirement is examined, it is found that a glorious self-sufficiency is envisaged, in which one will be at nobody's beck and call, answerable to none. Given that as a species we remain dependent on others longer and more totally than any other animal, our hatred and resentment of dependency is perhaps understandable, and our dream of a "financial independence" that will liberate us from all other dependencies, an all too human illusion.

Once the position of security has been established in the dream, it is possible to go on to the lusher pleasures of money. There is, for instance, the dream of *showing them all*. This was expressed by one man, as follows:

"As a boy, what I wanted was what others in my street had and I didn't have. I didn't covet a big car because people in my street didn't have big cars. I didn't think of big cars. What being rich meant to me was having the best house in the street. What it meant to me was *coming back and showing them all*. Showing them all that I was better than they were. It never got outside my street. I had no terms of reference outside my street. I didn't want to be a film star, nothing like that. I couldn't grasp that. Film stars were pure fantasy stuff.

"I remember once, at twenty-one, a man driving past in a beautifully tailored suit. What impressed me was the carelessness with which he treated that suit. I was in the tailoring business, I knew how much a suit like that cost. And that he could wear it so carelessly impressed me terrifically. That was the man I envied, the man who could wear an expensive suit carelessly. I didn't envy millionaires. There weren't any on my street."

The desire to triumph is invariably the desire to triumph over others, and in the dream that means the people in one's immediate environment. In the first place the aim may be quite modest: to be able to wear an expensive suit carelessly, instead of in Sunday-best manner. The dream becomes gaudier as the thirst for revenge increases. Now the dreamer imagines himself one day returning to his hometown and really rubbing their noses in his wealth. In the Dürrenmatt play *The Visit,* an enormously rich woman goes back to her place of birth, and it slowly emerges that in return for a bequest to the town, she is demanding the murder of an old man, who in his youth had been her lover, and had jilted her.

This is the classic dream of someone who has been slighted, humiliated, rejected. *One day, one day . . . Just wait.* Money is dreamed of as the agency of that longed-for revenge, whether it is only a matter of showing them, or of actually doing something. The superior hotel manager who refuses us a room, or the room that we want, is seen in the mind's eye in the moment of our vengeance, when we have bought the hotel and are firing him. There are millionaires who actually do this sort of thing: it is said that when the Greek shipowner Stavros Niarchos was refused the principal suite at the Ritz in Paris (because it was permanently reserved for Barbara Hutton) he instructed his agents to start buying up the hotel's shares, and he had got nearly 50 percent when the management found out, and promptly acceded to his demand.

To the extent that we feel powerless, we dream of money as remedying that condition. And in the fantasy, money can do anything; it can buy up the Ritz, or put to death a false lover. The delight with which people recount the often apocryphal stories of how this or that millionaire has used his money in some casually omnipotent way, expending colossal sums to achieve a small satisfaction, shows how deeply attached we are to this particular dream. The basically childish delight in such power is classically expressed in the story of Aladdin and his lamp, the rubbing of which can effect the downfall of an interfering Grand Vizier, or build a palace in the blink of an eye, or win the Sultan's daughter, and even, finally, bring our hero the Sultanship itself.*

Love is something else that money can bring in the dream. The composer Lionel Bart says: ". . . I hit it really big with *Oliver*. And I needed love. So I thought I could buy it. I had this desperate need to be loved, you see; and people I considered my friends could get the world out of me. Money was no object. I used to think that giving somebody an expensive gift was a foolproof way of buying their admiration . . ."[5]

The equation of lovability and wealth is long established in the reveries of young men, who by tradition are expected to go out and make their fortune before claiming the girl. The legend is that if they come back with the money, they will be loved. In practice, it usually happens that the girl takes somebody who stuck around, but still we entertain the notion that if we are rich we will have a better chance of being loved. This is not a cynical belief in the power of money to buy love—which is another dream—but a sort of faith in its magical properties, in its power to transform. Overnight stardom, with its concomitant shower of shekels, is similarly thought of as something that will make the person to whom it has happened more lovable. All the evidence of short-lived marriages and love affairs in that sphere does not alter the ingenue's dream that if she is rich and famous, people will love her in some way that will be infinitely superior to the tepid way in which she is loved now.

This dream is an aspect of the wider one of money as a transforming agent. The wish is to be somebody else, because being oneself is somehow disappointing, and it is thought that money can bring this about. As Cinderella rose from the ashes and became clean, so shall we, if we have enough money.

---

* Throughout the story, the power of Aladdin's lamp is very similar to the power of money at its most magical.

The great excitement that the idea of outfitting oneself in new clothes arouses is part of this fantasy of a money-wrought metamorphosis. It is a very ancient wish, to which religions cater by means of rebirth ceremonies, and by propounding concepts of resurrection and the transmigration of souls. In a more immediate and material way, it is something that we suppose we can achieve by winning the lottery.

The desire to be somebody else is rather strange, but in the fantasy it is thought that this other "rich me" would not merely have more money, but would be changed fundamentally, would be stronger, less fearful, more charming, wiser, less vulnerable, and so on. Money is endowed with magical powers. And arising out of this comes the belief that it can provide us with a kind of immortality. To the native of New Britain, the purpose of acquiring great wealth (in seashells) was that on his death "men should bewail, praise and honour him with feasts."[6] In the dream, money will make us great, and remembered, the way Alfred Nobel is remembered through his prizes, the way Ford is remembered through his Foundation. Thomas J. Watson, founder of IBM, put it directly when he said in 1933: "I want you to understand this company is going to go on forever."

And if not life everlasting in a material sense, then at least there is "the good life" here and now. Month by month *Playboy* magazine chronicles this dream in meticulous detail, and since its founder, Hugh Hefner, is evidently living it, disbelief may be effectively nullified. He is to be found, is he not, in "the remote-controlled, wired-up, electronic heaven which passes for Hefner's bedroom, squatting on a 7½-ft.-diameter revolving bed, with its cabinets at the rear, and a whole Wurlitzer of buttons at hand"[7] to summon any or all of the dozens of servants in permanent attendance. Somewhere below, the waterfall in the greenly lit indoor pool has begun to fall, and the "Woo Grotto" is awaiting its first occupant of the day. There's a private cinema, closed-circuit television, and a stream of celebrity visitors that includes Bob Hope, Norman Mailer, Mort Sahl, Elia Kazan, Dizzy Gillespie, Frank Sinatra, Budd Schulberg. If he wishes to move from his electronic paradise he merely has to step into his flying version of it, a DC9 that has: an elliptical bed covered with a spread of Tasmanian opossum skin, in Hef's private bedroom; a living room with Ampex 660 color videotape machine; a discotheque for impromptu dance fests; a conference area above the wings; and even a private side-entrance, in case a girl wants to slip out quietly, without being seen by everybody. It is not said whether a parachute is provided.

Judging from the number of people who read the magazine, the dream of living like that must be more widespread than one had imagined. There are permutations of it, which emphasize one or another aspect to a greater or lesser extent —there may be Roman baths instead of kidney-shaped pools, or the elliptical bed may be replaced by a white cashmere divan some fifty feet in circumference, which was Balzac's seduction couch.[8] There may be stroboscopic light shows or quilted walls, or whatever. The dream is of living in the lap of luxury, an expression that suggests the origin of the desire may be found in the state of blissful comfort that the small child sometimes knew in his mother's lap. With great wealth we will be able to abolish all work, rid ourselves of burdensome tasks and live for pleasure.

The novelist and TV playwright Robert Muller says: "Because one enjoys going to the South of France and staying in a fine hotel for two weeks' holiday one somehow imagines that such an experience indefinitely extended would be bound to make one happy. Of course, it wouldn't, but one thinks it would and says sighingly: 'Ah—if only we could live like this all the time.' "[9]

If, in the end, the luxury palls even in anticipation, then

there is a final and more deviously satisfying form that the dream takes, and that is of being the biggest, or the greatest. A former waiter, who opened up his own restaurant and did very well, wants to go on to have the biggest chain of restaurants in the land. He doesn't know why. "It's just that if you are a general, you want to be the greatest general, don't you?" he says.[10] Napoleonic ambitions are not always confined to the military. The dreamer of this fantasy sees himself with the ever-widening circles of his acquisitions spreading across the globe—newspaper chains, radio stations, TV networks, paper mills, insurance companies, car-rental firms, banks, airlines, oil, cinemas, hotels, supermarkets—he's going to have everything. Such is the gargantuanism of this dream that it stops only when the mind has finally been made to boggle at its own insatiability.

These are the common dreams of money. For some, they come to pass, with varying consequences. But there is a particular type for whom the dream will never be implemented—because he is addicted to the dream *as a dream*. A man on relief says that one of the things he misses most about his present situation is not having the money to bet at the race track as he used to: not that he expected to win, but it let him dream. This is characteristic of the type. The dreamer is someone who prefers his own imaginings to reality. The nineteenth-century French novelist Balzac was such a man. As his novels show, he had an extraordinary understanding of money, and was clearly hopelessly in love with it. He went in for all sorts of business ventures; he was involved in land speculation, in a printing works, in advertising perfume, in the reprinting of the classics. But all his financial enterprises come to nothing, despite the great knowledge of finance that his books show him to have had. One of his biographers, André Maurois, has suggested that the repeated failure of his ventures was due to the fact that when life created difficulties, he withdrew at once into his imaginary world, which he could control, and where the outcome was entirely in his hands. This is the traditional way of the dreamer.

He is found in all cultures. Arthur Miller's play *Death of a Salesman* is the tragedy of such a man. In the depression years after the First World War the cafés of Vienna and Budapest were filled with out-of-work men sipping their one cup of coffee all afternoon, and dreaming out loud of the fortunes they were going to make. Most of them dreamed their lives away in this fashion. The betting shops, the race tracks, the casinos, the patent offices and the waiting rooms of music publishers are full of such people. Everybody else knows that it's not going to happen for them, that they are wasting their time, but they are too deep in their fantasy to listen or care.

In their minds they take the dream to its impossible extreme; money is imagined on a scale that defies reason. Since the dreamer never intends to actually do anything, he need not confine himself to the feasible and practicable. His imaginings have the hallucinatory intensity of self-induced sex images. In those activities that promote the fantasy—playing roulette, for instance—the fantasist is often in a daze of prolonged undischarged excitation. Freud saw in the rituals of the casino, in the passion for play, the replacement of compulsive masturbation by the mania for gambling, and considered that the emphasis laid upon the passionate activity of the hands confirmed this.[11] Even more striking in this respect would be the hand gestures and facial expressions and cries that often accompany dice-throwing games, like craps.

People get themselves all excited about money; they work themselves up; they titillate themselves with visions of wealth. There is a whole subliterature that stimulates their desires without, of course, being able to satisfy them; it is to be found in advertising, in newspapers, in magazines, in films, in TV, in commercials, in fashion photography, in interior decoration—those gold-plated bathroom fixtures, those imitation leopard skin covers! Such images are so commonplace as to go unheeded on conscious levels; but, in the unconscious, they are food for the dreamer and serve to excite his gaudiest longings. They help to create an addiction to the images of money, and to produce a kind of voyeurism that finds satisfaction in spying on others leading their rich lives. In Nice, at the height of the season, you can see tourists standing outside the grand hotels, watching the people inside eating under the crystal chandeliers.

There is the person who goes to car showrooms and sits in expensive cars he knows he can't afford. There is the person who lets real estate agents take him around properties much too expensive for his means. There is the kind of woman who will try on clothes that she knows she hasn't the money to buy. There is the person who fills in coupons for round-the-world trips that he could not possibly take. By such means people whip themselves up into states of money excitement. They talk of what they are going to do when they are rich, when their ship comes in. What can be the source of such an addiction?

The psychoanalyst Ernest Jones has noted that there is among children great attachment to "reversal fantasies." They believe that as they grow older and bigger, their parents will grow smaller, which, of course, in a relative sense, is true. When these fantasies are closely examined, they are shown to contain dreams of revenge. Jones quotes the three-year-old girl who said to her mother: " 'When I am a big girl and you are a little girl I shall whip you just as you whip me now.' " A little boy of about three and a half used to say to his mother: " 'When I am big, then you will be little; then I will carry you about and dress you and put you to sleep.' "[12]

It seems that children deal with situations in which they feel small and helpless and at somebody else's mercy by reversing them. The sort of thing that they laugh at (Mickey Mouse, Charlie Chaplin) shows their perennial delight in reversals.

One way in which the child is constantly dependent on his parents is for things that he wants them to buy him. For they have money, and he hasn't. So he is forever having to say: When will you buy me this? and, Please buy me that; and, I'll be very good if you buy me the other; and, Why won't you buy me such and such? The rage of dependency is clearly seen when a refusal to buy a child an ice-cream cone or a toy car produces a fit of screaming.

Because of the importance that children attach to being bought things, adults buy them things as a way of controlling them. They devise systems of rewards and punishments, based on buying or not buying. "I'll buy you that if you're a good boy/if you take your medicine/if you go to sleep/if you stop wetting your bed/if you get good marks at school . . ." The child feels controlled by the adult's capacity to spend money, which he lacks; and being given to reversal fantasies he naturally enough imagines situations in which he will be able to control the parents by a money system of his own. The little boy who tells his father that he is going to buy him a racing car for his birthday is not necessarily motivated by an overflowingly generous heart; more likely he wants to control Daddy with the promise of the car in the way that he feels himself to be controlled.

Thus the money dream would derive some of its intensity and its habit-forming nature from its origins in the reversal fantasy in which the child is the rich one and Daddy the beggar.*

* In suggesting this as a source of the dream, I do not intend to imply that it is the only source.

Of course, dreaming has its uses; it can provide the scenario for action—but that is a different kind of dreaming. The continual indulgence in the dream *as such* inevitably brings about a dependence on it; such people whenever they are miserable, down, bored, will have themselves a money dream to lift their spirits. They will resort to one or other of the fantasies of wealth that I have described, and will in this way seek to bring themselves out of their low mood. They will gawk for a while at their self-induced hallucinations, will feel briefly excited and therefore cheered-up, and then with a sigh will revert to reality, which in these circumstances becomes increasingly intractable.

2
The Quest

There are some who make the dream happen, even though they may deny ever having had it. They may be fortune hunters, financial wizards, robber barons, or gnomes of Zurich, tricksters, oil tycoons, colonizers, overnight stars, or thieves. They may seek riches in a woman, or a deal, or a dodge, or in the depths of the earth, or in a notion. They have every kind of temperament, but there is a common denominator to them—it is the belief in the crock of gold, the buried treasure, El Dorado, the coup, the killing, the jackpot. This sort of person does not aspire to being well-off; he desires an inundation of money, wealth beyond the dream of avarice, more than he will know what to do with. This is his craving; and like other cravings it frequently overrules reason and morality, as in the case of a man like Sir Walter Raleigh, who asserted that "taking millions has never been regarded as a crime," and finally forfeited his life to this principle.

To strike it rich on this scale is something that has only become possible during the past century. Before mass industries sprang up, it was virtually unknown for a man to alter his material circumstances by his efforts alone. He couldn't *make* money; it was granted him by a monarch or a war lord, or it came in the form of booty, or was taken out of the earth or conquered territory. But the alchemists' dream of *creating* wealth where there was none before, of conjuring it out of nothing, or out of something without known value, has only been realized in the last hundred years. The aggregate of all the world's millionaires throughout the whole of history up till 1875 is fewer than the number now to be found in the United States in any one year.[1] It took the Krupps eight generations, starting in the sixteenth century, to obtain great wealth. By comparison Rockefeller did it in about forty years at the end of the nineteenth and beginning of the twentieth centuries. And in the present day Britain's whizz-kid financier Jim Slater, of the house of Slater, Walker, took just eight years to turn £2,000 of personal savings into an investment and banking complex valued at £220 millions on the stock market.[2]

Notwithstanding the skill or cunning involved in picking up this kind of fortune, it is in effect a windfall of the times. The Krupp dynasty thrived on wars; Rockefeller's oil wells gushed most profusely just as the motorcar started being produced on a mass scale (in the early 1900's) ; the asset-strippers take advantage of world inflation and soaring capital values to buy up old undervalued firms.

The natural energy in the earth, and the invention of machines to utilize it, has produced most of the great new wealth of the last hundred years. Though a few inventors did well, most of the fortunes went to the entrepreneurs who saw the commercial applications of fuel- and electricity-powered machines. Of the forty-two richest Americans named on *Fortune*'s 1957 list of Inherited Wealth-Holders, twenty-one owed their wealth to oil or the motorcar. The list included seven Rockefellers (oil), four Mellons (oil, steel, rubber,

etc.) , three Du Ponts (chemicals, motorcars, oil, rubber, etc.) ,
and four Fords (motorcars) . A list of *new* wealth-holders published at the same time was headed by the name of Paul Getty,
whose fortune comes from oil, and was followed by thirteen
others who owed their wealth to this source. Another four
owed it to General Motors. Ten years later, in 1968, *Fortune*'s
updated list was still headed by three men who owed their
wealth to oil: Getty, H. L. Hunt and Howard Hughes (the
Hughes Tool Company owned the patent of the drilling bit
that is used in oil drilling, and Hughes laid the foundations
of his fortune by hiring out the bit in return for a royalty on
any oil found) .

In Britain, too, the origins of the great nineteenth-century
fortunes were closely related to the tapping of the earth's
energy. Oil, coal, steel and the railways produced most of the
new rich, and their descendants joined the descendants of the
landed families in manning the vantage points of power. The
older wealth was more conspicuous in Britain because there
was more of it, but plenty of new fortunes were made. The
late nineteenth century and early years of the twentieth century favored the ruthless entrepreneur-capitalist because nations had not yet grasped the full value of their natural resources, or their public franchises, and were allowing them to
go to whoever grabbed them first. There were few controls at
this stage. The trust-breaking came later. The pace of moneymaking was gathering momentum in all parts of the world
where fuel-powered mass production was becoming established. Riches were not merely added to riches—they multiplied. With mass-production technology producing businesses
that doubled* in size every two or three years, a new quasi-

* In 1896 the Duryea Motor Wagon Company produced thirteen automobiles,
the first manufactured for sale in the United States; in 1900 the motorcar
business was not big enough to be listed by the United States Bureau of the
Census, but by 1905 it had grown to an industry with products valued at
$26,645,064.[3]

magical factor entered the calculations of capitalism: *the multiplier.* It has remained the most alluring aspect of playing with money. Here is an example of the sort of thing that can happen in the present day: "In 1962 the entire market value of Solitron was less than $1,000,000 and in 1967 the market value was more than $200,000,000. Solitron's earnings increased more than tenfold, but the market's opinion of that earnings increase made the stock appreciate 250-fold."[4]

Anyone who had put $10,000 into the company in 1962 would have turned it in five years into about $2.5 million. This was the magical multiplier in action. The stockmarket multiplies the annual earnings of a company by a given number to arrive at the value of its shares. This number—it may be as low as ten or as high as forty, or more—is partly based on real values, tangible assets, but it also is determined by past *rate* of growth and by the *anticipated rate of growth,* and in the latter category it is simply a matter of shares' having "sex-appeal." Those who possess it may soar to the top on the basis of nothing more solid than what is expected of them. And once shares have changed hands at inflated prices they can go on rising on the basis of what dealers call The Greater Fool Theory. You buy because however overpriced a share is there can always be found a greater fool who will pay even more. As an indication of the solipsism of the market, there was a report, on one occasion, which said that shares on Wall Street had risen because they had not fallen after some recent bad news from Vietnam.

A financial writer wrote in the London *Times* of one kind of financial operation (asset-stripping) that these operators "convinced themselves that they have discovered the secret for which medieval alchemists searched so hard."[5] And, indeed, when such methods are examined, they do seem to consist of a series of magic formulas for, in effect, "creating money."

Behind the magic is The Greater Fool Theory—as long as such a being can be found prices will continue to rise and everybody can go on making profits. Their capitalist's faith amounts to a belief in unending increase, the continual squaring of the number originally thought of, to infinity. The self-perpetuating structure depends on wants being created by the process by which they are satisfied, in Professor J. K. Galbraith's famous summary of the matter.[6] For the general multiplication of wealth to continue, it must be possible to increase wants ad infinitum. This means raising "never having enough" to the level of an economic imperative. A large body of opinion now holds that there must come an end to growth, not only because the earth's resources are being used up (it is argued that new sources of energy tend to be found when the need for them has arisen), but because there must be a limit to human wants in the material sense, which when exceeded produces the glutton society, feeding itself to death. Since this is a foreseeable consequence of continuing adherence to the multiplier principle, the question that is posed is: How has the desire for the fortune so overruled reason as to commit us to such a disastrous course?

In his study of the alchemists, the Swiss psychologist C. G. Jung wrote: "What to the chemist seems to be the absurd fantasies of alchemy can be recognised by the psychologist without too much difficulty as psychic material . . ."[7] It is an important insight that the obsessional desire for gold—the fortune—is primarily an expression of a psychic craving.

If this is so, it would go some way towards explaining how we have got on the path of endless increase. Because, while there is a limit to how much people can consume, own, use, there is no limit to the psyche's wants, as is indicated by the fact that God in most religions is limitless and infinite.

The visible god money in our time has come to symbolize so much that is desirable, that the fortune is sought for all sorts of unacknowledged reasons. As it is the highly publicized goal and ultimate reward to which almost everything in our culture is geared, people are not inclined by and large to question their money motive. Why look for other reasons when a perfectly good one exists? *Why pursue money? For the money, of course.* Its desirability is regarded as self-evident. The "rational nature of the irrationality of modern society," in Herbert Marcuse's phrase, makes it difficult to see anything strange or unnatural in the desire for the fortune. It is what everybody else wants, and that alone is enough reason for wanting it.

The strong tendency to deny *other* motives has to be overcome before insight can be achieved. Of course, people will be ready to agree that there must have been something mad about the alchemists with their giant retorts and kabbalistic formulations, desiring to make gold out of lead. In our time it *is* possible to make a fortune—out of property development, or by means of some *chemistry* that will produce a hit film, or by developing a copying process like Xerox or a camera like the Polaroid. Since it can be done, it must be reasonable to do it.

But this rationality becomes more questionable when one begins to consider the ultimate consequences of the multiplier principle on which the making of the fortune is based. In human terms, striking proof of the uselessness of the limitless fortune is provided by the case of a man like Howard Hughes, for whom money becomes wholly symbolic—the *deus ex machina* in his private theater of the absurd. In social terms the rationality, and even the reality, of money is questioned by some economists, such as the late Geoffrey Crowther, who spoke of "the creation" of money by banks. He wrote: ". . . the banks retain a very large power to determine both the quantity of money in existence and the persons into whose hands it shall be placed."[8] Consider, too, this formula for the making of a fortune: "The new entrepreneurs . . . generated a very large premium on the market price of their shares. And that premium made it easy for them to enlarge their takeover and exploitation horizons, so that, with p/e ratios of 20 on their own shares and p/e ratios of 10 on their takeover targets, they were able to achieve earnings growth by definition."[9] It is money growing on paper.

The alchemists were working on a hypothetical substance, the miracle material X, whose existence was generally assumed, even if nobody had yet succeeded in isolating it; the self-made millionaires work in paper values which are created by virtue of a common assumption that they exist. It reminds one of Rilke's unicorn, for whom "the possibility of being . . . was able to confer such strength, its brow put forth a horn."[10]

The kind of financial formulas that can create this sort of rapid wealth on paper, work not because they express some inexorable economic law, but because everybody concerned agrees that they work; they are an expression of deals of the mind, which all the participants have at that moment by tacit consent chosen to honor. If they all *changed* their minds, the paper values would disappear in a moment.

What does this *making* of money in the mind mean? What is actually going on in these ceremonies of profit? What is the game? The alchemists saw in base lead "something so bedevilled and shameless that all who wish to investigate it fall into madness through ignorance."[11] Psychologists speculate that when people deal with an unknown substance, or a commodity with unknown properties, they are impelled to project upon it aspects of their own unconscious, and to treat what they then see as an objective reality. This suggests that the characteristics the alchemists attributed to lead, or gold, or other metals, of which they had only emotional knowledge, may have been those of their own minds. Could it be that in the case of "shameless lead" they were talking of experiences in the leaden state of sleep, in other words of dreams? And from the reference, we may postulate that these dreams were of a "base" nature. The desire to transmute a physically impure substance into a physically pure and valuable object may have behind it the command of the superego to transform base desires into pure ones. In other words, it suggests that the desire to make gold is in the Freudian sense "overdetermined," i.e., has more than the single ostensible motive.

Such a conclusion is not difficult to accept in the case of the alchemists, since their "gold-making" was such an esoteric business; by comparison, making a fortune today is no longer wrapped in mystery—it seems to be a perfectly rational activity. The example of the alchemists is useful because in them the desire for the fortune had not yet become rationalized, and therefore was highly suggestive of underlying motives. The language of their theories hints at what gold and gold-making may have meant to them. In their abstruse treatises, the key to the whole process was supposedly the substance mercury, which was not simply quicksilver, but something possessing the qualities of water, fire, soul and duality. Jung defines it as follows:

"Mercurius, following the tradition of Hermes, is many-sided, changeable, and deceitful. Dorn speaks of 'that inconstant Mercurius,' and another calls him versipellis (changing his skin, shifty). He is *duplex* and his main characteristic is duplicity. It is said of him that he 'runs around the earth and enjoys equally the company of the good and the wicked.' He is 'two dragons,' the 'twin,' made of 'two natures' or 'two substances.' "[12]

In this many-sidedness is it not possible to recognize the

quicksilver spirit of money, of which Mercurius under his Greek name of Hermes was in fact god?

The modern fortune-seeker, like the hero of fairy tales, or the "blindfolded" figure of alchemical treatises, is unconscious of his motives as he seeks out hidden assets, buried treasure, natural gas, oil, copper, gold, building sites. He rationalizes what he does by reference to the self-evident desirability of money, per se, and consequently has no need to consider its meaning for him. If he believes that the money is going to change him, he feels confident that it will change him in the way he wants to be changed. He has no fear of money, since he has no awareness of its Mephistophelian role. Nor does he understand that the commitment to moneymaking becomes, as a rule, progressively more binding, that he cannot stop whenever he likes, as many a multimillionaire has found when the money has ceased to have any real meaning for him but *must* still be made.

The classic pattern is of someone spending much of his lifetime ruthlessly destroying or gobbling up rivals, sacrificing loves and personal happiness for the sake of his goal, struggling to overcome the hatred and opposition that his methods inevitably arouse, and finally, when he has got there, discovering that the money is of no use to him, that all he can do with it is give it away, which he then proceeds to do with the same fanaticism that he had brought to amassing it.

This was essentially the story of John D. Rockefeller, perhaps the most spectacularly successful of the great acquisitors, whose life exemplified the "blindfolded" state of such money-seeking. He had started at the age of sixteen as a bookkeeper, and by the time he was in his forties he had substantial holdings in sixteen railroads and nine mining companies; in industries making paper, nails, soda, timber; in nine banks and investment companies; in nine real estate companies; in six steamship lines; in two orange groves. And, of course, he had Standard Oil, the source of all his great wealth. From every part of his ever-growing empire the reports spoke of "wells roaring like Niagara Falls," of fields producing ninety thousand barrels a day, of bursters and gushers. Standard's oil was being transported in sampans through the waterways of China, in oxcarts along the Great North Road of India. Native chieftains lit their palaces with Standard oil. Mexican priests mixed it with beeswax and stearin to make candles. It was spreading throughout Europe, with companies set up in Britain (Anglo-American Oil Company Ltd.), Denmark, Germany, Holland. It was getting to Russia, Africa, South America. This was all before the motorcar. Then came the development of engines using petroleum as fuel, first in steam boilers, and on farms for pumping water and sawing wood, and later in ships, and eventually in motorcars. In the last years of the nineteenth century, Standard Oil's annual net earnings were climbing like this:[13]

1894: $15,544,325
1895: $24,078,076
1896: $34,077,519

In the first few years of the twentieth century, as the motorcar industry grew at an explosive rate, the earnings went on soaring:

1900: $55,501,774
1902: $64,613,365
1906: $83,122,251

It was a continuous bonanza, and the methods used to maintain it—and increase it—became part of the legend of the robber barons. There were secret deals; price-fixing arrangements; espionage; intimidation. The industrial emperors could impose their own terms. The Hepburn Committee reporting in 1880 spoke of "the colossal proportions to which monopoly can grow under laws in this country," and discovered that Rockefeller was able to transport his oil on the railroads on terms more or less laid down by him, which gave him enormous discounts (between 50 percent and 80 percent), resulting in the railroads' increasing their rates to other firms and to the general public, to make up their loss.[14]

There were, too, stories of widows bought out by the ruthless monopolist, of which the most famous was "the widow Backus case." According to her tale, Rockefeller had ruthlessly taken advantage of a defenseless widow, and appropriated her business for little more than a third of its value. It must be said that there are various versions of this story, and in not all of them is Rockefeller depicted with equal blackness. But the point to note here is that at the time it first became known, the widow's story was generally believed, because it appeared to be in character for Rockefeller to have done what it was said he had done. By then this side of him was well known. In 1905 a writer in *McClure's Magazine*, Ida Tarbell, was calling him "the victim of perhaps the ugliest . . . of all passions, that for money, money as an end . . . It is not a pleasant picture . . . this money-maniac secretly, patiently, eternally plotting how he may add to his wealth."

One of Rockefeller's chief aides complained bitterly of their image: "We have met with a success unparalleled in commercial history, our name is known all over the world, and our public character is not one to be envied. We are quoted as the representative of all that is evil, hard hearted, oppressive, cruel (we think unjustly), but men look askance at us, we are pointed at with contempt, and while some good men flatter us, it's only for our money, and we scorn them for it and it leads to further hardness of heart."[15]

This was the prelude to proposals for sharing profits with the oil producers and with Standard's own employees in order to "change the current opinion, which is now setting so strongly against us." Though Rockefeller listened to the plea of his old colleague, he did not implement any of his proposals, which clearly went against the grain for him.

In all this, his blind attachment to money was evident. At the same time it was no unmitigated pleasure for him. He often thought of it as a great burden that only his benefactions helped to lighten. One of his aides, Frederick T. Gates, was warning him in dire Old Testament tones: "Your fortune is rolling up, rolling up like an avalanche! You must keep up with it. You must distribute it faster than it grows. If you do not, it will crush you, and your children, and your children's children."[16]

Still he fought tenaciously and cunningly against the government's attempt to break up the Standard Oil Trust, which was making a return on investment of 1,400 percent per annum.[17]

He had little personal use for the money. His taste in clothing was extremely simple. His family could hardly get him to renew his suits when they were wearing out. He ate very sparingly; a favorite dish was bread and milk. The cuisine of his household was always plain; they never employed a French chef. He was a teetotaller and an ardent proponent of temperance, and considered that the Republic itself was imperiled by alcohol. And he was giving away his money at an accelerating rate. Starting with $2.77 in 1855, it became a quarter of a million dollars in 1887, more than half a million in 1891, more than $1,350,000 in 1892. In 1909 it was over $71,000,000; in 1919 it was $138,000,000 plus.[18]

On the one hand there was the grasping, greedy "money maniac," as he was described, piling it up; on the other, the philanthropist and benefactor giving it all away. It wasn't even as though his benefactions were in support of causes that he deeply believed in. He gave a great deal of money to education, for instance, but hardly ever read a book himself. His passion seems to have been largely confined to having the money pass through his hands.

From such a history an entire substructure of unconscious motives may be inferred. And insofar as Rockefeller's money mania was shared by others, who emulated him either in imagination or in actuality, we may infer that they too were activated by motives of which they were not aware.

The success stories of Rockefeller and the other great nineteenth-century industrialists set off a general money chase on an unparalleled scale. The opportunities were there, and also the examples to show how it could be done. To make his pile became a man's aim in life. There was no reason to question this. Particularly in America, because of its being a country that set such store by "sturdy independence" and "making one's way" as part of the pioneer tradition, there came to be a widespread belief that "the game is winning and getting rich and powerful, and nothing else."[19] Moneymaking and manliness were one and the same, and anything went; business was the testing ground of real men.

Real men like the Merritt brothers, hard-bitten fortune seekers in the tradition of the day. They were looking for pine timber in the Mesabi hills in Minnesota when they found their compass needles "spinning like whirligigs" and became convinced that the rocks held rich iron-ore deposits. By means that were not particularly scrupulous, but common at the time, the Merritts got control at the ludicrously low rate of less than a dollar an acre of much of the Mesabi lands. When exploration revealed rich deposits, the brothers organized the Biwabik Mountain Iron Company, without having a cent. They ran up colossal debts. They bought railroads by paying for them in time notes. And by fast talking and what their

biographer calls "maniacal eagerness" they got large sums of
money from financiers and investors. Setting themselves up
as the Lake Superior Consolidated, they issued stock for
$26,050,000. They had turned $2,000,000 of stock in mining
and railroads, most of which wasn't bought with their own
money, into five times as much in the stock of the new company. In this way they made about $10,000,000 for them-
selves.[20]

Such tales went to create a folklore of moneymaking. A
whole new human possibility was being presented; the chance
for everyone to get rich. This had not existed before on a
practical level, and consequently the dream of self-enrichment
had been contained by the reality principle. But now it was
something that could happen to anyone, and though in practice it still only happened to very few, the prospect of it
changed people's lives. It changed their aims and their way
of thinking. Inevitably, it affected the older and slower social
patterns of rural communities where no dramatic change of
circumstance could be expected from one year to the next.
Now there was the general restlessness of knowing that there
was money to be made somewhere, that others had done it.
What was required of a bright young fellow was get-up-and-go,
a term that expressed exactly what he had to do. He had to
leave. He had to go where the money was.

In the expanding, bustling cities of America the newcomers
in town were *all* fortune hunters. You went to the big city to
make your pile, one way or another. And the racy raffish
flavor of that life, and news of the opportunities it presented,
reached every part of the globe. In Armenian, Polish, Greek,
Italian, Irish, Russian, Lithuanian towns, people without
prospects dreamed of one day going to America and becoming
rich. The image of this blessed condition consisted of much
more than merely having a lot of money. All the various forms
of misery and oppression and constriction to which they were

subject disappeared in the vision. It was truly transmutation that was promised—a new life.

Wherever they came from, the newcomers to the big cities, having no roots, no old family ties, were bound to make money relationships with each other, since it was money that brought them together, and since money was their common interest. It was who you knew that counted in business, and so naturally you chose to know people who might be useful. Connections were what you had to have, and connections were what you went after. A person who wasn't some sort of a connection was a waste of time. But to know somebody who knew so-and-so, who knew the man who was the top man in such-and-such—this was interesting, important, exciting, *useful*. It wasn't that a man coldly and calculatingly chose his friends only from among those people in some way capable of serving his interests; it was simply that people of no use to him didn't interest him.

The other side of this particular coin was the intimacies that sprang up between people who were closely involved in moneymaking activities. Idealized as lifelong friendships, even as loves, they could crumble in a moment when their monetary basis disappeared. These were not necessarily cases of cynical opportunism; it was just that the *raison d'être* of these relationships disappeared when moneymaking paths diverged.

In the commercial hearts of the big cities, money became the object of worship; as in every religion the obeisances to the deity were quickly ritualized to the point where original meanings were lost. Moneymaking became, in its most highly refined form, automatic; it was done as a matter of course, on the basis of certain canons that were not questioned.

The gospel of the fast buck spread. Ordinary people became sharper about money. They were getting an eye for a profit. A great universal itch had been started. It finally got

to the grass roots through men like Bernie Cornfeld, who sold
the dream of "People's Capitalism" to the masses—jackpots for
everyone. You, too, can be rich and famous. In less than a
century the hope of sudden wealth, previously limited to the
mad genius, or the conquistador, had become generalized. A
man like Cornfeld knew how to play on this. He would hold
sales seminars and "safaris" at which the money-believer's
catechisms were thrown about: "Are you Wellington Winner?
Or are you Louie the Loser?" "Do you want to use the capitalist system? Or do you want to let it use you?"[21] With Cornfeld
himself as the model of the correct answer (complete with
châteaux, private airplanes, dolly girls, and powerful friends)
the trainee salesmen were in no doubt about wanting to be
Wellington Winners too. The quickness with which they got
the basic message is indicated by the story of the new salesman
who was told by an older hand that as a result of shrewd
investments and high commissions, the latter was worth over
a quarter of a million dollars. At which the Cornfeld-inspired
tyro quibbled: "But is that enough for people like us?"[22]

The Cornfeld method consisted of first selling his salesmen
on the idea of getting rich, and then having them sell their
prospects the same, if watered-down, dream. It was a very
winning system. In the late sixties Cornfeld's mutual fund
companies had almost two and a half billion dollars of other
people's money to deploy and invest. Cornfeld had amassed
over $100 million himself, and about a hundred of his lieu-
tenants had hit the million-dollar jackpot themselves. All of
this was achieved by systematically playing on people's money
itch. For the man of small means they produced figures to
show how he might turn $10,000 into $54,000 in ten years.
If this wasn't exactly a fortune in hard cash, it was going to be
achieved by something called "the millionaire's method":
the aura of big money was fostered, even if the reality was not.
The sell was a subtle variation of the pitch they had been

given themselves on their sales safaris. The fantasy of making a killing was promoted. What the prospect didn't grasp was that *he* was the killing that was being made, and the salesmen were the ones who were making it.

On the whole, people were taken in because getting rich was in the air. Everybody had heard of somebody's having done it. At one time you had to strike oil, and the chance of a wildcatter hitting a profitable field, one that would produce a million barrels, was 1 in 43; the chance of hitting a 50-million-barrel field that would make you rich was 1 in 967. So obviously this kind of bonanza was limited to the few. But Cornfeld promised fortunes to people who could keep their foot in the door, and they promised it to anyone who opened the door to them and had a few thousand dollars to put into the right offshore island. That this seemed credible to so many was an indication of how common and tenable an ambition getting rich had become.

Formerly, a man thought of building up his business as a lifetime's work. People didn't expect to make a fortune overnight. But now they did.

A single deal, a development in Wigmore Street, brought Sir Max Rayne a million pounds. Over a period of fourteen years his company London Merchant Securities rose in market value from £300,000 to somewhere in excess of £50,000,000, and over this period he was responsible for generating a further £50,000,000 for associated companies.

Rayne described to me how one of the early deals happened:[23] "I was totally unknown. I had no financial resources worth speaking of—possibly a few thousand pounds I could have commanded from various sources including my own savings. The Church Commissioners were proposing to sell their Paddington Estate—including a property at Eastbourne Terrace—at auction. The surveyor acting for them happened to be a friend of mine and, in idle conversation, I suggested that it

seemed wrong for the Church to sell this site, that they ought
to be involved in the development of it. He said that seemed
to make sense to him and how would I go about it? With my
architect I produced a scheme—literally in forty-eight hours—
showing how it could be developed physically, with estimates
of cost, assessments of rental values, and sold the idea. The
object of the exercise was to persuade the Church Commissioners to retain an interest in the development potential
which they would otherwise have forgone." Rayne's company
put up £1,000 and supplied the know-how; by 1967 the profit
on this one development was £5.6 million.

There were many such fortunes to be made in England,
and at least a hundred men—and the Church Commissioners
—benefited spectacularly from the continuous inflation of
capital values. One man, Harry Hyams, made a personal fortune estimated at over £42 million on the basis of capital
appreciation, while keeping some of his principal buildings
empty and unlet. In his case the money motive is seen at its
starkest. At the other end of the motivational spectrum, the
Church Commissioners, once initiated into the game, went
on to use the Eastbourne Terrace development as a model
for a wide range of similar enterprises, thereby, as Rayne
points out, "greatly increasing the revenues available for
distribution to the clergy." Rayne, one of the best of the
developers, appears to have been more concerned personally
with seeing his financial and architectural vision vindicated
than in the actual money, much of which he quickly disposed
of to a wide range of trusts and foundations principally concerned with the arts and medicine.

This is how another man, Harvey Karp, made his fortune,
as told to me in his own words:

"Our company was making toilets, recirculating toilets,
which were little chemical plants actually, that went into the
707s and the DC8s and the Lockheeds.

"We'd built up a company with an excellent reputation, with a very good following in Wall Street, and with a profit rise each year that was quite impressive.

"At that point the urge to merge was rampant. And we found a company that we liked, a very old and fine company. The largest stockholder wanted to dispose of its holdings. We negotiated to acquire the company for some $15 million, *which was about three times our net worth.* It was a fascinating negotiation. What we did was we went to the Bank of America, in California, and said we'd like to buy this company, and this is its record. Its record was unusually fine. It had been in business since 1888 and had made money every year right through the Depression. Very solid company. Making electrical installation equipment.

"The bank looked at the record, and we said, If we could get an investment banker to agree to take a certain number of our shares and market them to the public would the Bank of America lend us the $15 million? And the Bank of America said yes, if we got a broker they approved.

"So we said fine, give us such a letter, and they did. They said they'd lend us $15 million, *and we had a net worth of $5 million.* With that letter we went to an eminent investment house and to a second investment house, because we had developed this concept of never relying on any one investment bank, or any one supplier.

"So we got both companies to agree to underwrite an issue for us. We then went up to Boston to negotiate the final terms. Now, at that time our stock, which my partner and I had acquired for $4 to $5 a share, was worth $25 a share. If we had been able to sell our stock at $25 a share in order to finance this $15 million purchase we'd have been happy. But what happened was that soon the word of our agreement became known, and the price of our stock started to move up, moved up to $35 a share. We were delighted. As we got closer and closer to making the deal our stock moved up to $45, to $55, and we finally sold the stock to the public at $64 a share. Our net worth jumped from $5 or $6 million to $26 million. We were the minnow swallowing the whale. And so in one fell swoop we were into the big time.

"In making one deal we'd taken us up from $25 to $64, taken our net worth and increased it by 400 percent and our sales by several hundred more percent. And our earnings were more than doubled.

"Were the stocks really worth that much? In talking about the market price of stocks, you are talking about something that is just not definable. Our stock shot up before we had bought the other company, in anticipation of it.

"As a result of this acquisition we became a glamour company, people felt that we had an extraordinarily good product in the sanitation field and the fastener field, and that in addition to that we would be growing externally through acquisitions, and at the time acquisitions was the fad. People were attaching high-earnings multiples to companies that were engaged in the acquisition business. It seemed like the way to get rich fast, and indeed it was. If you have a piece of paper stock certificate selling at thirty times earnings and you buy another company with that paper, and that other company is selling at ten times earnings, you are going to get rich. That is the basic formula for all conglomerates, why acquisitions worked well for many people.

"At this point I was thirty-seven—it was 1965 to 1966—and with this one action had made another $2 million for myself personally.

"I felt that I had made a major personal coup and that I had the money game pretty well in hand."

Three years later, when the company was at the height of its value, having by then acquired some dozen or so others, and having some forty plants in five countries, Karp got out,

resigned his positions of president, secretary, director, treasurer, took his money, by then $10 million, and quit the game,
or that particular game.

This sort of business acumen is condemned by many people
—but it is also enviously admired. Against their better judgment, people thrill to the success stories of financial wizards
who produce millions out of a hat. A young financier, John
Bentley, got his break when he produced a scheme that would
return £100 million for an outlay of £2.5 million. He had
found an insurance company, Scottish Life Association, capi-
talized at a mere £2.5 million, which controlled book investments worth £40 million, and had hidden reserves of another
£60 million. He persuaded Jim Slater of Slater Walker to
mount a raid. They had bought up 8 percent of the equity
before the company's board found out what was going on.
They were stopped; but the shares they had bought doubled
in value. It was the start of Bentley's high flying.[24]

Charles Bluhdorn put together Gulf & Western by piling
one acquisition on top of another, from auto parts and zinc
mining to the screen rights of *The Godfather* (they came with
Paramount, which he had picked up on the way) .

The popular belief, fostered by the widely disseminated
clichés of success, is that all you need is an idea. You only have
to think of something, as Dr. Edwin Land did in inventing a
camera that develops its own pictures in seconds; it made him
a personal fortune estimated to be around $185,000,000. If
one could think of a way of making an automatic shoe-
polisher that also spreads on polish without dirtying your
trousers! Or buy a company with the money of the company
being bought—which people apparently have done, since a
law was brought out against it in Britain. Or you can make a
killing in cocoa, if you happen to know that the cocoa tree is
about to be stricken by Black Pod, or that Ghana is about to
go up in flames—time it right, and you can buy at 23 cents

and sell at 70 when the calamity has occurred and the confectioners are screaming for cocoa. Or you can buy on margin. Or you can buy in time notes on a rising market in the expectation that what you have bought will be worth more by the time you have to pay for it.

New ways of making fortunes are being mooted all the time, the methods varying from the clever to the crooked. Once this was something decent people didn't do—quadruple their money at a stroke. At least, you didn't talk of such things in polite society. But in the new permissiveness there are circles where people talk of little else; gone is the shamefulness of wanting to make a lot of money quickly. In fact, those who do it, the asset strippers, the conglomerators, the "shell" operators, the international speculators, the wheeler-dealers, the showmen, the entrepreneurs of pop, the promoters of sex festivals, the whole gallery of fortune seekers have become the heroes of our time. We may call them anti-heroes, as a way of putting ourselves morally in the clear; but from the sheer attention they receive it is evident that people identify with them, whatever they do. The obloquy that used to attach to anyone who was good with money ("a bit of a Jew") has gone; the bad image about which Rockefeller's colleague was so concerned no longer exists.

Few today would look askance at any multimillionaire, nor is there much sign of anyone being held in contempt for the way he has made his fortune. Quite the contrary, the ruthless pursuit of money is now regarded as the most generally appealing form of adventure. A novelist like Harold Robbins treats it as such and regards the businessman "as a modern knight, jousting for supremacy," an outlook many people must empathize with, judging from the sales of the books. He is no longer represented as someone with "an ugly passion," as Rockefeller was; nowadays an asset stripper like John Bentley is depicted in terms that were formerly reserved for film stars. To complete the revamping of the image, all that temperance and bread and milk are out.

A man who has made $5 million says categorically: "The men who make a great deal of money are the men who are sexually most highly potent."[25]

What makes people go into the money game in the first place? Walter Gruber was a journalist who had worked for *Newsweek* in Washington, covering the White House, the State Department and the Senate side of Capitol Hill. He knew the important people. He was a friend of the then Senate Majority leader, Lyndon B. Johnson. He'd had two private interviews with President Eisenhower. In 1961 he quit journalism because "I was tired of writing about the people who made things happen. I wanted to make them happen myself." So he decided to become a financier. He went to ten Wall Street firms asking for a job. The first question they all asked him was "How much money do you have?"; the second question was "How much money does your father have?"; and the third question was "How much money do your close friends have?" After Gruber had answered those questions, "Zero," "Zero," "Zero," he was told he was unemployable. But in the end he persuaded one firm to take him on at thirty-five dollars a week, working in the mail room, delivering the letters around the firm. One day he met the Austrian ambassador on Madison Avenue and heard of some difficulties Austria was having raising a loan of $12½ million for a hydroelectric development in the High Tyrol. He told the ambassador: "Your Excellency, there's no problem. Come to my office on Wall Street on Monday and I'll get you your $12½ million."

Negotiating the Austrian loan was how he began as a financier. Today he is an investment banker who acts as financial adviser to very rich men interested in getting richer still. He has been in a position to observe the men with a passion for money at close quarters. And this is what he says about their motives. "People go into the game of making money for three or four reasons. First, because there is nothing else they can do. Secondly, because of the power. And third, out of greed. That's what dominates a lot of the action. And then a lot of it is just because it's a game. It can be likened to backgammon or horse racing or anything else that motivates people in the game-theory sense. They like the *game. I* like the game. I'll give some cases. One man is acquiring more and more money because he really wants to build an empire. As far as he's concerned there was the Greek Empire, the Roman Empire, and *his* empire. He wants to take over. He doesn't care about the actual commodity he is dealing in. It is putting it all together and making it the biggest that counts for him. That's one kind of fellow, and he wants to do it because he wants to be a very big cheese. The second fellow has social ambitions. He wants to be invited by Dukes. And that's all: he just wants to be rich enough to be asked to certain houses. The third fellow is an outstanding stockbroker who is probably one of the world's five best backgammon players, and he plays for $5,000 a point, and one of the fifty best bridge players, and he's only in it for the game. He starts in the morning with the racing paper, makes his horse selection for the day, goes to the Stock Exchange, spends a few hours at that, leaves, spends the afternoon playing backgammon, spends his evening playing bridge. It's all part of a life pattern that consists of playing games, one no different from the other. And the techniques are the same. When he's trying to take over a company it's a backgammon game played with bigger chips."[26]

More and more businesses as well as individuals are becoming jackpot-orientated. Even such a colossal concern as IBM subscribes to the ethos of "the killing."

"Few people realize," says Michael Merritt, a senior research analyst with the International Data Corporation in Newton, Massachusetts, "the gamble IBM took on the 360s (A range of computers from small to very large, entirely upwards compatible, so users would not need to rewrite all their programs each time they changed mainframes). To design, develop, manufacture, market and finance a whole line of computers in IBM style takes literally billions of dollars. When IBM announced the 360s in 1964, top management gambled the life of the company *on that one product line.*"[27]

The key factor in such operations is that everything is gambled on one best seller; and increasingly businesses, even the largest, are becoming geared to conducting their affairs on such a principle. The auto industry has become a jackpot business, depending on models like the Mini or the Mustang to clean up. This is also true of the aircraft industry. One airplane design can make or break a great corporation. Rolls Royce crumbled because of the TriStar engine. Polaroid became a supershare, but Zeiss Ikon had to stop making cameras, though they were of indisputable excellence. The pharmaceutical industry's jackpot-orientation is obvious from the resources put into developing a "morning after" contraceptive pill. It was also revealed in the thalidomide tragedy, which occurred largely as a result of the fact that the original German manufacturers ignored warnings about the side effects of the drug in their determination to find a winner. The movie business has always been a jackpot business, but nowadays the jackpots get bigger and fewer, so that the destiny of a company can hang on a single film. It is thought that *The Godfather,* for instance, will eventually show profits of $80,-000,000 for Gulf & Western Industries. This is a substantial addition to the earnings of even a large conglomerate. The other side of the story is that a failure like *Hello, Dolly!,* in which about $20,000,000 had been invested, can sink a company. It almost sank Twentieth-Century Fox, which got by on the skin of its teeth because of the unexpected success of *M*A*S*H*.

A jackpot business is a business that concentrates enormous resources on producing a single article or model that will prove to be of such overwhelming popularity that it will make up for the losses incurred on all the other articles that have flopped. There are still many businesses that are not of this kind. They provide a range of products or services for which there is a market, and do this at a price that will give them a margin of profit on everything sold. Farming, transport, engineering, textiles, building homes, medical services—these are some areas not yet subject to best-seller fever.

In all these lines people can make a good living, can indeed get rich, but not suddenly, and not on the basis of a single product or a single idea. This does not mean that it may not come. There is no way of greatly multiplying the profits from raising beef, but researchers have found ways of making high protein foods in the laboratory, and if they came up with a really delicious plastic beefsteak, that would be a jackpot. Medical care can be highly profitable, but it is cure-alls that make millions. Computerized medical checkups could become big moneymakers. And there is a doctor who claims to have found an effective cure for coronary heart trouble; he is traveling all over the world setting up clinics that will have the concessions to use his treatment. Already rejuvenation treatments are big business. The funeral business is not yet a jackpot business, but if post-mortem freezing catches on, *that* will be.

In practically every field, people are looking for a formula, a key, that will make them rich. There is a deep restiveness about merely earning a living, providing a service, supplying an article of use. Of course, the inherent contradiction of this mass desire for wealth is that everybody can't be rich; the only sense in which richness can be experienced is in relation to somebody else. Thorstein Veblen in *The Theory of the Leisure Class* says:

". . . The desire for wealth can scarcely be satiated in any individual instance . . . no general increase of the community's wealth can make any approach to satiating this need, the ground of which is the desire of everyone to excel everyone else in the accumulation of goods . . . the struggle is substantially a race for reputability on the basis of an invidious comparison . . ."

The fact that the desire to make fortunes has become widespread since Rockefeller does not render it any more rational than it was in his case, though new social mores may bestow upon it the appearance of rationality.

The sort of enterprises that are most immediately associated with fortune-making on a spectacular scale are those which have often involved the destruction of forests, the hunting of animal species to extinction, the exhaustion of natural resources—perhaps the exhaustion of space itself. An Elizabethan colonizer like Raleigh was interested in new territories for the gold he could dig out of them, and once they had been emptied of their treasures he went off in search of other places to plunder. A company like Rio Tinto Zinc did pretty much the same. When there was a uranium boom in 1959 it began a mining operation at Lake Elliot, Ontario, that left a thousand-acre wasteland where nothing could grow. Under pressure from the Canadian government, the company attempted to grass and reforest the great mud lake, but without success.

At the time of the great Poseidon share boom, when prices sometimes doubled overnight, the public galleries of the Sydney and Melbourne stock exchanges were full of wildly excited investors, fighting to see their shares being traded. A former Wall Street stockbroker has said that at such times you can literally feel the greed tide rising. It can be seen, too, in the frenzy of shoppers on the first day of a major sale as they fight each other for the bargains.

What is expressed in all these activities is greed of a peculiarly elemental kind. It has been defined as a greed for more than the subject needs or the object can give. It is an emotion that does not know enough. As in the case of Rockefeller what is so ferociously acquired one day might well be given away the next, in the way that many a woman who has battled tooth and claw for some bargain at a sale never wears it, or gives it away.

3
Origins and Consequences

The key to understanding this kind of greed has been provided by the work of the psychoanalyst Melanie Klein. Her developments of Freudian theories and her imaginative new insights into ancient problems are arguably the most significant contribution to psychological knowledge since Freud's own work.

Mrs. Klein's* insights arose out of her analysis of very small children, with whom she developed a play technique, which she used in conjunction with orthodox analysis. By analyzing the meaning of the child's play—his use of toy figures, cutting instruments, water, paints, pencils—she was able to reach levels of feeling more primitive than language. The younger the child being analyzed, the deeper she was able to penetrate into the fantastic world of the infantile unconscious. She wrote:[1]

* Though the center of the Kleinian movement has been in London, there are now Kleinian groups in Spain, Brazil, Argentina, Italy, Portugal, Australia and the United States.

"We get to look upon the child's fear of being devoured, or cut up, or torn to pieces, or its terror of being surrounded and pursued by menacing figures, as a regular component of its mental life; and we know that the man-eating wolf, the fire-spewing dragon, and all the vile monsters of myths and fairy-stories flourish and exert their unconscious influence in the phantasy of each individual child, and it feels itself persecuted and threatened by those evil shapes . . . The real objects behind those imaginary, terrifying figures are the child's own parents . . . and those dreadful shapes in some way or other reflect the features of its father and mother, however distorted and phantastic the resemblance may be . . ."

Before, with few exceptions, psychoanalysts had not explored the deeper layers of the unconscious in children, such exploration being considered too dangerous. Mrs. Klein, in the course of analyzing children as young as two years and nine months, obtained a direct picture of the phantasmagoric world of unconscious feeling. She described what she discovered in words, since "we cannot translate the language of the unconscious into consciousness without lending it words from our conscious realm," but emphasized that the infant felt these things "in much more primitive ways than language can express."[2]

What she discovered in very small children has great significance in enabling us to understand those infantile structures of the adult personality that are covered up in us by many years of self-disguise. In particular, her interpretation of the origin of elemental greed is of great relevance to the understanding of the acquisitiveness and possessiveness that in adulthood take the form of moneymaking.

Mrs. Klein came to the conclusion that the infant, having formed part of his mother in the prenatal state, has an innate feeling that there exists outside himself "something" that will give him all he needs and desires. "Under the dominance of the oral impulse," she says, "the breast is instinctively felt to be this source of nourishment and therefore, in a deeper sense, of life itself."[3]

The child in the womb has had all its needs taken care of; it is part of an idyllic union, which with the violence of birth comes to an end. The lost unity is the beginning of anxiety. With the trauma of separation the newly born child is embarked upon a life-and-death struggle for survival. From the beginning, it fears the annihilation of the self at the behest of the death instinct, whose operation, in the Kleinian canon, is innate. Hunger is its first representative, and when that is appeased, the breast—or its symbolic equivalent, the bottle— is felt to be good. But when the breast in some way is frustrating (the milk does not come fast enough, or plentifully enough, or not when it is most wanted), then it is felt to be bad. Faced with this fundamental duality, and the first bitter experience of its contradictory feelings, the baby splits its world; it divides its objects into good and bad, according to whether they satisfy it or not. This process, essential to its development at that stage, turns "the bad breast" into one of the devouring monsters of its fantastic inner world, and the "good breast" into a kind of guardian angel.

In this way, the emergent ego seeks to cope with the dangers that beset it. Inevitably, what such a split leads to is great exaggeration of both the "badness" and the "goodness" of the breast. It is out of this rudimentary organization that the next step occurs: the concept of a breast that is so "good" it will satisfy the ego's needs forever. This is what Klein called the "phantasy of the inexhaustible breast." This is the Promised Land, flowing with milk and honey, based on an image of what it was like *once,* inside the mother. Whether it was actually like that is another matter. Professor Norman Morris, a leading English obstetrician, says that the fetus in the womb may sometimes be under stress, and in the latter stages of pregnancy, when it may be short of oxygen, almost certainly is.[4] And Melanie Klein says that the universal longing for the prenatal state may well be based, in part, on idealization of the unity with the mother. Thus, perhaps, our unconscious memories of the womb are of an imaginary place, and express the tendency of the human mind to conceive of nirvana states of total contentment, peace and satisfaction that have no equivalent anywhere, and have never been known.

In these early vain yearnings for such a place and such a condition, I suggest we can see the beginnings of the desire for limitless riches. If this is so, it would explain why when great wealth *is* obtained it is never enough. If what has been sought under the guise of making a fortune is really an "inexhaustible breast" such as the baby's earliest wishful imaginings had conceived of, then it is obvious that all the money in the world cannot provide it. As Freud has said, *money* is not an infantile wish,[5] and this is why it cannot give us happiness; it beguiles us because being the most interchangeable of all commodities it can so easily be made to *stand* for other things, including "an inexhaustible source" such as we once craved. Because of its interest-bearing aspect, money is the nearest thing to such a source that we can put our hands on. Untouched capital can give us income and never be exhausted. Only in the psyche can we find something that comes closer: a bountiful and loving internal object created out of the imago of the mother.

But the kind of fortune seeker we are postulating is someone not very inwardly directed, who has a minimal awareness of internal reality, and must therefore seek all his satisfactions in the external world, in things that are the nearest equivalent he can find to the much-desired inner states of which he is hardly aware as such. However near an external source comes to appearing to meet his inner requirements for security, safety, love, it never can do so entirely, and this accounts for the way in which money doesn't satisfy. It does not satisfy insofar as it is a *substitute* for something that the infant greatly desired and could not have.

The tendency to reclusiveness that is sometimes a concomitant of great wealth, may be an attempt to recreate that imaginary condition of total isolation and total safety and comfort of the womb. There are millionaires who go to some lengths to try to produce those conditions. They live in luxury apartments, where everything is provided, so that they do not have to budge. A staff of servants is at their disposal twenty-four hours of the day to satisfy all their demands and needs. Instant gratification is the order of the day. In this luxury cocoon, they have created an artificial inexhaustible breast, and feel safe. Such is their dependence on it, and attachment to it, that exposing themselves to what they cannot control is something they avoid as much as possible.

When this reaches the extremes it has in the case of a Howard Hughes, it becomes obvious to everyone that there is something sick about such a way of living. In its milder and more common forms, it passes as "rich man's eccentricity." But even the most fabulous penthouse, the most devoted valets, chauffeurs, butlers, secretaries, cooks, mistresses, cannot in the end live up to nirvana nostalgia. It was not that good even in the womb; what has been so painstakingly reproduced is a kind of material artifact of a mental artifact.

A further complication arises in that the greatly desired flow of wealth quickly palls; the unstemmable bonanza seems to have a curiously jading effect on people. They become blasé; with limitless wealth, money becomes meaningless. "Money to burn" sums up this state of mind. If the origins of this craving are as I have suggested, then there is a very surprising explanation of why this kind of money turns out to be so unsatisfying and is sometimes actually despised for its unlimited abundance.

The displeasure with an excessively rich source has its parallel in a curious discovery of Melanie Klein's: she found that not only did the baby hate being frustrated, but, also, there sometimes appeared to be resentment of "the very ease with which the milk comes." This resentment of the good—biting the hand that feeds you—is one of the most puzzling and disturbing features of human nature. It is often observed that great kindness is rewarded by insults, hatred, contemptuousness; that generosity very often evokes ingratitude. This seemingly inexplicable phenomenon is accounted for in the Kleinian concept of envy. According to this, we envy that which does us good for the goodness that it is capable of doing. The more we long for something, the more value do we attribute to the capacity to satisfy that longing, and therefore the more do we envy the person who has that capacity. We desire to be fed, loved, sustained, supported, and so we envy the other person's ability to feed, love, sustain and support us. The better he does it, the more is he envied. And this envy has to be understood in its most fundamental sense: Dr. Elliott Jaques has pointed out the etymological root of the word in the Latin *invidia,* from the verb *invideo,* which means to look askance at, to look maliciously or spitefully into, to cast an evil eye upon, to envy or grudge anything. Envy wants to spoil the good, even when that good is being done to us. When we say of others that they are "too good for us," meaning it as an angry rebuke of their insufferable excellence, the tone of voice and the facial expression express exactly the envious resentment of their real or hypothetical goodness, which sometimes simply cannot be stood.

One can have an embarrassment of riches. If money has been too much desired, a wholly disproportionate value will be attributed to the source that provides it in such great abundance, as the breast is hated for the ease with which the milk flows: the sheer limitlessness of the source becomes too much envied to be borne, and a kind of protective blasé condition sets in. This is simply a way of devaluing the source in order that it need not be envied so much. The other side of Rockefeller's money-grabbing was that he felt oppressed by the money pouring in; it was a great burden, he said, alleviated only by his benefactions. Envy of the limitless source is alleviated by becoming that limitless source itself.

This point can be emphasized by postulating a reverse situation. A person who does not attach great value to money does not regard the source of it as so desirable that he envies its desirability; and so he does not feel impelled to become such a source himself, which means that he doesn't need to give his money away. This supports the paradoxical state of affairs that those who have most greedily desired money are sometimes the ones who feel most compelled to give it away. The identification with an inexhaustible source is a new way of explaining this phenomenon. The fact that one can continue to be such a source even after death is a factor too.

In the light of all this, it can be seen why making a fortune should often turn out to be such a curiously double-edged business, hardly ever affording the satisfactions and the pleasures that were so gaudily imagined in the dream. Some people are driven mad by money, some are destroyed by it, some are confused by it, have their heads turned or their hearts hardened; others are simply disturbed by money, or disappointed by it. A few thrive on it. The equivocal nature of the fortune must be related to the mixture of motives that has gone into its making.

A frequent discovery of the person who has *hit it* is that he cannot seem to grasp his new wealth. Mario Puzo, when he had made $1,000,000 out of *The Godfather,* complained that he had never actually *seen* this mythical sum. And many people in his position have found that, despite what their bank accounts say, they don't feel rich. Paul Getty once said, in a television interview: "I've never felt really rich—in the oil business others were all much richer than I was." He meant Texaco, Gulf Oil, BP, Shell, Standard Oil. The comparison may be a false one (comparing his personal wealth to the corporate wealth of great companies owned by thousands of shareholders), but it undoubtedly expresses his *feeling,* which, of course, is not a matter of quantitative differences in wealth, but clearly has other sources. Nothing could illustrate the power of these other sources so strikingly as the situation of the richest man in the world not feeling rich. It shows that the fortune seeker who is trying to realize "the phantasy of the inexhaustible source" in terms of money must fail even when he has in fact acquired limitless wealth. All the oil, the mansions, the statuary, the paintings, the wives, the private zoos, the fame, have not altered the misanthropic cast of Getty's face—it is the face of a man not given to ecstasies. In Citizen Kane tradition he appears to be dimly aware of some loss to which he cannot put a name.

It is the fairly common discovery of people who have made a lot of money that the anticipated satisfaction eludes them. Victor Lownes, Hugh Hefner's chief lieutenant in the European side of the *Playboy* empire, has made a personal fortune of $5,000,000. Among other things, he plays the stock market, and sometimes he wins. He says: "It happens to me that a flyer I take turns out, and I make a couple of hundred thousand dollars. One gets a feeling of considerable elation, and in a way it's kinda silly because it doesn't bring me anything I couldn't have had before."[6] In that sentence is expressed both the mysterious euphoria of the win, and the letdown of discovering that it is after all only money.

Another person who can testify to this experience is the author John Pearson. Some years ago he wrote a biography of Ian Fleming, and several American publishers were bidding for it. "One day," said Pearson, "my agent held a Dutch auction at the Ritz and when he came out the price had gone to around a quarter of a million dollars, and I remember walking up Regent Street and looking in the shops, and thinking, What can I buy with it? And suddenly there was nothing that I wanted."[7]

Such a state of mind doesn't usually persist—people do find things to buy (often it is only by spending it that it is possible to obtain a sense of *having* the money). The significance of Pearson's experience is that it expresses a common *feeling* about the unreality of sudden money. What will it buy? What good will it do me? And is this good good enough? And if not, how much more do I need in order to feel really good? Victor Lownes speculates on this matter as follows:

"Okay, Hef has a DC9, and I don't—every time he wants to go anywhere he has to plan it a couple of days ahead of time, got to get the pilots, they got to arrange their schedules, and I say: Am I not better off? All I've got to do is go out to the airport and get on a plane. Am I not in a way more mobile than he is? On the other hand, it's nice to have your own DC9. It's a luxurious means of travel, and you have the meals served on the plane that *you* want to have on the plane. It has the satisfaction of status, and other people admiring it, and you can invite your friends to go with you, which is an expansive and fun thing . . . I shouldn't mind having all these things, I shouldn't mind having a castle, or a house with forty servants like Hef has in California. I don't *hanker* for it, because I can rationalize it as an encumbrance. I can see both sides, I can see that I would like to have it, and I can see that I am able to rationalize not having it. So that I am left happy, as it were. It would be terrible to want it and not be able to have it and not be able to rationalize not having it. I am always looking for a bigger house, and I actually go out looking. I have estate agents who phone me and say they

believe they have just the right house for me. I always put in
too small a bid for the house. You see, I recognize that it's a
whole new bunch of problems if I get the house. It's stepping
up to a whole new level. Sometimes I think I'd like to step up
to that level, other times I think, What for? it's just an
encumbrance."[8]

In such ruminations one finds an ambivalence about money
and what it can bring that is not found in the dream or in the
quest. How can we account for this? Intense striving for anything produces a high state of tension, the relief of which in
the moment of achievement is felt as supreme pleasure. Freud
wrote, "What we call happiness in the strictest sense comes
from the (preferably sudden) satisfaction of needs which
have been dammed up to a high degree and it is from its
nature only possible as an episodic phenomenon. When any
situation that is desired by the pleasure principle is prolonged, it only produces a feeling of mild contentment."[9]

The fortune seeker is in the position of someone bent on
obtaining the money high as a permanent state; this turns out
to be impossible because "we are so made that we can derive
intense enjoyment only from a contrast and very little from a
state of things."[10] The man who has made his fortune finds,
in the words of Goethe, that "nothing is harder to bear than
a succession of fair days." A great deal of money is even harder
to bear because it is thought (by all those who are still seeking it, and therefore to some extent by the person who has
got it) that it *ought* to be satisfying, enriching in a real sense,
and the fact that it isn't is felt as a personal failure. This
applies only if the money has been dreamed of as some sort
of panacea in the first place; but of course the fortune seeker
does look upon it in this way.

There is another way in which money commonly fails; it
not only fails to bring certain promised forms of happiness,
it also puts to an end previous forms of happiness. The

novelist Lawrence Durrell once said, "The trouble with making money is that it enables you to pay other people to do for you things that you had previously enjoyed doing yourself. When I had no money I got great pleasure out of building a wall around my house in France. When I got some money for the film rights of my *Alexandria Quartet* I was able to pay somebody else to build the wall, and as soon as this was the case I no longer enjoyed doing it myself."[11]

The ramifications of this are almost limitless. As people get more and more money, they are relieved of all sorts of tasks that they had previously derived satisfaction from doing themselves. Cooks, chauffeurs, gardeners, nannies, private tutors, social secretaries, assistants, aides, can in the end deprive the newly rich of a large proportion of what they once regarded as their lives.

There is a story of a man who loved boats and the sea, and eventually got his own luxury motorboat on which he used to take people on charter cruises. It was a life that he loved, and since he was an extremely capable skipper he was always in demand—so much so, that soon he was having to turn down business because there weren't enough months in the year to accept all the charters he was offered. So somebody said to him, why don't you buy another boat, and offered to put up the money. The second boat also did very well. And soon the skipper had a third, and then a fourth. In a matter of a few years he was running a prosperous cruise and charter company. But now the job of running it took up all his time, and he hardly ever went to sea himself. Money had turned the sea skipper into a glorified clerk.

Many an architect has had the experience of becoming so successful that he finds himself doing less and less designing, becoming instead an administrator and costing clerk. In this way the original love is sacrificed for the sake of the higher return, which people feel unable to refuse because the whole burden of social propaganda is to the effect that the money is what counts. It requires a unique kind of resolution to be able to turn down a prospect of higher profits for the sake of keeping the more satisfying and rewarding work—and this is often the case even when the person's present earnings are more than ample for his needs, and going for the higher returns has no meaning other than fortune-seeking. The belief is that the fortune will give him something once dreamed of. It is this type of person who is shattered when it doesn't. He finds that he has made the sacrifice of his real love for some illusory concept of richness.

These are all instances of money not bringing an expected satisfaction or spoiling a previous one; there are also times when its effect can be positively damaging.

It is always difficult to prove that any one thing in somebody's life is related to any other thing, but there is a kind of mysterious appositeness that can often be noticed in these matters, which gives one reason to reject the explanation of pure coincidence. It does seem unlikely, for instance, that what happened to Rockefeller in the heyday of his acquisitiveness was purely coincidental. From 1890 to 1896 the earnings of Standard Oil were rising from $19 million to $34 million a year, and he was getting his reputation for grasping and greedy ruthlessness, which led one writer (Ida Tarbell in *McClure's Magazine*) to say "he has turned commerce . . . to war, and honeycombed it with cruel and corrupt practices." There is a kind of Dantean justness in the fact that at the same time, between the ages of fifty-one and fifty-seven, he suddenly aged; he became stooped and portly, his face took on deep lines, and he lost all his hair, as a result of the nervous disease known as generalized alopecia. After 1890 he was constantly complaining of nervous fatigue and of digestive ailments. It is no use attributing these ailments to the stress of struggle. In 1890 he was already sufficiently invulnerable financially to be able to give away $303,542, and in 1896, $1,881,649.[12] However unlikely it may seem, one has to allow the possibility that the bonanza itself was having the adverse effect: the money trauma.

Before going on to examine what the causal factors might be, it is worth noting a more readily understood variant of this phenomenon: the person who "drives himself mad" in the course of making his pile. Money was almost certainly a factor in Lord Northcliffe's mental breakdown. In Paul Ferris's *The House of Northcliffe* one sees the extent to which the British press baron's manias fed on his wealth. He could speak and act with indifference to other people's feelings and rights because of the protection that his great wealth afforded him. It even "protected" him from any possibility of medical attention for his deteriorating mental condition, since men of such wealth cannot be told that they are out of their minds. However disgracefully, and insanely, he behaved, there were people prepared to put up with it, in effect to collude with him in representing his actions as sane. Money, by freeing him from conventional constraints, removed whatever checks to his manias there had once been. His nephew, Cecil King, for many years chairman of the *Daily Mirror* group of newspapers and magazines in Britain said:[13] "I was brought up amid several uncles who had made themselves multimillionaires and exceedingly miserable. Like some people took to drink (and they took to that too), they took to making money."

There is continuous evidence in newspaper stories of people suffering money traumas. A headline in the London *Times* read: "Man who tried to give fortune away found dead." A young man, Michael Brody, the inheritor of a fortune which he tried to give away, had been found dead in Ashokan, New York. He had apparently placed a hunting rifle between his knees and shot himself in the head. Another headline read:

"Success killed business man." David Crossley, a Londoner, was building up his business a little too rapidly. He became anxious and depressed, and killed himself. The coroner said: "This business succeeded quite considerably and the effect has been to put him under pressure and this caused depression." Other headlines tell of "recluse who had $150,000 but lived in $4 room," and of "Recluse's $400,000 Estate found after he is buried in Potter's Field" and of a theft victim who "rues fortune left in closet."

Anthony Sampson wrote in his *New Anatomy of Britain* that after Jack Cotten had formed the biggest property company in the world, he began to show increasing signs of megalomania, and ill-health; in 1963 he sold all his shares, and died the next year.

Lionel Bart, the composer of *Oliver* who made millions and lost every penny, said: ". . . being wealthy was more than I could cope with."[14] A disc jockey, Simon Dee, for a while found himself "riding the wild horse of success" but money threw him: "I didn't know where I was . . . it was a spiral, an incredible spiral, but I couldn't handle it, of course . . . I didn't understand money . . . it was just fantasy . . . like a chameleon adopting the colour of its environment we adopted the colour of our income . . . money is such a corrupter of morals, God it corrupts people . . ."[15] He ended up broke, and on the dole. The novelist Michael Crichton said:[16] "And suddenly you find yourself with a lot of money and you must make some accommodation to it. My response initially was to pretend that none of this had happened. I didn't spend any money . . . I sound like this experience is a curse. I don't think it's a curse. I think it's great. It's worth it. I *think*." He added: "I don't think there's any question: you can get wrecked by this success. It opens up all kinds of corrupting power . . ."

Even animals, who under normal circumstances have nothing corresponding to a money system, are capable of being "corrupted" in this way. The zoologist Desmond Morris did an experiment that introduced the "profit motive" to apes. He first of all got them to draw and paint, and he found that they were doing lovely things. Then he started rewarding them with peanuts for their work. Morris said wryly: "Soon they were doing any old scrawl to get the peanuts. I had introduced commercialism into the ape's world, and ruined him as an artist."[17]

How are we to account for the fact that something so eagerly desired by so many people, and believed in as a kind of cure-all, when obtained should have a range of effects varying from the disappointing to the traumatic? What is the psychological mechanism that produces the backlash? Must it always happen? And if not, what are the requirements if the fortune is to be of benefit rather than harm?

Light is thrown on these questions by the work of Dr. Elliott Jaques. Jaques combines several disciplines: he is a doctor of medicine, a university professor, a practicing psychoanalyst, and the inaugurator and consultant of a special management project at The Glacier Metal Company in Britain. Bringing together the knowledge derived from these various roles, he has come to the surprising conclusion that we each know unconsciously exactly how much we are worth, and that trouble occurs when there is a departure from this self-evaluation either upwards or downward. He writes:

"When overpayment . . . is experienced for any length of time, guilt and anxiety set in. Compulsive expenditure with purchasing characterised by waste and ugliness ensues—expenditure described by the economist as naïve ostentation beyond the norm of conspicuous consumption. Or an equally compulsive hoarding may occur."[18]

Underpayment, as one would expect, also has its particular

consequences, but we are here concerned with the question of why overpayment—as it is manifested in the making of a fortune—should have an adverse effect. By what criteria can one arrive at the awareness of having been overpaid? What *is* too much, and how can we know that it is?

Jaques has formulated a highly original theory on the basis of which the work load carried by an individual, and therefore the level of reward to which he feels himself to be entitled, can be measured. Basically, what he says is that the burden of work may be defined in terms of the length of time that the individual carries sole responsibility for his task; he calls this "the time-span of discretion." He found that "people at the same time-span feel entitled to by and large the same pay; the longer the time-span the higher the payment to which they feel entitled." Why should this be so?

The real work burden that anyone has to carry is uncertainty. The more uncertain the outcome of something, the harder it is to bear. This is because uncertainty means the deferment and the possible loss of the desired gratification. Small children are almost totally incapable of such deferment —they want it now. Later, longer periods of uncertainty become tolerable. Jaques says you can actually get a good indication of a child's future capacities from the age at which it is able to forego some immediate gratification in favor of greater gratification the next day. Further development then becomes a matter of being able to increase the length of time that one is able to bear postponement of gratification. What we call leadership or initiative or strength of character or, for that matter, innovative genius is fundamentally a matter of being able to carry the burden of decision—that is, not knowing the outcome—longer than others. Small children engaged in a task require immediate reassurance that what they are doing is right, approved of, or desired. We recognize this by providing them with more or less constant supervision. The teacher or parent giving his decision (even a negative decision is a relief) enables the child to venture on the next period of uncertainty.

In some people these periods are never greatly increased. In adult life they constantly have to be supervised, reassured, led, urged on. They can carry only a light burden of work. Jaques says: "The psychological sensation of weight of responsibility is just as 'real' a sensation as the sensation of warmth. We have all experienced it. We know when we feel the weight is too heavy, and we feel worried, oppressed and overburdened. Equally we know when the weight is becoming lighter, and when it has become too light; oppression and worry turn into relief, which turns into boredom and lack of interest . . ."[19] Jaques believes that it is possible to measure the differing sensations of the lightness and heaviness of the work burden in terms of the length of time a person has to shoulder it by himself without the relief of somebody else's intervention. And he believes that what is felt to be proper payment is related to this time-span.

What we generally regard as the higher and more difficult tasks in life are those that call for the longest periods of sole discretion. A window-cleaner's work is very soon subjected to the inspection and judgment of others; a shoeshine boy's time-span of discretion is even shorter. But as we move up the scale of tasks, we find that people have to "carry the can" for progressively longer periods—the foreman for longer than the workman; the manager for longer than the foreman. A managing director may have to bear two- or three-year periods of uncertainty before his work is vindicated or found wanting; a Prime Minister or President, five- or ten-year periods, or longer. As work becomes more demanding, the period of time that elapses before its outcome can be known increases. Certain statesmen, leaders, artists, innovators will *never* know the outcome of their work; only history will be able to judge it, and this is the supreme burden. A genius is someone who "operates in a time-span longer than his own span of life."

It is a theory of considerable originality, and Jaques has empirical evidence to support it. He claims to be able to "time-span" any individual on the basis of fairly simple questioning. He asks him to write down on a piece of paper the earnings to which he feels entitled on his present job, irrespective of whether he is getting more or less in actual fact. Then he asks some questions about his work, that is, he finds out the length of time this person carries sole responsibility for his tasks, and on this basis he is able to deduce within a small margin of error what level of earnings the man has written down as being his proper entitlement.

The significance of Jaques's theory in the present context is that if we know the weight of the work burden that we carry by comparison with others, we also know what our proper reward should be in relation to them. This means that if we are rewarded grossly beyond our entitlement, we suffer a variety of stress symptoms because we feel ourselves to be cheating others of their due, and fear their revenge. This would explain why making a fortune is so often productive of paranoia. To counter these persecutory fears, the rich man has to make himself still richer, so as to make himself invulnerable. But the richer he gets, the more he has to fear from those whom he is depriving of richness. This is the way to reclusiveness or megalomania, or both.

We might say that the trauma of wealth occurs when there is a sudden deluge of money out of proportion to the work put in, using the term "work" in the strict sense in which we have defined it. This is why artists, writers, show-business people, gamblers, speculators, promoters, all those liable to overnight riches, are so peculiarly prone to this kind of trauma: in their hearts they feel they are not worth it; they feel themselves to be cheats and frauds who are going to be found out, who are going to be brought down in the end and punished for their hubris. The fact that they may have arrived at a *false* sense of their own worth, because of their particular neuroses, either grossly undervaluing or overvaluing themselves, is a further complication. Some people can survive sudden money because in their gargantuan capacity for self-aggrandizement they can make themselves believe they are worth it. Their awareness of not being worth it is banished into the depths of their unconscious, and only manifests itself in the form of psychosomatic illnesses of the kind that afflicted a Rockefeller, or in self-destructive behavior of the kind that many successful show-business people resort to. Typically, such people feel better when they have got rid of some of their money.

The question then arises: Can someone ever be justified in feeling that he is worth millions, and therefore be immune to the adverse consequences of making a fortune?

Jaques says that the entrepreneur's work* is taking the risk of whether or not what he produces will be wanted; this is the uncertainty that he has to bear. And insofar as his risk is big enough, his return can be in proportion without being felt to be excessive. The difficulty of measuring a proper return for anyone engaged in entrepreneurial work is that the entrepreneur sets his own tasks, and therefore it is extremely difficult for anyone else to tell how much risk he is really taking, and over what period of time. But in theory, at least, it would be conceivable that someone who engenders projects the ultimate consequences of which will not be known in his own lifetime carries such an enormous work load that even limitless financial rewards are not felt as being fraudulent.

What kind of pattern can be extrapolated in the case of such an outcome? First, it may be assumed that the *money*

---

* In Jaques's definition, anyone in business for himself—i.e., not a wage earner —is an entrepreneur. Thus writers, artists, musicians, would be entrepreneurs.

was not too greatly desired, was not endowed with magical curative properties. If nothing magical was expected of it, it can be appreciated for what it does bring, instead of being despised on account of all the things that it doesn't. The true risk-taker will have a large capacity to tolerate uncertainty, a fundamental factor in all creative work; this being so, he will not be looking to money to alleviate the anxiety of not knowing, he will not try to buy assurance for himself, and he will not go in for any of the follies or vanities whose purpose is to prop up a shaky self-esteem. If he is not dependent on money in a neurotic way, he will be able to use it coolly as an instrument of his purpose, and derive from that the satisfaction that comes from the effective and accurate use of any powerful tool.

The concept of "good" and "bad" money is borne out by certain emotional feelings that are more or less general. The universal disdain in which usury is held reflects the awareness that money made out of money (with the minimum of risk and no creativeness) is a barren kind of profit. Equally, the *rentier* and the absentee landlord are poorly thought of, because whether we realize it or not, we regard unearned income as the lowest sort. On the other hand, we tend not to begrudge the inventor his royalties, because we recognize the investment he has made in terms of the risk that his invention will not turn out successful.

We appear to have an innate sense of what form of money-making is "good" and what form of it is "bad." Aristotle sought to define the basis on which such a judgment was arrived at.[20] He considered that getting a livelihood was in accordance with nature. It was part of what he called household-management. The natural way of making money was for the purpose of obtaining those things needed in order to live one's life. Hunting and piracy are justified "where people are living the life that their need compels them to. Getting a living in this self-supporting way is clearly given by nature herself to all her creatures . . ." If people seek goods that are necessary to their lives, this is not unnatural "because the amount of property of this kind which would give financial independence adequate for a good life is not limitless . . ." Therefore a certain kind of property-getting is the natural duty of those in charge of a house or a city. But there is something else, that he calls "moneymaking," which is the pursuit of limitless riches, and this he considers unnatural. "Because it closely resembles the form of acquisition we have been discussing, many suppose that the two are one and the same. But they are not the same . . . one is natural, the other is not."

What he considers unnatural is moneymaking to which there is no limit because wealth and getting money are themselves the end. "All those who are amassing wealth in the form of coin go on increasing their pile without limit . . . the end is sheer increase. Some people . . . imagine that increase is the function of household management and never cease to believe that their store of money ought to be hoarded or increased without limit." He condemns interest because it is "money produced out of money" and of all the ways of getting wealth "this is the most contrary to nature."

But Aristotle also emphasizes the importance of the motive. To illustrate this, he tells the story of the philosopher Thales who proved that someone of his calling can also be a practical man.[21] By utilizing his knowledge of the stars he was able to foretell an excellent crop of olives while it was still winter. He raised a little capital with which he paid deposits on all the oil presses in Miletus and Chios, in this way securing an option on their hire. It cost him only a small amount, as there were no other bidders at that time of year. Then when the time of the oil harvest came, there was a sudden demand for oil presses, and since he had secured rights in all of them he was able to hire them out for any amount that he chose to ask.

Thus, concludes Aristotle, even philosophers can get rich. And he advises that the best way of getting rich is by securing a monopoly. Thales is not censured because getting rich "is not his object in life."

Thales' method is indistinguishable from any other money-maker's, but his motive is different, and it is the motive that defines the act. Similarly, Kierkegaard's knight of infinity, who hasn't two pennies to rub together, reflects: "Yes, if the money were needed, I dare say I could get it."[22] Motive is everything, and this is in line with modern psychological thought. Whether a man is crushed, corrupted, destroyed, driven mad, or revitalized by his fortune is largely a matter of his motive in seeking it.

4
Uses

What can the person who has made a fortune actually get for his money?

In 1971, an Iranian oilman named Henri Sabat paid $415,800 for a fragile-looking Louis XVI table and became the owner of the most expensive (and most useless?) piece of furniture in the world.

Back in 1895 when George W. Vanderbilt came into his fortune at the age of twenty-six, he built himself a French Renaissance château, near Asheville, North Carolina, at a cost of $7,000,000. It had 250 rooms, which in design and furnishings copied the grandiosity of Fontainebleau and Versailles. Rich Americans have often shown a penchant for shipping the splendors of a bygone Europe across the Atlantic, to fix up their Californian or Texan places with a little imported class.

Paul Getty, who is careful about telephone calls and once sent ten dollars to a nuns' charity, bought Titian's "The Death of Actaeon" for a little over $4,000,000—but in the end was not allowed to send it out of Britain. A Velásquez, "Juan de Pareja," went for $5,544,000.

For $7,125 you could have got a jeroboam (equivalent of six bottles) of Château Mouton Rothschild 1929, which would work out at about $170 a glass. You could have got a 16½" × 12½" Van Gogh still life of a vase of flowers for $320,000. If you had produced a banker's card guaranteeing that you had $2½ million you would have been allowed to bid for the world's third-largest uncut gem, the Star of Sierra Leone (970 carats) when it came up for auction. For about $250,000, you might have got a Henry Moore bronze. You could have had a Moorfields carpet designed by Robert Adam for $23,000 and a T'ang dynasty horse for $20,000 to $25,000. For just under $100,000 you could have had the best state-room on the *SS France* on its journey around the world. All this, in the recent past.

In the thirties, when everything was cheaper, you could have got an entree into the higher levels of American politics for a mere $25,000—this was the amount that Joe Kennedy contributed to Roosevelt's campaign fund. (He also lent the Democratic party $50,000 and raised a further $100,000 among his friends. He was aggrieved when Roosevelt did not immediately offer him a post in his government, though he did later get the job of American ambassador in London.) [1] By doubling the outlay, you could have got a sure thing. The sugar magnate Henry O. Havemeyer testified to the United States Industrial Commission that he habitually contributed to both political parties, thereby ensuring the certainty of protection of his interests.

You could also ensure that you would win at tennis—or any other game. It was generally known that the newspaper magnate William Randolph Hearst expected to win when he played tennis, and he usually did. Considering that he carried his insistence on winning into old age, and that his way of playing was not to move very much but, so to speak, to will the balls to come to him, his opponents had to exercise considerable skill to ensure that he always did win.

It has been said about the very rich that they are the same as other people, but their toys are bigger. Sir Max Rayne is intrigued by a watch that is said to be the most expensive watch in the world. "Not because it is the most expensive watch in the world, but because if what they claim for it is true, it sounds like the most accurate watch in the world . . . of course nobody needs that much accuracy. What I am interested in really is perfection . . ." His attitude to the use of money is that if he employed a hundred people to look after his personal needs, to see that he was clothed and washed and fed, that would be inexcusably extravagant, because it would be a wastage of human resources. "But," he says, "if I go out and spend £20,000 on a painting I have merely re-arranged the position of a certain paper sum of money, which has not involved any kind of wastage of anybody's resources."[2]

The expenditure of money in the pursuit of perfection is the traditional sport of the rich. And, of course, they don't have to wait. Their money enables them to *have it now*. The film maker Otto Preminger once went into a gaming club and seeing that all the places at the baccara table where he wished to play were occupied, offered one of the players $500 for his chair, rather than wait until one became vacant.

The rich can make others fit in with their plans. If they change their minds, a lot of people simply have to change their schedules. "Having money," says one businessman, "gives you the right to say 'tomorrow' to people. If you step off a plane for an appointment, and are feeling tired, you can pick up the phone and say, 'Let's make it tomorrow.' " The rich are not perturbed about doing that sort of thing to others, and whether it is a business conference or a social appointment, a party, a dinner, the opera, a ball, a wedding, a safari, they do not hesitate to cancel if they are not in the mood. They can delegate the everyday frustrations of life to someone else to deal with. A man with a progressive view of women's rights explained that in his household his wife was of course as free as he was to pursue her professional and other interests. And who looked after the household? "Oh, we get a woman in who does that," he replied.

At its most recherché, the life of the rich becomes a work of art, with money as their paintbrush. Where they spend their summers or winters, how they redecorate their houses, the kind of food they serve at dinner, the clothes they wear, the guests that they mix at their parties, the people that they marry or sleep with, their dogs and their children and their protégés—these are the materials and the choices out of which they construct their masterpiece. When Scott Fitzgerald said "the rich are different from the rest of us" he did not just mean that they have more money. Certainly, the rich can be enticing to the outsider, as the following vignette of the high life may or may not show.[3]

Principessa Marizina Odescalchi, the beautiful thirty-eight-year-old daughter of an Italian match tycoon, was brought up in a castle, looked after by an English nanny and educated privately in Switzerland. She lives in Rome in a fourteenth-century palazzo, has a castle thirty-seven kilometers from the city, another in Turin, a house in Cortina, and an apartment in Paris. In Rome she will spend hours lying on a big bed covered in guanaco fur telephoning friends and financiers, buying and selling shares, talking to Cabinet Ministers, arranging parties, or arranging to go to them. While she attends to such matters, a young man, "who looks like a younger Maximilian Schell," attends her. He is someone she met at a party at Cap Ferrat last summer, and he has been around ever since. Her husband the prince does not live with her. They are friends, she explains, but do not live together. They have

an arrangement. Sometimes they meet for tea in one of
Rome's fashionable teashops. Her husband also lives in a
palace, even grander than hers—Bernini did it, she says. And
he has a castle in the country, too. What does he do? "Nothing." He spends his time shooting. Deers and wild pigs and
pheasants. She and her friends are apparently very charming,
and they vote for the Fascists because they are terrified that
if the Communists came in their entire life might go. Without their money and their titles (already officially abolished
but still usable socially), what would they be?

"Without money I'm nothing," says Glenn Turner, an
evangelical American moneymaker, who sells do-it-yourself
courses on how to be great and make fortunes like himself.
He teaches people to stand before their mirrors and say each
morning: "I'm so great, I'm so great, I'm so great," until they
have mesmerized themselves into believing it. Thousands of
people pay thousands of dollars in the hope that Turner will
make them great through money. He plays on the feelings
and fears that make a certain type of man say: "Don't give me
all that bullshit about Professor Einstein, how much did he
ever *make?* My business earns more money in one year than
all your Professor Einsteins put together earn in their whole
lifetime." In such utterances it is not difficult to catch the
forlorn cry of someone frightened by his own sense of nothingness, and desperately trying to counteract it by telling himself
how great he is because he makes money. What is really
envied by such a person, what makes him feel nothing and
therefore in need of the therapy of riches, is that he believes,
rightly or wrongly, that there are some people who have the
truly valuable life-stuff—courage, ability to face up to and
master vicissitudes, creativity. His real or imagined lack of
these qualities means that he needs money to buy not only the
material comforts, or the sybaritic life, but, most importantly,
a sense of himself. He can buy fame.

Victor Lownes says of Hugh Hefner: "Hef needs to be a famous person. Fame is important to Hef. Being recognized on the street is important to him. We spent $1,000,000 for a television show which is not a commercially successful thing, but the exposure that it gave to Hef personally as the master of ceremonies on this TV show week after week gave him a certain kind of identity that no publisher has ever had in America. I mean, nobody would recognize Henry Luce, were he still alive, if he were strolling down the street, but Hefner and his pipe is preeminently recognizable. Now Hefner really needs this kind of recognition. I have a lot of friends who are recognizable celebrities in the film world and it gives them an extra quality; they have a certain electricity, plus that it's sexually attractive too."[4]

The rich and famous person doesn't have to explain who he is, because everybody knows. The late George Sanders claimed he was so forgetful that he not only forgot other people's names, but also his own. "Fortunately," he said, "since I was well known, they could always tell me who I was." The celebrity is spared the irksome form-filling aspects of life—he does not have to begin every encounter with a ritualistic fencing to establish who he is and who the other person is, and who has to defer to whom. Since his identity has been previously established, there is no danger of an embarrassing mistake occurring, such as somebody failing to realize his true standing. Also, the alleviation of their fear of the unknown makes people respond more warmly, more trustingly, to a well-known person; he is not a total stranger. This, in turn, is agreeable for him, for it generates the sort of superficial warmth that is conveyed in the smile of recognition, and he can derive from that a comforting sense of being loved or well liked. It is also useful insofar as people who know you, or think they do, tend to give you better service, because they already have a sort of relationship with you on the basis of their imagined knowledge. The rich man who is also famous derives the benefit of that. Hotel doormen and managers, waiters, taxi drivers, bell boys, telephone operators, and public officials, and all sorts of other people, treat him in accordance with the image they have formed of him. They may like him or hate him on the basis of what they have heard, but in encountering him they will almost certainly treat him as someone of importance.

Fame, then, is a way of counteracting the deep dread of being nobody and nothing. The person who lacks an inner sense of identity, because he has ruthlessly jettisoned his identifications, dispensing with once-admired models that now hold him up, such a person having no inner knowledge of who he is, must get it from outside. To be famous is to be somebody, in the familiar phrase of countless movies. It affords confirmation of one's existence, something that one movie star could only get from seeing himself on the screen, and this applied to his private life too. The man who is rich and famous needs the publicity so that he can turn to reports of his doings and activities to know that he is alive and well.

Money, of course, is famous for opening doors. Even the doors of the Kremlin respond to it. When the banker David Rockefeller (Chase Manhattan) took his family on a visit to Russia some years ago, he received a message that Khrushchev would like to see him at the Kremlin the following afternoon. The two men had a long talk. In 1973 Rockefeller opened a branch of the Chase Manhattan at 1 Karl Marx Square, Moscow.

Nobody is in any doubt about the kind of power that money can exercise. Sir Max Rayne says, "I remember as a young man I used to think that it was appalling for any one man to have £1,000,000 a year of income to dispose of, because of the power that gave him." Today, through his trusts and foundations, Rayne is in a position to dispense money on this scale. "One can make one's opinions felt," he acknowledges, "and I can indulge some personal predilections. For example, I can decide that it is important for the National Gallery to buy a Cézanne, and I can do something about that. But in Britain money does not give you direct power in the way it does in America. What goes on there is frightening. Money power is exercised on the highest levels."[5]

In the wake of Watergate, nobody would question that. What is perhaps less realized is the extent to which money can be used quite legally and respectably to affect events. A House of Representatives Report of 1962 revealed how the Ford Foundation used tax-free earnings in direct competition with tax-paying banks to lend money to selected companies at preferential rates of interest. In one case, this was as low as 2.65 percent on a $3,000,000 twenty-year loan.[6] In this way, clearly, the normal process of commercial competition can be interfered with. It is possible to favor one company at the expense of its rivals in the field, who have to raise money at the usual rates of interest and whose goods therefore are likely to cost more. Simply the movement of money, when as in the case of the Ford Foundation assets amount to billions, can be carried out for a specific purpose.

Then, too, there is the fact that recipients of foundation grants must be ideologically acceptable to the donors. Foundations that make grants to universities, museums, research institutes, hospitals, study groups, have an important say in the type of study that will be pursued and in the appointment of personnel; in this way money can determine the broad course of action that will be followed. It was largely the money of Rockefeller foundations that financed the Kinsey Report, whose social consequences have been immeasurable.

Without suggesting that such money power is necessarily used in a Machiavellian way, it is evident that by means of grants, subsidies, secret financing, a particular bias can be given to events. The Central Intelligence Agency, for instance, makes use of foundations as a cover for some of its tendentious financing activities, meant to contribute to the realization of specific long-term objectives.

All positive uses of money depend on the possession of considerable skills. Professor Jaques, rebutting the notion that any fool can spend, insists on the contrary that it takes abilities of the highest order. He says,[7] "The Ford Foundation employs the highest level of people in the United States to give money away." And he believes that on a personal level, too, spending money in excess of a certain amount is work, calling for as high a level of ability as making money. "I've been through the exercise of assessing the amount of work it takes to spend $250,000 a year. You're in business. You're in the spending business."

The distinction that Jaques is making is between spending and squandering. Anyone can get rid of money in wild and reckless ways, and criminals are famous for doing so. It is spending money so as to derive some real use from it that is hard. Jaques talks of "the quality of spending," and he says that spending becomes senseless squandering when the amount of money that a person has is greater than his capacity to spend it.

"The lottery winners, what do they do with the £200,000? What do they do with it? They can't spend it, can they? They may *squander* it. So you go out and buy a £15,000 yacht, so what? What the hell do you do with it then? What they discover is that if you buy an expensive yacht you've got to know how to hire people. You have to be able to employ a staff. And if you, as an employer, don't have a greater capacity than your staff, what happens is that you get taken for a ride. This is what happens to your gold strike people. They can't control their money, they don't know what to do with it, so they are swindled."[8]

Among the positive uses to be derived from money by some-one possessing a high capacity for spending, enlightened patronage is perhaps the most valuable. Great patrons like the Medicis of Florence enriched the entire world. The same can be said of three aristocratic Viennese patrons who pro-vided Beethoven with a regular income, since his music did not earn him enough to live on.

The use of money for entertaining, for the creation of artistic, political or scientific circles, where ideas can develop out of a particular social mix, has been one of the more useful functions of great hosts and hostesses. In a few cases, such use of money in party-giving would deserve to be called inspired.

Also, money is very useful inasmuch as it frees the person who possesses it from the pursuit of money. It was a million-aire President of the United States, Franklin Delano Roose-velt, who brought in the far-reaching reforms of the New Deal, which caused the dyed-in-the-wool rich to accuse him of being a Communist and a traitor to his class. Likewise, John F. Kennedy, as a Senator, was sufficiently free of personal monetary considerations to be able repeatedly to vote against his own financial interests, on oil and gas issues, for example.[9] A few wealthy men of this type have benefited mankind by what they have done with their money, but it is rare, since wealth and the ability to use it are only coincidentally related.

Finally, what must be regarded as the most characteristic use of money today is as a barometer of success. The size of the purse determines the prize-fighter's rank. *Succès d'estime* can be a rare delicacy, but it is tame compared with full-blooded money success. Norman Mailer, hoping for an enor-mous sale for his 1955 novel *The Deer Park,* was "waiting for the quick transfusions of a generous success" to lift him out of a feeling of emptiness. When the big sales did not material-ize, he felt, "I had no magic so great as to hasten the time of the apocalypse . . . something God-like in my confidence began to leave, and I was reduced in dimension if now less a boy."[10] It is a frank admission of what is sometimes expected of money success, and on this occasion was not obtained— though he got it all later.

The superstar must get his million-dollar fee to feel God-like. The money coming in is a communication of esteem in a language that cannot damn with faint praise, cannot hem and haw, equivocate. Money can't change its mind. It is the chieftain's headdress, and you can't argue with it. As such, it is sought most fervently by all those whose self-doubts make them crave official confirmation of their position. At the same time, it is the hallucinogenic that can lift depressions or arouse to action and the opiate that can quieten and calm.

PART TWO
Money Types

5

The Romantic

It is put forward in this section that there exist definite money types. Nobody would dispute the existence of the miser type and that he is what he is because of his character make-up, rather than circumstances. My argument is that other less extreme money attitudes also arise out of character and produce the type of person who must hustle for a living, or the type who must idealize his moneymaking as a romantic adventure, or the type who must hide his sense of shame about money by assuming the mask of the company man.

I am postulating these basic money types: the romantic, the company man, the collector, the hustler, the double-dealer, the criminal, the gambler, the loser, the non-player. Of course, nobody is wholly of one type rather than another; everybody has opposing traits in him. When I describe someone as a money romantic, this does not mean he may not also have something of the criminal or company man in him. It means only that his *predominant* characteristics are such as to place him in the category of the romantic. Overlapping is bound to occur. There is also movement from one category to another. The romantic may become a loser. The hustler may become a criminal. The company man may tear off the mask of the company and strike out for himself, reveling in the romance of moneymaking. All the categories that I am postulating are open-ended and fluid; but I believe it can be shown that there are patterns in people's money behavior which can be related to their character make-up, and that there is a sufficiently constant correlation between character and behavior to justify speaking of money types.

The first of these, in the typology that I am putting forward, is the romantic, by which I mean someone who idealizes and overestimates his beloved, in this case, money. "Let me kiss thee," said Volpone to his gold, exemplifying the displaced ecstasy of the type, "thou being best of things, and far transcending all style of joy: such are thy beauties and our loves."[1]

If the fortune, generally speaking, can have the meaning of an inexhaustible source of whatever it is that the individual craves or needs, to the romantic it is predominantly a source of love. To him money is applause, vindication, approval, the expression of fate's favoritism. He is someone who derives from monetary reward the kind of joy that others obtain from being in love, or from their children, or from the love of God, or from art, or from devotion to a cause or calling, or from recognition.

The Alfred Krupp (1812–1887) under whom the fortunes of the Krupps made their biggest leap forward was someone for whom money was overvalued in this way. When Krupp's mother, who had doted on him, died, he wrote: "Two things alone can move me, honour and prosperity," and as this event involved neither, he turned quickly to the firm's new line in teaspoons. So tied was he to the business that when he finally married, he built his wife a home in the middle of his steelworks. From a little glassed-in lookout he could peer out and observe the workers coming through the factory gates, and make a note of any latecomers. Clouds of oily grit and soot had soon put his bride's trousseau past saving and stained all their fresh linen, but what did that matter, since he was making so much money? The action of the heavy steamhammers smashed all the glasses on the sideboard and made the *Gartenhaus,* as it was euphemistically called, tremble. But to Krupp it was the sweet music of moneymaking. When his wife, on one occasion, asked to be taken to a concert, he replied: "Sorry, it's impossible! I must see that my smokestacks continue to smoke, and when I hear my forge tomorrow that will be music more exquisite than the playing of all the world's fiddles."[2]

This is the essence of money love. A person in the grip of it sees himself as a merchant adventurer, or an oil king, or a cattle baron, or an empire-builder, or at worst as a *prince* of thieves. The Canadian-born press baron Lord Beaverbrook, a bold apologist for the buccaneering spirit of business, gave an indication of how such men looked upon their moneymaking. He wrote:

"A man must feel those early deals right down to the pit of his stomach if he is going to be a great man of business. They must shake the very fibre of his being as the conception of a great picture shakes the artist. The money brain is, in the modern world, the supreme brain. Why? Because that which the greatest number of men strive for will produce the fiercest competition of intellect."[3] The American dream is founded on these principles.

If popular culture regards making good, in financial terms, as the supreme achievement, the romantic folly of this notion has been the consistent theme of the critics of that culture.

Probably the key novel of the American dream turning bad is still Scott Fitzgerald's *The Great Gatsby.* Its theme is the confusion of love and money. Gatsby, the poor boy from nowhere, falls in love with Daisy's voice, which is "full of money . . . that was the inexhaustible charm that rose and fell in it, the jingle of it, the cymbals' song of it . . . High in a white palace the king's daughter, the golden girl . . ." From the beginning, love and money seem to be somehow interchangeable. Gatsby believes he can win Daisy by making himself enormously rich. It is the illusion upon which he constructs his life:

"The most grotesque and fantastic conceits haunted him in his bed at night. A universe of ineffable gaudiness spun itself in his brain . . . Each night he added to the pattern of his fancies until drowsiness closed down upon some vivid scene with an oblivious embrace."

Bob Guccione, the Brooklyn-born founder-photographer of the *Penthouse* girlie empire, is a man who has made the universe of ineffable gaudiness a daily and nightly reality. Starting from nothing, he has in a matter of a few years created a business valued at $75,000,000, and proudly declares that it is all his, as he has no bank loans, no backers, no stockholders. In the U.S., his magazine sells over two million copies, and is the fastest-growing publication in American publication history, having achieved this sale in less than three years. For every five copies sold by *Playboy,* which has been established for twenty years, Guccione's magazine sells three.

His story is in the tradition of the romantic pioneer-entrepreneurs like Henry Ford, even if the area in which his pioneering is taking place is the pubic region of the female body. *Penthouse* girls are said to lead the market by opening their legs wider and fingering themselves more overtly than their *Playboy* big sisters. At any rate the formula, which includes a sexual advice column by a former prostitute, and readers' letters about their experiences with ropes and whips and plastic macs and rubber underwear, has evidently worked, and Guccione will now pay a photographer $2,000 for a centerfold of pictures, though mostly he takes them himself. The first girl he ever persuaded to take her clothes off for his camera he paid fifteen dollars, which was all he could afford at the time. For that amount he got the pictures for the entire first issue of the magazine. He had taught himself to be a photographer overnight, literally in a few hours, after having had the basic principles explained to him by a professional friend. A man of forty who wears hand-embroidered shirts split to the waist, with long gold chains dangling down the deep décolleté, he speaks in a soft Brooklyn accent and looks rather like Victor Mature playing Samson.

At the invitation of the Communist government of Yugoslavia he has created a forty-million-dollar gambling and leisure complex on the island of Krk designed to draw the foreign big spenders. Launched by stripping *Penthouse* pets and bouquet-carrying Communist officials, the entire operation was something even Gatsby in his most grotesque dream could not have conceived. But in the updated fantasy the inherent contradictions of such a venture dissolve in "a Xanadu of glittering buildings . . . for international cognoscenti . . . in the land of Tito."

The defining characteristic of the money romantic is that he sees himself not as a hard-headed businessman coining it, but as someone with a mission, and a destiny to succeed, be it in the field of opening up new trade routes, or colonizing new territories, or offering the world a more succulent hamburger, or providing a service of sexual therapy.

Guccione says:[4] "The attitude that the world is buying tits, so we'll give them tits, is one that some of our competitors have, but it is totally alien to me, and it is because of my attitude that I succeed and they fail. The reason for the extraordinary success of *Penthouse,* which is now 4½ million copies worldwide, is that I would never put anything in it that I cannot morally justify to myself. I am quite a moral guy. *Penthouse* is entirely an expression of my attitude. I come from a very strong tightly knit Roman Catholic family. I was brought up to have genuine respect for women, which reflects in the magazine. I was told that every older woman is somebody's mother and every young girl somebody's sister. If you look at the magazine closely you will see that women are not just blatant sex objects as they are in other magazines, but are handled with great dignity, although they are shown in an explicitly sexual context. It has to be possible to justify the magazine to myself and the public. There has to be a release of any guilt feeling. The printing is of especial good quality. The paper is good. The layout is good. The editorial matter is good. Whatever is done, is done with taste. The public wants to be able to buy a magazine without feeling guilty about it. Why *Penthouse* and *Playboy* achieved such high sales is because people feel they can buy them with impunity."

It might be Louis B. Mayer talking about the family picture. Such is the romantic's capacity for self-idealization, and for turning *any* business into a crusade. The elevated sentiments are not allowed to interfere with the business of making money. Guccione, as proprietor and photographer, knows what sells his magazine. Many of the picture spreads are taken by him in his penthouse apartment, a place of mirrors, Spanish carved oak, latticework, wrought iron, and screens. Here the girls strip off, posing against rented theatrical props, used to suggest a variety of erotic settings.

To Guccione, the theorist of concupiscence, it is essential that his model, who is often a nonprofessional, be sexually aroused by the situation of undressing for a strange man and showing herself off in attitudes often designed to be suggestive of masturbation. But, says Guccione, laying down the law, the photographer must never screw the model, because then her sexual excitement is dissipated on the photographer instead of being captured by his camera lens for the reader. The girl has got to look unsatisfied so that the reader can satisfy her in his fantasies. Considering that some of these photographic sessions last four days and involve the enactment of complicated clothes fetishes, such strict adherence to the rules is an example of how the romantic can subordinate all other passions to those of moneymaking.

Like any daring entrepreneur, Guccione will take chances. One time he had a lesbian picture spread, "in very good taste," but somewhat ahead of its time insofar as it showed the girls belly to belly and simulating cunnilingus, among other things. It got the magazine banned in one chain of bookstalls in America, and lost Guccione 400,000 copies. But in keeping with the romantic spirit, he has his eye on distant horizons and feels the risk was worth taking. He enunciates his credo in these words: "I try to lead the market, I try to be on the side of progress. I have an aesthetic that others in the field don't have. I have no stockholders, I have only myself to live with. Money to me is merely a barometer of success. I'm a builder, a creator, I'm an empire-builder. I've already got more money than I can consume in a lifetime, and all my grandchildren. I keep on going because I'll never be satisfied. I want to own radio stations, I want to own television stations, I want to own newspapers. I just want to go on building, building, building."[5]

The commodity being sold varies, but the romantic's capacity for self-idealization remains the same, come what may. To the car boss Donald Stokes the merger of his company, Leyland, with the gigantic BMH (formerly British Motor Corporation) was in the national interest, and he had no compunction about using shock tactics to oust the man who stood in his way. Sir George Harriman, head of BMH, was slowly maneuvered into an untenable position and then told "to get the hell out of it." In the moment of capitulation, as he was about to sign away his power and position, the defeated car chief became ill, and was rushed to the London Clinic. There, his blood pressure was found to have risen to an alarming level. He was ordered total rest for a fortnight. After being found at the Clinic next day in a state of semi-consciousness, he finally signed.[6]

To Stokes, who later became Lord Stokes, such business techniques were justified by the higher end of serving British industry.

A great deal of the pollution and despoliation of the environment that goes on today is done by romantics under the pretext of extending the boundaries of human knowledge, or harnessing the earth's energy, or creating wealth, or giving expression to the human impulse to discover. Bernie Cornfeld, who at the time of writing sits in a Swiss jail, on remand, told his sales force not to think of themselves as salesmen or even business executives, but as missionaries, philanthropists, statesmen.

This type needs to make himself believe in the romance of money, and he usually succeeds. At the great business conventions in America strong men have been known to weep at the excellence of sales figures. Company songs move the executive to devote his life to his company, as soldiers were once inspired to die for their country. The speechifying, the grand openings, the status symbols, the pretty secretaries and the serious young Harvard aides, the call girls to supply the warrior's well-earned rest—all the trappings of wheeling and dealing are designed to foster the romantic image of money-making. Salesmen become "hunters." An IOS report spoke of a sales competition in the final stages of which "1216 hunters hit the final clearing—and never in Big game history has there been such a jungle jangle jingle."[7]

Without such a self-image of derring-do, many an executive couldn't face himself. He has to make business, per se, glamorous and worthwhile, irrespective of what is being made or sold. Otherwise how could he make and market vaginal deodorants, a business with annual sales in the United States worth $50 million, which the Food and Drug Administration has decided serves no useful hygienic purpose, and can be harmful. How do people live with themselves if their life's work is making and selling cigarettes? Where one's products are of little use, or actually harmful, the normal satisfactions and pleasures of creativity and of service to others have to be replaced by romantic myths about the glories of money-making.

Milton, in *Paradise Lost,* speaks of men taught by Mammon, who ". . . with impious hands/Rifl'd the bowels of their mother Earth/For Treasures better hid . . ."

The romantic conceals from himself the other side of his money motive. He sees only the grand design of his ambition, and does not scruple at the nasty details of his method. If the quest for El Dorado requires it, then so be it.

What is the etiology of such a type? If, as has been posited earlier, the desire for great riches arises in the first place out of the infant's longing for some external source that will meet its needs forever, then we might conjecture that the romantic money-seeker is someone who once knew such a source and ever since has been trying to find it again, as Raleigh once "saw" El Dorado across a high mountain pass.

The remembered perfection is of a past time of preeminence, of having once held dominion over all sources of supply. The rich breastland was his! And full-up with milk, he was rich as Croesus.

In the voracious go-getting baby, with its great possessiveness, the future millionaire and monopolist is foreshadowed. The technique of the crib will be somewhat refined and developed, but already in the first months of life the basis of such a personality is apparent—the desire to own and control an inexhaustible source; the confident belief in one's powers of doing so (by means of a deft tongue) ; the ruthless elimination of rivals; and the idealization of the special relationship to the breast as a great romance. To be so richly fed, to be so indulged, must mean a deeply loving mother, which presupposes great lovability.

To have been so perfectly loved once makes for a perfectionist, someone forever looking for the reinstatement of his ideal, and since real people can rarely come up to it, he will often seek to find his fulfillment in money. Such a person needs to always be richly rewarded in order to have the sense of being loved; he will seek such rewards in the world—and attach the highest motives to his quest.

Finding oil, or gas, or silver, or gold, or uranium, or developing a product that sweeps the market, or pulling off a great deal—whether such successes have any intrinsic value or not—makes him happy, because to him these are the rewards of a loving fate to a favorite son. What he seeks is not so much the condition of being rich but the experience of enrichment, and so he will be venturesome, he will want to make his companies grow into ever larger units, he will maximize profits, he will open new trade routes. He has a mission, whether it is bringing a certain kind of Southern fried chicken to the masses, or making the world a more sweet-smelling place to live in by means of his aftershave lotions. His skyscrapers improve the skyline, and his empty office blocks are his monuments. Even in the face of the overwhelming superfluousness of the riches that he accumulates, and the uselessness of the things he makes, he can never have too much. Can one have too much proof of love?

While he has not yet succeeded, but is within reach of ultimate success, the illusion of a goal is powerful prophylaxis against many ills. The unrealized objective tranquilizes, and keeps the vision intact. But once possessed, the romantic's love object is invariably disappointing, and then you get the man who has everything crying plaintively: *Is this all?*

It is true that some manage to escape the disillusionment with money and die with their faith in it intact. In their case it is often observable that they seem to thrive on the intensity of their hates and feuds; their vendettas keep them going. While they have powerful enemies, they have no need of friends. They have devised a system whereby everything that is still imperfect in their lives may be attributed to some outside force. With his profound unconsciousness of his own deeper motives, the romantic is particularly adept at engaging in the sort of trade wars and business struggles and conflicts of personalities that can serve in lieu of internal conflict. In this way he is saved from ever doubting himself, or his goal.

This type of man leaves behind him wrecked marriages, discarded mistresses, lost friends, abandoned associates—nothing is allowed to stand in the way of the attainment of his vision.

Such is the mesmerism of the type that he can usually persuade others to sacrifice themselves on his behalf, as Raleigh was able to induce Lady Raleigh to let him sell their personal property to finance his last vain search for El Dorado.

This type of person has the capacity to get others to do his bidding. If he often seems curiously free of burdens it is because of his genius for making others carry them. If he seems above the vulgar, wearing constraints of everyday life, it is because of the presence in his circle of an unseen victim, someone—a partner, a friend, a mother, a wife, a mistress— who out of strength, or a masochistic inability to refuse, or blind love, takes the consequences of his ruthlessness, suffers them in his place. The bride that Alfred Krupp housed in the midst of his steelworks soon began to "moan and twist her hands," and she spent the rest of her life going from doctor to doctor and from spa to spa in search of some cure.[8] It is often found that the "magnificently" obsessed pursuers of fortune, with their superabundant energy, which exhausts everyone else, have invalid wives, or unbalanced sons, or sick partners, or daughters driven to some extremity.

We can guess that this type of man was a child who, by a mixture of threats (of which the most effective is that of dying), tantrums, and sheer strength of purpose, imposed his will upon family and friends, who, like many later conquests, went along with him for the sake of a quiet life. One can imagine that he must have early on acquired a taste for getting his own way; and it was always his last territorial demand. ("Just give me another chocolate and it's the last thing I'll ever ask." "But you said the last one was the last." "Yes. I want another last one.") The habit of winning must have become ingrained in such a child, and not to win must have had for him the aspect of a gross miscarriage of justice.

If there has been built up in such an individual the confident expectation that his demands will be met (because they always were in the past), he will bring to his everyday relations the grand certitude and authority of one born to rule. In technical terms, such a person has never properly worked through what Melanie Klein calls "the depressive position," which is the adjustment to reality and loss that an infant makes in the course of normal development. Having never learned to lose, winning becomes the only tolerable condition of life for him, and if he does in fact win he becomes confirmed in his inner belief that he is a special person, entitled to special privileges as a right. Is it not evident from the way everyone defers to him who he is? And, of course, they do, for they find his certitude, and his unquestionable position, deeply comforting. The great relief of a commanding presence is that the burden of decision is removed from oneself;

and where there is somebody of evident superiority to decide on one's behalf, it becomes almost a matter of course to let him do it, to turn to him.

The pain of being wrong, or in the wrong, is what most indecisive people cannot bear. They want to be supported in whatever they do, so that if it goes wrong they can say, "But you told me to." He tells them to, gladly. When things do go wrong, they do not go wrong for him. When a film of Otto Preminger's received a very bad press, he was asked what he thought of the critics. "If the critics did not like one of my films," he declared with supreme aplomb, "it is not my problem. It is the problem of the editors who employ them." This is essentially the attitude, and it marks him out from those who are shaken by the force of circumstance, put off-course.

The romantic has the advantage of all people in love—a willingness to go to extremes. Where somebody else would stop, decide it's not worth it, that it's only money, *he* goes on because to him it is El Dorado. Although this often has disastrous consequences, it has to be said that there are certain enterprises that can only be carried through by someone of this temperament. The man who goes looking for oil in the sea bed, or in Alaska, or like Alfred Nobel seeks to find a *stable* explosive (killing his brother in the process), or invents motion pictures, or the alternating current in electricity, must possess at least a touch of romantic madness—he must be able to conceive of the inconceivable, and bring it to fruition.

Nikola Tesla got the idea of how electricity could be made to flow in *alternating* currents (something regarded by everybody else as impossible) from watching a sunset and recalling a poem of Goethe's.[9] This made him a rich man (for a time), and inaugurated the era of electrical gadgetry in the home.

In later years his ideas became more and more fantastical,

not to say mad. But he was utterly convinced of his rightness, and he pursued his clear visions without respite. In the end he ruined himself, and died broke.

The romantic—be he visionary inventor or pioneering entrepreneur—is sure he can grasp the great prize, though, as in the case of Gatsby, it is all the time receding before him.

6

The Company Man

In contrast to the romantics, there are those who exemplify the dry-as-dust aspects of money, who deny its power to inflame the senses, and declare that it is just a numbers game. They are usually found among the company men, the gnomes of Zurich, the actuaries, the administrators of funds, the men who would rather remain anonymous.

There are recruiters from big business firms who have had the unnerving experience at some American universities of interviewing hundreds of students without once being asked about salary.[1] These serious young men give the impression that they would not allow a question of money to determine their choice of job, even when they are going into finance. Somehow the making of money for others, for which they would claim to have some special gift, is separated from the notion of making money for themselves. The former is a duty, or skill, or responsibility, the latter a somewhat embarrassing personal matter.

Some years ago *Fortune* magazine discovered that ". . .

money is no longer a prime incentive in getting a good day's work out of the boss . . . What is happening today is that the bosses of business (i.e., those high-class hired hands like presidents, vice-presidents, treasurers, and division heads) are in the confused process of discovering for themselves what experimental psychologists and a number of sages have known for a long time: money isn't everything . . ." What he really wants, concluded the magazine, is 1) recognition of achievement; 2) dignity of position; 3) autonomy of management; 4) rewards paid in leisure. Money didn't figure at all in the list. Odd, considering that this same man was required to devote himself to moneymaking *on behalf of his firm and shareholders* with unparalleled ferocity if he was going to get any of that dignity of position or leisure. How can someone work up a real head of steam for making money for others while remaining indifferent to money as far as he, personally, is concerned? This is the contradiction that the type embodies.

The interesting thing about him is that although he isn't interested in money, and doesn't discuss it, he is often very rich. In the professions, he manages to get the highest fees without ever mentioning filthy lucre. He simply puts in his bill. As far as your dealings with him are concerned, money might play no part in it. Partly because of his lofty disdain for the whole subject, the possibility of querying his bill or offering him less has to be discounted. If you have seen a French priest being paid for a baptism, with the notes changing hands as if it isn't happening, you have a model of this kind of transaction.

It must be a factor in a person's choice of career whether or not he can tolerate bargaining about his own worth; if he can't, he will tend to choose one of the professions or lines where fees or charges are either laid down (as in the scale of charges for architects, solicitors, etc.) or not questioned, as in the case of doctors. Or he becomes a salaried employee in a big company and gets the rate for the job, which exempts him from having to negotiate his pay.

To this kind of man there is something deeply shameful about discussing his own finances. The TV reporter Alan Whicker, who has often shown an almost obsessive interest in other people's money, refused point-blank to talk about his own. "It's rather like asking a man: What sex position do you use?"[2] he protested. A well-known author, who has made a fortune out of one book, first agreed, then refused to discuss the matter, on the grounds that he wished to be known for his ideas, and not for the amount of money he had made out of them. A very famous French singer once gave an extensive interview in which she spoke freely and intimately about her love affairs. Later, asked how much money she earned, she replied in an offended tone that some things were private.[3]

Gore Vidal has spoken[4] of how good American families discuss the suitability of a possible husband for their daughter. Where does he come from? Who are his people? they ask. Do we know them? Does anybody know them? What *sort* of people are they? This kind of thing can go on for weeks before somebody finally blurts out: "But, my dear, they don't have a penny." The convention is still not to admit that this is a consideration.

In all these instances one observes deep personal inhibitions about money, and the commonest way of dealing with them is by transferring all such matters to *the company*. For many people the company, even when they constitute the whole of it, is a separate entity; it is something outside themselves, and therefore a useful repository for feelings that the individual does not care to own. "Put it on the company" is the common expression that also states an underlying psychological principle. It is a process whereby the individual does not acknowledge certain of his acts: the company is a sort of pseudonym or incognito for him. Where he might shrink from asking an extortionate price in his personal capacity, in the guise of the company he feels able to do so. People who hate to quibble about money themselves have no trouble in saying, "The company would never pay that." It is very different from saying, "*I* would never pay that." And if a large sum of money does have to be paid, such people feel easier if the company pays, even when they *are* the company. There are those who can sign company checks for hundreds of thousands of dollars but will contrive never to pick up a restaurant bill that has to be paid out of their own pockets. There are rich men who go around without any money in their pockets and borrow from office staff, who are told to "charge it up."

The restaurateur Alvaro said that the way people could bear to pay the sort of prices that they do pay at his restaurants is by signing the bill and having it sent to their company.[5] In some cases they are one-man companies, but even so it's different when the company pays. Getting the bill allowed against tax comes into it, but is not the whole explanation. Whether it is a matter of paying or being paid, the various anxieties and misgivings that attach to such transactions can be mitigated by "doing it through the company." One is not so personally involved. The company becomes the private person's persona. Behind it, he feels safer. Emotions associated with money that are experienced as dangerous or shameful are transferred to the company. Triumphs (dangerous because of the feared retribution from the defeated) become the company's; and so do setbacks and catastrophes; in this way moneymaking is depersonalized.

The kind of person who finds money deeply troubling turns it all into numbers. These are the people "who don't live any differently now" and "are not a bit changed" and "simply don't act like rich people at all." They pay themselves a comparatively modest salary and live on that. In this way they defend themselves against the anxieties that their acquisitiveness produces. In effect, they assert: We have not grabbed these millions for ourselves; we have little more than you. Jim Slater, who built up a financial empire of £220 million, takes a salary of £21,250.[6]

That the company may be an effective cover for one's own money motive was borne out by what was said by a major British industrialist.[7] Though he had welded together the present mighty combine (turnover of over £900 million) by his own dynamic efforts, and had shown a ruthless devotion to efficiency, he did not, he said, consider the amassing of personal wealth as particularly desirable. He had not set out to do it (although he had done it), and he would much rather have written the *St. Matthew Passion* than be who he was and have what he had. In keeping with the character type, he preferred to remain anonymous. He is a patriarchal figure, a man imbued with a sort of moral fervor for moneymaking. The way in which he spoke of it was reflective of the company man's ethos. The office in which he sat, and from which he controlled an organization employing 200,000 people, was uncluttered; his desk was clear, his manner unhurried. A middle-aged secretary was the only person in immediate attendance upon him. There was absolutely no "atmosphere"; the dramatics of big business were nowhere in evidence. He claimed his work was not something he enjoyed. Most of it was almost routine. What it largely consisted of was sitting at his desk reading reports. You had to take in a tremendous amount of information to be able to reach judgments.

This was the anti-romantic view of moneymaking: it was a duty, a task, in no way exciting or pleasurable; just something that had to be done.

In speaking of himself and his attainments he was often modest to the point of self-deprecation. "In particular circumstances where particular opportunities arise, one is not entirely oblivious to the advantages which might accrue." Only when he spoke of "the company" did any kind of passion for money inform his words:

"A business is a living organism, it goes on. One knows the business will last longer than any individual; it has a life of its own; it has to be treated as a thing apart. The business should not be treated as an extension of somebody's personality, somebody's ego still less.

"The purpose of industrial activity is to meet the needs of people, their wants and desires. My job is to satisfy those needs and wants and desires by providing a value to the consumer that is greater than the cost of production, and from this point of view profit measures the extent to which my activity is creative.

"The creation of wealth is to satisfy a want at a value greater to the person being satisfied than the cost of satisfying it."

By means of such formulations, sometimes neat and precise, sometimes circumlocutory, but always impersonal—like mathematical theorems—he defined the meaning and purpose of business activity.

"I would always be worried about making personal value judgments that affected the business as such, even if I am the whole thing, though I might prefer to sell the whole thing rather than continue with something I don't like. The successful running of a large organization has a moral base. All the people in it must see that it is behaving responsibly and in a moral way. Because otherwise they'll all behave purely selfishly."

Step by step, he developed his philosophy. He took it to be his duty to earn as much money as possible for the shareholders and to provide as much employment as possible for the working people, and he would feel this way if the money were entirely his own, or if it were entirely not his own (i.e., the State's). The law laid down what wants could or could not be satisfied. In principle, he believed that any want, the satisfaction of which was permitted by law and could be achieved at a profit, was one that he was entitled to satisfy. "Whatever I personally might think about a given thing, one has a duty to people who work in the business and to share-holders. If I were to say no, I would not make armaments, the consequences might be that people would be put out of work, the country might lose exports, all sorts of undesirable side effects would follow. Yes, I would make armaments. I would not regard myself as either morally or commercially justified in refusing to do something that I personally happened to object to. If I don't like the system, I must get out of it."

As a Jew he might have certain feelings about supplying war materials to Egypt, but he could not let his own natural feelings interfere with his duty to the company, and therefore he *did* supply war materials to Egypt. In fact, the company was obliged to take heed of the Arab Boycott Office's injunctions in the matter of supplying strategic materials to Israel. These were business considerations and in no way connected with his personal feelings in the matter. The company imposed binding obligations upon him as upon its other servants, and these he had to carry out, not as a matter of preference but as a matter of duty. He used the expression that he was "compelled to do it." The fact that he was in a position to wield considerable power one way or another did not give him the right to exercise it. Who had that right? It was a matter for the public conscience.

Profit was the indication that the business was running healthily, that it was functioning. In the current year, his company's profit pre-tax came close to £80 million, which was a substantial increase on the preceding year, and so everything was functioning. But it was only to the extent that it testified to successful functioning that he regarded money-making as a measure of success. The amassing of personal wealth he would not consider a measure of success at all.

Given such belief, people will be ready to go to astonishing lengths to serve the company's impersonal money motive. One result is the commonly observed split between a man's character at home and in the office. At home he may be modest in his needs, frugal in his appetites, considerate of others, a cat lover, a conservationist, the pillar of the local community, a generous contributor to deserving causes. But seated behind an executive desk in the office of a big company, and given a title, he becomes transformed into a monster of acquisitiveness, a ruthless manipulator of the destinies of others, a plotter, a schemer, an employer of spies and *agents provocateurs,* a user of graft.

He is not doing it for himself. It's for the company. The gobbling mania is *its.* *It* needs Avis car rentals, Sheraton hotels, Scott's fertilizer, APCOA garages, Wonder Bread, Morton frozen foods, Hartford insurance, etc. *It* requires the downfall of the Marxist government of Chile.

Harold S. Geneen, the Chairman and President of ITT, described by an Assistant Attorney General of the United States as "the most acquisitive corporation in the nation's history," is by all reports a man of modest tastes, nearing retirement age, living in a cloistered world of figures. Wherever he goes he is followed by a man wheeling crates of files after him; such is the inescapable nature of paper work: accounts, budgets, market analyses, costings, surveys, market research.

Geneen's salary and bonuses alone are close to $1,000,000 a year, and with all those crates of paper work following him about, his opportunities for spending such a sum must be limited. What is the purpose of it all? Operating profits shall increase every quarter: that is the single overriding aim, and it has been achieved for fifty consecutive quarters. To this cause staff are expected to sacrifice, if need be, their outside interests and their family life. An executive says: "You feel you are working for an order and not just a mortal company."

The aim of the company system is to make the employee lose his own identity in the corporate image. He becomes an IBM man or an ITT man or an RTZ man or Shell man. It has been observed that people who rise in such organizations have a common persona, and eventually they *become* what they appear to be.

By binding its executives to its "organic needs," by getting them to identify with its aims, by granting them indulgences for their actions, by giving their endeavors "meaning," by relieving them of guilt, and by offering them the immortality of money, the mystique of the company works in the way that God once worked.

At IBM there are no trade unions, no strikes, no labor disputes, no wage claims, even. The workers are totally fulfilled in their identification with the company's aims and achievements. All possible dissension is spotted well in advance by safety systems that can isolate a man who isn't realizing his objectives before he knows that he isn't. Supervisors, one to every ten employees, take on the role of confessors and company psychoanalysts. In any case, the employee has to have survived extensive psychological testing to have been accepted in the first place. The result is a labor force that completely identifies with the company and is unquestioningly committed to always increasing its profits ($1,279.3 million in 1972) to a new high in the next year.[8]

Such enormous profits are held to be exorbitant by many, and in 1972 there were lawsuits against IBM, accusing it of wielding illegal monopoly power, including one instigated by the U.S. Department of Justice. IBM's products are held by experts to be overpriced. The ordinary individual can hardly judge this kind of claim, but he can see that an IBM electric typewriter costs at least 30 percent more than a comparable, and some would say superior, Adler. There is good reason to think that IBM is able to use its dominance of the market in order to call the tune. On a personal level, this would be regarded as being greedy, grasping, extortionate. But under the cloak of the company this sort of thing can be done without anyone's feeling personally ashamed, a Shylock, a dirty profiteer. It isn't personal. It is being done in the interests of a greater entity.

But this mystique is capable of demystification. The company is not a "living organism" with its own imperatives, but, in this context, a creation of mass projection. The pretense that it has a life of its own enables the company man to find a kind of refuge there for the split-off parts of his own nature. The company becomes the exponent of his alienated impulses. Everything that is most fearful in himself is put into the company. His hates, his greeds, his trickery, his dishonesties, his ruthlessness, his criminality become the company's, leaving the other part of his divided self purged for a life of bourgeois respectability. The law in America and some other countries actually recognizes this split. "While the courts have decreed in their wisdom that corporations are 'persons' and are entitled to all the protection of persons, it is a fact that one cannot jail or execute a corporation. And officers of a corporation, being quite different persons, cannot, it seems, justly be held responsible by a careful Congress for the acts of the corporation."[9] Similarly, in Germany at the time of the trial of the manufacturers of thalidomide, the prosecutor pointed out that "the question of *individual* responsibility for each act is still open."[10] In West German criminal law, guilt was concerned fundamentally not with the unlawful behavior of a group, but referred to unlawful acts committed by individuals. And in this case, the prosecution said that "the individuals accused as members of the said collectivity were victims of the existing group pressure."[11] In the end, the prosecution against the individuals was dropped, even though the prosecutor had charged the company with negligence, with failure to inform the authorities of side effects, and with exerting pressure on medical journals to prevent or delay reports hostile to thalidomide.

Accounts of the trial indicate confusion between company responsibility and individual responsibility. Even the prosecution was compelled to subscribe to the split whereby what the company had done was distinguished from what the individual officers had done collectively. Clearly the problem was that as individuals these men—doctors, scientists, chemists—were respected people, and the court found it difficult to identify them with the ruthless money-seeking action of the company. The confusion is understandable since the psychological process whereby an individual forsakes some part of his autonomy in order to incorporate himself in a group is still only dimly understood. Jung says that group experiences take place on a lower level of consciousness than the experiences of individuals. "If it is a very large group, the collective psyche will be more like the psyche of an animal, which is the reason why the ethical attitude of a large organization is always doubtful. The psychology of a large crowd inevitably sinks to the level of mob psychology."[12]

This notion of the way groups function would suggest that the particular group known as the company can function rather like a mob. And the significant thing about a lynch mob, for example, is that the individual in joining it and losing his own identity, frees himself of moral restraints. In the peculiar and characteristic state of being alienated from himself he is able to commit terrible acts without feeling them, that is to say, without feeling responsibility for them, and therefore he can do them guiltlessly. There appears to be a mechanism which enables the mind to project part of itself into a sort of pooled consciousness, for the action of which it can then deny personal responsibility.

In the light of this, the role of the company can be seen more plainly. On the mob principle, it can enact the individual's greed—the desire for more than the subject needs or the object can give—without his having to suffer the consequential retribution.

While there is a sort of gain in instinctual freedom (as in the mob or the orgy), there is a corresponding loss of individuality, for a part of oneself has been given up, and sacrificed to an impersonal force. "Projections into group life," writes Elliott Jaques, "are the main cause of the diminution of the effectiveness in individuals . . ."[13]

On the one hand it is possible for men to go in for ruthless moneymaking and not feel bad about it; on the other hand, in the process, they become a faceless company-mob.

7
The Collector

What is indicated by the mystique of the company, or any of the other ways of denying the sheer "moneyness" of money, is the profound sense of guilt and shame that it arouses in some people. So much so that they feel obliged to disguise its nature—to turn it into mere digits. These they collect every bit as avidly as the romantic his gold; they have a real passion for those electronic print-outs with the serried zeros. They love to see the numbers add up, multiply, perform feats of parthenogenesis on the page. They adore to watch their money reproduce itself in a series of immaculate financial conceptions. The reproductive capacity of money lies in its interest-bearing attribute, and it is this aspect of it, the fact that money breeds money—that such people find particularly to their taste. They love the elegant beauty of such cool self-reproduction. Ferdinand Lundberg reports in *The Rich and the Super Rich* that there are old Boston families with $100,000,000 invested in tax-free government bonds, paying 3 percent, which gives them $3,000,000 a year. But they do not treat this as income. They reinvest the $3,000,000 and live on the income from that. In this way their capital is growing at the rate of more than $3,000,000 a year, and is never in any danger of being used up, or even used. Such people live quite modestly—on, say, $90,000 a year—in relation to their actual wealth.

They are the *unobtrusive* rich. ". . . they own only *small* yachts, and drive only *old* (but well-maintained) cars and are accustomed to wear old but *expensive* clothes of the first class so that they look quaintly dowdy."[1]

They are not interested in the flamboyant accouterments of money; nor in its power to affect events; nor in its capacity to buy sybaritic pleasures; nor in its capacity to corrupt others. They are not interested in any of its many uses, but only in having it: in possession. For this, the figures on a page are sufficient satisfaction. In this form, money has an abstract beauty and cleanness. It fulfills its natural functions unseen, in the dark of a computer's inside, where the shameful act can be done unwitnessed, and only the profit print-out testifies to its having taken place.

The origins of this dry passion are especially unacceptable —indeed shocking—to conventional sensibilities. "Perhaps the most astonishing of all Freud's findings," wrote Ernest Jones, "—and certainly the one that has evoked the liveliest incredulity, repugnance, and opposition—was his discovery that certain traits of character may become profoundly modified as a result of sexual excitations experienced by the infant in the region of the anal canal."[2] And one of the main character traits so modified is the attitude to money. Incredulity. Disgust. Revulsion. The great industrialist who appeared in the previous chapter—the one who preferred to remain anonymous—had to contain his abhorrence of such an unseemly connection between his activities and the act of evacuation in order to even consider the matter. When he did so, he quickly rejected any possibility of his moneymaking being related to something filthy. Certainly it is offensive to the grandiosity of the capitalist spirit to imply that what is being made with such great pride and self-importance is *shit*. And worse, that it is an erotic defecation, that the satisfactions of money-making are akin to erotic excitement of the anus, i.e., that they are a displacement of genital love. Indeed, Freud believed that where the anus was retained as a principal erotic zone, as in the case of male homosexuals, there should be less evidence of such *symbolic* forms of anality as moneymaking.*[3]

How does such a theory arise, and what is the evidence to support it?

Freud does not postulate any prime force in human affairs that was not originally a bodily force, arising out of bodily needs. It is obvious, therefore, that since the bodily functions are all vulgar, in the sense that they are common to everyone, and somewhat crude in their primary purpose, the connections between them and their cultural sublimations (business, art, homemaking) will inevitably be dismaying to that aspect of our natures that perpetually wishes to rise above itself. Refusing to be bamboozled by our affectations of superiority, Freud arrived at his theory of "the anal character," which is a cornerstone of modern psychology and affords the classic explanation of the interest in money.

As was often the case with him, he was struck first of all by the anthropological material, and by the myths, fairy tales and popular superstitions which seemed to be in agreement with what his delvings into the dreams and unconscious thought processes of his patients revealed: a connection between money and excrement.

"We know," he observed, "how the money which the devil

---

* It would be interesting to find out if, in fact, there is any evidence to suggest that homosexuals are less actively interested in moneymaking than heterosexuals. One's general impression is that this is indeed so.

gives his paramour turns to excrement on his departure, and the devil is most certainly nothing more than a personification of the unconscious instinctual forces."[4] He found, too, that there were superstitions that associated the finding of treasure with defecation. There was the story of the *Dukatenscheisser,* the excretor of ducats. In Oriental mythology gold was often regarded as the excrement of hell. Mammon is the Babylonian version of Manman, which was another name for Nergal, the god of the underworld.[5] Then there was the expression "stinking rich," an odd conjunction, but explicable in terms of the secret fecal meaning of money.

On the basis of these clues, the connection was pursued by Freud and other practicing psychoanalysts, and more and more evidence came to light to support the original notion. This had first been put forward in 1908; ten years later it was considerably developed by Ernest Jones. He pointed out that defecation constitutes one of the two greatest personal interests in the first year of life, and that "all later tendencies are considerably affected by earlier ones." This infantile interest, and pleasure, is one of the first to suffer repression. "The psychical energy accompanying the wishes and sensations relating to the region is almost totally deflected into other directions."[6]

The fact that a baby's stools are his first *products,* and that they tend to be received by the mother with expressions of approval (when they are well-formed and not too frequent or infrequent) gives them early on a value; they are things given to the mother, and they seem to please her. Moreover, the actual act of defecation affords a pleasure of the sphincter, which some infants store up by postponing the motion. Sándor Ferenczi, a Hungarian psychoanalyst, and close associate of Freud's, called this the first savings. Amount comes into it. Small children will say with pride, "Look, what a lot I've done," or rather shamefacedly, "I haven't done very much." The number of individual pieces produced is also a source of interest, leading to some of the earliest forms of counting.

At the same time, defecation, because it involves muscular effort and produces a tangible and visible result, gives children a sense of their powerfulness, something enhanced by the warnings about not touching because it's dangerous or dirty. In this way, the child gets to feel that it produces powerful and dangerous stuff in its anus, which people are afraid of, and at the same time attach great importance to and also treat with some secrecy. One child patient entertained the fantasy that he had the entire universe in his anus, and it is a common belief of children that this is where babies come from.

Defecation is also one of the functions which the infant is able to use in order to exercise control over others; by conscious effort of the sphincter, either in expelling or retaining, he can keep parents waiting *until he decides.* This is emphasized by certain common jocular expressions, such as referring to the toilet as "the throne." The psychoanalyst Karl Abraham points out that the Spanish expression for defecation is *regir el vientre*—"to rule the belly."

It can be seen that this natural function has many meanings not normally admitted to consciousness. It was Ferenczi who traced the step-by-step conversion of an infant's preoccupation with its feces to the adult's preoccupation with his finances.[7] He suggested that the first modification of the original interest occurs when the child begins to find the smell of his feces disagreeable; it is at this point that he transfers his interest to a substitute that has the same qualities of moistness and stickiness and dirtiness, but without the smell: mud. This, too, as a result of frequent admonitions—"It's dirty, leave it alone"— is in due course abandoned as a play substance and replaced by more approved-of substances like plasticine and sand. Eventually, playing with sand also comes to be regarded as messy, for the child tries all the time to return to the repressed substance of his interest by making holes in the sand and filling them with water. Then comes an interest in stones, when sand has been abandoned as too messy. At this point, the child becomes a collector, he finds interesting pebbles on the beach and makes piles of them, fills his pockets with them, takes them home, and evidently attaches value to them. The German expression *"stein reich"* (stone rich) points to the connection between this kind of playing and later capitalistic hoarding. The advantage of stones as things to be collected is that they represent a stage of transformation not reversible, for it is not possible to add water to them and make them messy. So, at this point, the original meaning has been thoroughly banished into the unconscious. From stones the interest turns to marbles, which have the advantage of also being shiny, and now these are collected with great delight. At the same time coins may engage the child's interest, and later stamps.

By this time the original interest in collecting in the bowels has undergone such drastic modification that we have the good-as-gold little stamp collector, so approved of by parents, instead of the collector of "dirty things." The transition to money is almost complete inasmuch as stamps are both worthless, in a real sense, and extremely valuable insofar as other people also have a passion for collecting them. Thus we see how, by common agreement, the worthless bit of paper becomes a greatly valued collector's item. The stamp, being both worthless and valuable, combines in one form the original object of the collecting mania with its final sublimation. Stamp collecting is thus the penultimate stage of the transformation process. The next stage is money. Now the worthless aspect, which can still be recognized in the case of the stamp, has been completely denied, and something unequivocally valuable has replaced it in conscious thought, its worth-

lessness only manifesting itself in what then seems like irrationality, like certain forms of getting rid of money, which
approximate to the defecation of worthless stuff.

"Pleasure in the intestinal content," Ferenczi wrote, "becomes enjoyment of the money symbol, which, however, after
what has been said is nothing other than odourless, dehy-
drated filth . . ." The dynamic of the whole process has been
the desire for something that has the unconscious meaning
and significance of the original possession (feces) but has
been purified. In this context one is reminded again of Bernie
Cornfeld's rumination about "the strange purity of money."

From this, it can be gathered why a certain type of person
finds money embarrassing and shameful, won't talk about it,
and contrives to reduce it to the ultimate abstraction—numbers. These "numbers men" are collectors of money, with all
the characteristics of collectors. Karl Abraham says that the
stamp collector who deeply feels the gap in his set of stamps
is not so far removed from the miser, who, according to popular notion, counts and gloats over his gold pieces. And one
may also be reminded of the corporation president who frets
over the lack of one group of companies that has not yet been
incorporated within his orbit. All *collecting of money*—
whether it is storing it in banks, or in properties, or in any
other safe repository—appears to be of anal origin, and with
it goes the tendency to the appropriately termed "tightness"
and wholly absurd forms of economizing. This was most
strikingly illustrated in the case of one of Abraham's patients,
a rich banker, who instructed his sons to retain their feces for
as long as possible so as to obtain the maximum benefit from
the expensive food they ate. That is perhaps an extreme
instance. But the desire of the very rich to ensure that they
get their money's worth, even when the effort involved is
wholly disproportionate to the amount at stake, is well
known. Rockefeller was once in a restaurant with his family,

where he ordered chicken for all of them. At the end, when the bill came, he found he had been charged for two chickens. He felt sure they had eaten only one, and so he called for the plates to be brought back and meticulously set about counting and assembling the chicken bones so as to establish how many chickens they had, in fact, been served.

"Numbers men" are characterized by an inclination to "sit on" their wealth and watch it grow; the common expression suggests the natural function from which it may well derive. But they will tend to splurge in sudden bursts for which they have "saved up." Thus such people display the puzzling characteristic of being obsessively mean much of the time, and suddenly giving way to bouts of extreme generosity.

Another of their character traits is that they are interested in using their money in order to establish control over things. A child may seek to control his parents by the opening and tightening of his sphincter; these "anal" money types control those around them by the opening and closing of their purses.

In the classic "anal character" described by Freud, there are three main characteristics that go together: excessive orderliness, parsimoniousness and obstinacy. These characteristics are often found in the "numbers man." The type is famous for his orderliness. In business affairs he is offended by disorderly inefficient structures to such a degree that he will gladly sacrifice human considerations for the sake of order. The closer human work can be made to the absolutely determinable action of machines, the happier such people are. Their passion for efficiency is realized perfectly in the production line, with human action reduced to some simple controllable action like tightening screws. Men engaged in such work at Ford complain that it is boring, demoralizing and degrading; they put up with it because the money is good. The manufacturers say that if everything is reduced to simple repetitive actions, lasting less than a minute, it is easy to train anybody to carry them out. The possibility of mistakes being made is minimal. In America attempts are being made to reduce the job time to fifteen seconds, so as to make the process even more foolproof. On the other hand, Volvo is experimenting with doing away with production lines, believing that there is something inhuman about reducing men to automatons. The difficulty is not, as is claimed, financial, for there is evidence of incalculable industrial advantages when human dignity is considered and job satisfaction increased. The real trouble lies in the fact that the production line has such enormous appeal to the obsessive orderliness of the "anal character," who tends to be the type from which management is largely recruited. The element of the unknown, the uncontrolled, is antithetical to the modern business mind, which requires that every contingency must be measurable and predictable. This, of course, is a misconception: absenteeism, strikes, malingering and health breakdown play havoc with schedules, and render most predictions meaningless. Professor Ivor Mills of Cambridge says that emphasis on ever-increasing efficiency is counterproductive in that it puts workers under such pressure that they become ill, or resolve their tensions by strike action. He says that society would work better if it made more allowance for natural human inefficiency.

But the "anal character" will persuade himself that everything is going well because his desk is tidy, his papers are up to date, his statistics and charts give him a detailed picture of what is going on, or so he believes. These are the people who become efficiency maniacs, who are always doing their arithmetic, which is to say, bringing their particular form of cost-analysis to bear upon any and every move that is contemplated. In this way all decisions are reduced to a question of cost effectiveness. This appears to be sound—financially, at least; but what it leaves out of account are the side effects on individuals, and the cumulative effect.

Nevertheless, there are some obvious advantages to this kind of character. In many lines of work orderliness is essential, and if we want banks and insurance companies and investment houses, we need "anal characters" to run them. Romantics are not suitable for such dry-as-dust work. As the anonymous captain of industry has said, at the top level of management the work, however momentous, is a routine, and a person given to sudden ecstasies cannot do it. It has to be done by somebody who sits cogitating on facts and figures, and arrives at decisions on the basis of them alone.

This character type has another aspect that our social system finds useful. Ernest Jones discovered that such people have a sense of "oughtness," which means they endow all their actions with moral force.[8] They bring this to moneymaking, so that it becomes a positive duty. Everybody is acquainted with this type. He is always appearing on TV and being quoted in the press, speaking in the most high-minded way of tasks that face the nation, of impositions that the individual must accept, of economic necessity, of "only alternatives," and of the otherwise grim realities that face all of us. This person has an overwhelming sense of "mustness," which leaves no room for argument. In the character-forming situations of infancy such a person has had it ingrained in him that "he must always" or "he must never," and whatever these imperatives applied to at the time, he has retained the habit of doing what he *must* do. His mind has acquired order as a must, and therefore he inflicts this order upon everybody else. In his dedication to duty, to precedent and the principle of the thing, one can recognize the small child whose earliest forms of discipline were imposed by moral bludgeoning. There's a right way and a wrong way, he will inform you, and early on he learned the right way, and this has given him a taste, and a justification, for imposing it on others willy-nilly.

Of the two other main anal character traits isolated by Freud, *obstinacy* takes various forms in the field of money-making, such as doggedness, perseverance, solidity and *conservatism*. All these traits have their usefulness within the limits of certain financial dealings and institutions. The old established insurance companies are the custodians of enormous sums of money. The Prudential had assets in 1969 of two thousand million pounds, and every week another two million is added to what it has to invest. It is obvious that it is useful for the men who handle this money to have the character trait of *retentiveness*, or they might use such vast sums of money in too venturesome a way, which could be disastrous for people who are relying on predicted profits for their retirement. Therefore it is appropriate that the men who run these companies talk of their duty to policy-holders, and of their fiduciary role, and that they usually try not to get involved in the power struggles of industry, despite often being the investors with the decisive holdings. They seek to determine their actions and investments entirely on a basis of balance sheets and price/earnings ratios. Their rather slow-moving approach provides a useful counterbalance to the whizz-kids and the high-flyers. The disadvantages of such a character make-up is the reluctance to do anything that hasn't been done before—that is, the obstinacy of not budging from an existing pattern.

The third of Freud's triad of anal characteristics is *parsimony*. This is manifest, for instance, in Paul Getty's installing a pay phone box at his Sutton Place home in England, so that guests will be spared the embarrassment of not being able to pay for their calls. Or there is the pathological case of the miser, treated by Karl Abraham, who would not do up his fly buttons, so as to save the buttonholes from wearing out.[9] (He

had other motives too, as one might suppose.) The unwillingness to part with money is shown in such behavioral common-
places as a reluctance to pay bills. Such people have to receive
constant reminders to make them pay up, and it is always
unpleasant for them to let go of any of their money, however
much of it they may have.

The connection here with neurotic constipation is amply
documented. Stinginess and miserliness, perhaps because of
the absurd extremes to which they are taken in practice, are
more obviously of neurotic origin than some of the other
traits of the "anal character" which have been to a much
greater degree rationalized in our social system. Abraham
points out the commonplace occurrence of a husband bitterly
opposing some expenditure proposed by his wife on the
grounds of not being able to afford it, and then "of his own
free will" giving more than was originally asked for, some
tortuous rationalization having meanwhile taken place
whereby he has convinced himself, in the light of such and
such, that the expenditure is now desirable, and positively
moneysaving in the long run. There are people who will buy
toothpaste and soap *in bulk* because it enables them to get it
for wholesale prices. There is the *Consumer Report* fanatic
who is perpetually calculating best buys, whose mind is a
veritable table of comparative values, and who can spot a
hidden price loading faster than you can say profiteer. These
are all people for whom life problems are quickly convertible
into sums; they make numbers out of everything, and thereby
believe they have acted with absolute logicality and sound-
ness, since they have not allowed themselves to be swayed by
impressions, or by impulse, or by advertising, or packaging.
They have got to the essence of the matter, by doing their
arithmetic.

At heart this is a belief in the magic science of numerology.
It is based on a deep faith in quantitative calculations, and

this, in turn, is related to a denial of the source of interest in money.

One might say that the salient characteristic of this mania to collect, whether it be money, or the waste matter of the body, or stamps, or companies, is the bestowal of one's love on something nonliving; it is the deflection of eros from a human object to an inanimate one, just as the original pleasure of the anus is a kind of sucking of dead matter in place of living flesh.

8
The Hustler

The form of moneymaking referred to as being in the rat race is characterized by the fact that those in it say they are only in it in order to make enough to get out. When they have made their killing, they will quit. Nobody actually *wants* to be in the rat race; yet very few ever succeed in getting out of it, no matter how many killings they make. There are reasons why this should be so, but first we must consider the type of person who gets himself into this sort of situation.

He freely admits he is in it for himself, that he is in it to make money, and that the way you make money is by beating the others. He does not purport to be striving for the general good, for the national interest, or to improve the lot of mankind. He copes with his guilt by admitting it openly, by despising himself if need be, and by treating the rat race as an inescapable condition of life.

The term "hustler" fits him because it expresses the moral uncertainty that we feel about his activities. At one end of its meanings, "to hustle," in the American sense, means to proceed rapidly or energetically, to be go-getting and aggressive in business, to be enterprising, determined to succeed. But then we see these on-the-whole-admired attributes shading into more doubtful ones: to "hustle" also means to push, to coerce, to force one's way; and before we know it, the meaning has changed to "to earn one's living by illicit or unethical means," to "obtain money by aggressive and illicit means," "to induce someone to play in a gambling game in which he will have little chance to win." And now a hustler is "a person who employs fraudulent or unscrupulous methods to obtain money, a swindler, a prostitute."

The hustler is someone about whom our feelings are divided. We react to him with a mixture of admiration and disapproval, but in both positions with considerable empathy, for we tend to believe, at least at some point of our lives, that, good or bad, to hustle is what we have to do. For if the rat race *is* the condition of life, then the hustler is its hero. If it is *all* a rat race, then one has no alternative but to hustle.

The hustler is a kind of realist. He knows the basic statistics of life and doesn't kid himself. He knows that the average life expectancy of a new business in America is six years; that the failure rate for new businesses for the first four decades of the century was 85 percent;[1] that in a culture so overwhelmingly attached to success, the actual experience of the vast majority is failure. He knows, too, that there is no such thing as People's Capitalism, that if all the privately owned wealth of America were shared out equally among the 103 million adult population they would each have about $10,000 in worldly goods, i.e., not more than a few sticks of furniture, an old car, clothes, and some personal belongings.* That is the wealth of

* These figures may seem surprising. They were arrived at in a study by Professor Robert J. Lampman of the University of Wisconsin for the National Bureau of Economic Research, and published by Princeton University Press in 1962. Professor Lampman wrote: "The personally owned wealth of the total population in 1953 amounted to about $1 trillion. This means that the av-

the richest country in the world at the richest moment in time, divided equally. Even if he does not know the figures, the hustler knows this in his bones. But he also knows there are more millionaires than there ever were before.

The last authoritative estimate in the United States, based on Department of Treasury figures, put the number of millionaires at about 90,000 in 1965. The Federal Reserve Board and Census Bureau said that in 1962 there were an estimated 200,000 families with assets of $500,000 or more. Allowing for the rate of inflation during the past ten years, there must now be in excess of 200,000 millionaires. In 1953 there were 27,000 millionaires in America, which suggests that over the past twenty years something like 170,000 families have moved into the mythic millionaire category, which is an average rate of about 8,000 every year. This is a statistic that interests the hustler much more than the failure rate. If 8,000 could make it, so can he. He knows that money is not something that can be shared out fairly and equally; and elevating this fact of life into an ideology of opportunism, he is determined to be the one in a thousand who can have what the others cannot.

This is the attitude that the hustler adopts. He does not subscribe to the romantic claim to be improving man's lot, nor like the "numbers man" does he de-monetize money and turn it into innocent numbers, having more of which than someone else is then a purely numerical distinction. The hustler knows what it's all about, he knows it's unfair, he is aware of demanding more than he is entitled to, but he's going to have it, because his wants are so great. Like the Casanova or the gourmand he will justify himself on the grounds that his appetites are bigger.

In the eighteenth and nineteenth centuries, the hustler operated in the salons of the aristocracy. It was called getting

erage gross estate for all 103 million adults was slightly less than $10,000. The median would, of course, be considerably lower."

into society then, and it was precisely described by Balzac in
A Harlot High and Low:

> Moreover, feeling the need to be adopted by so powerful
> a family, and impelled by his intimate counsellor to
> charm Clotilde, Lucien had all the courage of an upstart:
> he appeared five days out of the seven, he gracefully
> swallowed the affronts of envy, he outfaced impertinent
> stares, he answered banter wittily. His assiduity, the
> charm of his manners, his obligingness in the end neu-
> tralized scruple and diminished obstacles. Always wel-
> come at the house of the Duchesse de Maufrigneuse . . .
> idol of Madame de Sérisy, highly regarded at Mademoi-
> selle des Touches's, Lucien, happy to be admitted to
> these three houses, learned . . . to conduct his relations
> with the greatest reserve.
>
> "One can't devote oneself to several houses at a time,"
> his intimate adviser told him. "A man who goes every-
> where is nowhere the subject of lively interest. The great
> protect only those who vie with their furniture, those
> whom they see every day, who become necessary to them,
> like the divan they sit on."
>
> Accustomed to regard the Grandlieu drawing-room as
> his battlefield, Lucien reserved his wit, his epigrams, his
> news and his courtier's graces for the time he spent there
> in the evening. Insinuating, affectionate in his manner,
> warned by Clotilde of the reefs to avoid, he flattered
> Monsieur de Grandlieu's little manias . . .

The hustler today operates in a way that is not dissimilar.
Consider the case of a man, Doug Hayward,[2] who has become
one of the most fashionable men's tailors in London, and is
the part-owner of one of the smartest restaurant-clubs in town.

He comes from a working-class background. His father was

a boiler cleaner. In his late twenties, while working as the manager of a tailoring concern in Shepherd's Bush, it occurred to him that in order to succeed you had to play *their* game. He'd had some glimpses of how "they" lived because his wife's sister was married to a film director, and he was occasionally asked along to parties. People talked to him sometimes, but nobody listened to what he had to say.

It was at this point that he decided to go into business on his own and to set about making himself successful. First, he had to change his working-class accent, and by conscientious mimicry of the sort of people he met at the film director's house, he succeeded in doing this. He also learned how to say things, and the sort of things to say. For example, you said you were in business in Pall Mall (which he was by then), but you did not mention that your business was a basement room without a window, measuring 6′ × 6′.

When, through a friend, he was summoned to the hotel suite of a somewhat quirky film producer, he had learned enough to realize that to be successful you must give the appearance of being successful, but not *too* successful. He had learned to understand the desire of the great to patronize. Great film producers tend to suffer from Pygmalion complexes even in relation to their tailors, and wish to feel they have created them. The hustler is not someone to deny somebody else a satisfaction he craves.

The tailor's clientele grew. He made suits for film stars. He learned to charm. He never asked people to come to his premises (the basement room would have been a giveaway) but instead always visited them in their homes, sensing the unease that men for some reason feel about going for tailors' fittings. In their own homes, over a sociable drink, it was made painless. They tended to order suits by the half dozen.

Later, when this side of his business was thriving, he opened a restaurant club to which all the famous people who came to him to have their suits made came to eat; and then a barber's, where these same famous people came to have their hair cut.

The key factor in his success came with the realization that "in the group in which I was playing the difference between a marvelous suit and a good suit was minimal," and that what counted was being around, having a personable appearance, charm. "We are in an age when people are adoring faces arranged in the right order. The 'little tailor' may be great, he may be better than me, but he's got less chance. I saw the opening and I took it."

Once he was in, it was a matter of "creating a fashionable person who says the right things at the right time and is in the right place at the right time. You have to be seen with the right people. It's very difficult to avoid being a flatterer. It's very difficult to retain dignity in that role.

"If you really consider it a game, what you do is you play the game, as long as you retain *some* dignity, as long as you don't sell yourself totally.

"I sacrificed my first marriage," he is obliged to admit. "I was never there. I used to leave at eight in the morning and come home at eleven at night. I'd be going around being sociable. Have a drink, sit down, have a chat. That was part of my business, part of selling myself. There may be people there who are potential customers, who know somebody who is a potential customer. Chance for me to impress them, that was how the business built up."

Today he is fast moving towards wealth, his business interests having spread to property, catering and other entrepreneurial ventures.

He says, "As long as you are energetic, alive, and don't slip an inch you can keep doing what you are doing for a long time. But those same people that patronize me now are waiting to pounce. You say that to them and they say, 'Oh, don't be silly, we're the most loyal,' but those same people won't go near the —— [a previously fashionable restaurant club] now because they feel that's bad news now, being seen there would dirty them somehow. I have no illusions about it. There's no future in that. So I formed a company with two other men and we're dealing in things I don't have to know about, where I don't have to know the customers personally."

He said he intended to keep at it another four or five years, and by then he'd have made enough to be able to quit. He would then go into politics.

The hustler, like Arthur Miller's *Salesman*, is "riding on a smile and a shoeshine." But unlike the failed *Salesman*, the hustler knows how to turn on the smiles of others. If not this way, then that way.

Our tailor, having established himself by his gift for making himself liked, understood that this was no foundation for continuing success. He was not going to put himself in the position of the *Salesman* where "when they start not smiling back—that's an earthquake"; no, he kept them smiling long enough to diversify, to get into lines where others will need to seek his smile in order to ride high.

In the most general sense, the hustler is a go-getter, someone possessed of an inexhaustible energy for the game, whatever it may be. He is forever running, doing, trying, maneuvering. He is the wheeler-dealer and the promoter. Whatever his field, it is characteristic of him that he will always abandon a given position in order to take up a more advantageous one. His freedom of movement, which is his pride and joy, is due to having no binding commitments. His attitude is to play life by ear, to sound out every situation for the benefits it can bring *him*. He is naturally quick, and to the bystander this quickness is the very essence of glamor.

Granting, then, his great secret appeal for all of us, it is not surprising that the hustler so often finds himself in show business, or in the media, in advertising, PR, promotions, or those businesses where the line between what is allowed and what is not allowed is moveable, and the force of charm, personality and panache can get things moved *his* way.

His cool unscrupulousness may evoke the disapproval of our moralizing natures, but at the same time it excites our latent love of the *taker*. Against our better judgment, we can't help half admiring someone like Arndt Krupp, founder of the Krupp dynasty of German arms manufacturers. Four hundred years ago, when plague was sweeping through Essen and everyone was getting out from the city as fast as possible, he coolly began buying up the land of the fleeing citizenry, who, of course, were in no position to hold out for a price. The land obtained by these means is still in the possession of the Krupp family today.[3] Something very similar happened during the London blitz. One developer, who later, not surprisingly, became a millionaire, used to ring up his agent after a night of heavy bombing, and say: "Take off your coat, roll up your sleeves and go out and buy. Did you hear the bombs last night? There must be some bargains around this morning."[4]

There is a kind of brutish daring about such dealings; to take advantage of the disasters that have befallen others is hardly admirable, and yet there is something that we relish, against our will, about a man mad enough to buy piles of rubble, on the theory that if his country wins the war the bomb sites will become enormously valuable for rebuilding, and if his country doesn't win, everything is lost anyway.

When the war was over, this kind of man became a genius at finding loopholes. If the law restricted new building licenses to existing structures that were a hazard to public safety, he made bloody sure, as one such developer put it, that *his* structures *were* a hazard to public safety, if necessary by going around with an ax the night before the District Surveyor called.

Wherever private gain and public good are to some extent in conflict, and a system is worked out to protect the general interest without jeopardizing individual endeavor, there are people who can beat the system. Some of the most successful architects are not those who can design the finest buildings and make the most farsighted changes in our physical mode of living, but those who know the bylaws and regulations so well that they can get around them. The new building now occupied by New Scotland Yard holds twice the number of people that the local planning authority had regarded as being the appropriate density for the area. There is a ratio of site-to-floor space of 7 to 1, when zoning rules allowed a maximum of 3.5 to 1. The developers had simply exploited, as many others had done, certain provisions which allow an old building to be enlarged by up to 10 percent of its cubic capacity. This means that, allowing for the much more wasteful use of space in the old building (wide stairs, high ceilings, large rooms) and adding on 10 percent extra capacity on top, rebuilding gave them practically double the former density.[5]

It is just one of the many perfectly legal ways of flouting the law. One architect was so good at this sort of thing that the planning authority said they had to wait for him to discover the loophole in order for them to stop it up. By means of such cleverness, people can make large sums of money. For example, in the United States, you can drill for oil with "tax dollars." Oil producers are allowed to deduct $27\frac{1}{2}$ percent of their gross income as a "depletion allowance" (with certain provisos). This means that out of a gross income of a million dollars, $275,000 will be tax-free in many cases. The cost of drilling dry holes is completely deductible. If you have a very high income, you try your luck with what are known as "tax dollars." "A tax dollar," one operator has explained, "is the name given to money that would normally be paid to the Internal Revenue Service." Anyone who strikes oil using tax dollars keeps $27\frac{1}{2}$ cents of each dollar tax-free. Add to that the other normal tax concessions, and the oil investor ends up paying no tax on thirty-five cents of each dollar. If he hadn't invested in oil and just paid his taxes, only 10 percent of each dollar would have been tax-free. If the investor loses, hits a dry well, then the whole of his losses, including "intangible expenses," are deductible from his gross income. For anyone in a high tax bracket, it is government-subsidized gambling. The way it works out in practice was illustrated in a speech in the Senate in 1957 by Senator Paul H. Douglas, of Illinois, who gave the figures of the net incomes of twenty-seven oil and gas companies over a ten-year period, and of the federal income taxes they paid. One company with a net income of $21,029,648 paid $1,252,000 in tax, or 5.9 percent, compared with the general corporate rate of 52 percent. Another company, with a net income of $4,477,673 in 1951, paid $404 in tax, which, the Senator pointed out, was less than what a married couple with three dependents and an adjusted gross income of $5,600 would pay. Another company which made $12.5 million not only paid no tax at all but had a tax credit of $500,000.[6]

To go in for this sort of smartness, one needs to have the hustler's love of pulling a fast one, for which some have a taste and others no taste at all.

This essential difference in character can be illustrated by what happened between two inventors, George Westinghouse and Nikola Tesla. Both men possessed extraordinary talents. At the time when the only form of electricity was Edison's direct current system, which could carry electric current only short distances from the powerhouse source, Tesla invented his "polyphase alternating system." This could carry a thousand times more electrical energy, and deliver it across vast distances. The genius who invented this had been working as a day laborer, unable to get other work, although he had previously worked for Edison. Edison hadn't seen any advantage in Tesla's alternating current. But Westinghouse had. He heard of the invention, went to Tesla, and offered him a million dollars for it. For the time, 1887, it was an enormous sum. In addition, the inventor was to be paid one dollar per horsepower generated. Not a man of business, Tesla sold away his patents, and later agreed to forego his royalties as well. Still, it may seem that a million dollars wasn't bad. Yet his biographer, John J. O'Neill, calculated that in foregoing his royalties Tesla lost around $12,000,000. He died broke, and today his name is largely forgotten, whereas Westinghouse is immortalized in refrigerators and other electrical appliances, the commercial viability of which depended on the alternating current system that Tesla invented.

People admire what a Westinghouse does because it's clever to make a fortune out of somebody else's brainchild, and clever is something we can all imagine ourselves being, whereas one can't imagine being a genius without being one. This is the essence of the hustler's great appeal—that he does something that we all feel we could do too, given the chance. Could we not all have done what a beautiful California lady publicist did? At the time when commercial TV was about to be launched in Britain, there was general pessimism about its chances of being profitable. But Suzanne Warner was sure it couldn't miss, and said so to Lew Grade, then just a theater agent. In fact, she told him, if he could find one million pounds, she could find another two million to get the project going. How was the delectable Miss Warner (then still in her twenties) in a position to offer £2,000,000 to Grade? Well, Miss Warner had a doctor with a very fashionable practice, and among his fashionable patients was a senior partner in the merchant bank of Warburgs. Miss Warner was the sort of girl who didn't miss a trick, and she got an introduction through her doctor to this banker. And being a persuasive girl (she was not a top publicist for nothing), she convinced the banker that there was a big future for commercial TV in Britain. She got him together with Lew Grade, and impressarios Val Parnell and Prince Littler, and out of this coming together emerged one of the largest of the new TV companies —ATV, now run by *Sir* Lew. Suzanne's cut of the founder's shares made her a substantial fortune.[7]

Some years later when it came to reallocating the licenses, an even more high-powered operator, David Frost, telephoned Sir Arnold Weinstock, managing director of General Electric Company, and without benefit of introduction (not needed on that level of fame) put to him a proposal for setting up a consortium to apply for one of the commercial channels. "Arnold's reaction was delightful," David is reported to have said. He was prepared to come in. With one backer lined up, David proceeded to go after the others he needed. Some turned him down, but he was not easily put off, and in the end succeeded in obtaining backing from the Imperial Tobacco Pension Fund, Lombard Banking, Pearl Assurance, London Cooperative Society, Magdalen College, Oxford, the publishers Weidenfeld and Nicolson, and the paper group, Bowater's. In this way the package was put together, million by million, until the capital of £6,500,000 needed to launch the company had been raised. With the ITA's acceptance of the consortium's application—it became London Weekend Television—David's personal holdings in the equity of the company immediately rose from a nominal value of £75,000 to something around £400,000.[8]

So far we have depicted the hustler at his more benign, as go-getter and opportunist. But there is another sort who has parallels with a very old figure in human affairs, the trickster. Essentially he is somebody who gets something for nothing, by some trick or device. In the mythologies of all ages there are many such figures. Of one Jung writes: ". . . his body is not a unity, and his two hands fight each other. He takes his anus off and entrusts it with a special task. Even his sex is optional, despite its phallic qualities: he can turn himself into a woman and bear children. From his penis he makes all kinds of useful plants."

This is the turncoat par excellence. He has long ceased to know what his original coat was.

What can be the etiology of such a character? From the skill with which he milks every source of sustenance we may conjecture that he was the sort of baby who pretended he hadn't had his food and so got fed twice. Or he discovered some way of making the rules that applied to others not apply to him. He must have been the type of child who, by a mixture of cheekiness, charm, flattery and cunning could always get his way. It must be assumed that he resorts to these methods because for him they are the only way, and such a state of affairs must mean that he feels unable to rely on people's lovingness to support him, perhaps because of a lack of lovingness on his part towards them.

It may also be due to an actual lack of lovingness in his environment, in which case his scheme for survival by means of trickery and cleverness will be justified by events. He will discover again and again that life is based on mutual exploitation, that there is no such thing as altruism, that nobody does anything for nothing. Since a large part of life *is* based on such principles (he's not the only trickster) he will have no difficulty in finding the people and the milieu to prove his theory, and so he will become confirmed in his belief that he has to outsmart everyone. He cannot entrust himself to the benevolence of others, because having so little of his own he

can't believe that anybody else has any. It is in this situation
that he puts all his faith in money, the only thing he can trust.

At least with money he can be sure of getting what he
needs, he has ample evidence of *its* efficacy, and as for the finer
things of life, he admits that perhaps they can't be bought,
but one day, as soon as he has made enough, he is going to get
out of the rat race and devote himself to the good work he is
really cut out for. He will spend more time with his family,
he will travel, ease up, educate himself, listen to music, go
into politics and change the rotten system so that others don't
have to do what he did. These ambitions are perpetually deferred until he has made enough. But enough never arrives
somehow, and even if he makes the pile he's always told himself he's going to, he can't stop now, after all he has sacrificed.
He can't quit when the tide is with him at last, when luck is
on his side. Life is short, he might never get another chance
like this one. And so it goes on.

Naturally, with money having this kind of hold, being vital
to the person's whole well-being, almost anything will be
done to get it, and from mere opportunism the hustler will
graduate to rougher stuff. Then see how he glitters with the
glamor of being on the make, and those who can't stand the
pace still can't help admiring him, can't help feeling a certain
masochistic satisfaction in the way that they are loosened from
around his neck at the critical moment. Ah, they sigh, falling,
feeling the weight of their own encumbrance no longer holding him back, ahh, now he is free of us, there was no holding
him. Thus do abandoned wives, friends, partners, colleagues,
respond to the dust that the hustler leaves in their faces, admiring the untoward speed of his departure. "If it was us,
we'd do the same, good luck to him." Of course, there is envy
and hatred too, and the hope that he will fall, and a kind of
conviction that in the end he will. But, basically, there is the
belief that he's right, and that his is the only way.

"Fuckin' big bastards, that's what the Beatles were," says John Lennon. "You have to be a bastard to make it, and that's a fact."[9] It is a notion that many others in that line of business would uphold on the basis of observation; subsequently what is seen to happen becomes glamorized as a necessary condition of success, and from there it is only a small step to *loving* the bastard. Whether it is Balzac's Lucien Chardin in *A Harlot High and Low,* or John Braine's Joe Lampton in *Room at the Top* and its sequels, or their real-life equivalents, we react to such types with fascination, because we recognize in them a part of ourselves that we tend to suppress, not daring to give full sway to our self-aggrandizing instinct, as they do. There is, of course, something enormously exhilarating about throwing off moral scruples and going all out in pursuit of life's goodies. The consequences come later. In the actual moment of making it, or feeling one is about to, which is the more characteristic situation of the hustler, it feels great.

Consider this frank confession from Norman Podhoretz's *Making It* of how he engaged in the office politics that eventually brought him the editorship of *Commentary:*

"After storming out of the *Commentary* offices that day, I went to the offices of The Boss's boss to announce my resignation and in the course of explaining to the head of the AJC's [American Jewish Committee] personnel department why I was quitting, I heard myself saying things I had never had any conscious intention of saying. The Boss, I said, was running the magazine in a spirit altogether alien to the way in which it had been run by Cohen . . ."

He went on to make various charges, and later realized that he was committed to "a power struggle whose seriousness and reality showed in nothing so clearly as in the dirtiness with which it had opened . . ." Later he reflected on his conduct of the struggle: "Not only had I won, but I had conducted the battle over a period of six weeks as skilfully as the most seasoned pro—lining up support and sympathy from all the right quarters and behaving myself with just the right combination of diffidence and fervor."

Now it is no longer just a matter of being around, and being liked, but of removing somebody else. For one person to get on, somebody else has to lose out. This aspect is illustrated by the case of an American businessman who went to see a potential investment partner at his house. Going through the proposed portfolio, the businessman saw at once the outline of the other man's character, depicted in the spread of investments. He could see his follies and foibles reflected in the shares, and immediately decided against the partnership. But he liked the man's house, and asked if he'd consider selling it. The man said he didn't want to sell it, but for a price he might. The price was too high, and the businessman didn't make an offer. When his wife said to him she really would like to have that house and perhaps they *should* pay the price, he replied, "We'll have it. At our price." Six months later he got it at a very reasonable figure. How could he have known this? He explains, "I knew from the guy's portfolio that he was going to be in trouble, and that *then* he was going to *have* to sell that house, and that when he did he'd be coming back to me and would be grateful for my offer."[10]

And so the hustler got his house, and is very happy there with his wife and family; for it is not in the hustler's nature to lament the misfortunes of others by which he has benefited. He comforts himself with the knowledge that they would have done the same to him.

And so the game gets rougher. The Beatles, according to John Lennon, took it out on some of the people who worked for them and with them. "They took a lot of shit from us because we were in such a shitty position,"[11] he says. The implication of this remark is quite clear; those who have the power of success behind them feel entitled to assert their kingship and exact the subservience of others as their due. And the others take it because the kings throw them free drinks and women and money. The Beatles were the Caesars, Lennon says, and their hangers-on were ready to take a great deal not to have to give up the privileged position at their feet. The picture here presented is of the sort of ruthless world of which it could certainly not be said that all you need is love. At the same time it is clear from the acridly self-critical tone of Lennon's reminiscences that a lack of something was perceived at least by him, that early on he was having reservations about the fun of living like Roman emperors.

The Beatles were not doing anything unusual in taking advantage of their position. The practice is general. Walter Winchell, the originator of the big-time American gossip column, put many forms of pressure on people, such as pressuring girls into sleeping with him in return for a mention. He made and destroyed people for the sheer pleasure of it, and because it was good copy. He was rewarded by being for a long time the highest-paid journalist in the world. He lived at the zenith of the hustler's world, which he both chronicled and exemplified.

Such people operate on the basis of being what they call realists, of seeing that that's the way things are, and *they* are not going to be the mugs. Of course, from their point of view, life *is* like that, and everything confirms it. They *do* live in the jungle. It *is* screw or be screwed, and only a fool does something for nothing. The fact is that they create their own world, which they take with them everywhere, and everything that they believe of it is true as a self-fulfilling prophecy is.

To those in it, it must have looked like the whole world, the whole of human nature. For the most basic law of the psyche is that you breathe in what you put out, and if you have soured the air, everything tastes sour to you. Freud wrote: ". . . the ego thrusts forth upon the external world whatever within itself gives rise to pain."[12] This is the basis of projection, and it means that people attribute to others those aspects of themselves that they cannot bear. It is a device of the mind whereby a danger from within, from part of the divided self, is put outside, where it is felt to be that much less dangerous, because of being that much further removed. It is a way of giving external form to a formless threat from within. The person who is threatened by a ruthless part of himself makes it into the ruthlessness of the world in which he lives, against which he then seeks to defend himself by becoming even more ruthless than "they" are. But in making himself that which he fears, he makes himself more fearful to himself; and so again he has to project this great inner fearfulness, and the world becomes even more fearful, even more threatening and ruthless, and he has to become even more ruthless to be able to deal with it.

Consider now that great numbers of people are doing this, and it can be understood how ghosts become real and are seen by many people at the same time. If those threatened by the ruthless parts of themselves project these parts upon each other, you have a rat race, and it is perpetual; it can never be won because, by definition, it can only be won by somebody more ruthless than everybody else; and such a person's ruthlessness would be so great he would have to project it, making the world ever more menacing.

Unlike the romantic who in his hubris grasps the prize, and then incurs the envy of the gods (paranoia) and becomes "the mad millionaire," the hustler is smart. He sees to it that he never actually gains so much that he has to cope with the fury of the dispossessed. The hustler maintains his equilibrium by keeping in constant balance his powers of triumphing over others with their capacity for retaliation. It is this balancing of forces that gives to the rat race its characteristic feeling of static struggle, that for all the desperate expenditure of energy, nobody is actually moving very much. For if somebody moves ahead too far, he immediately becomes vulnerable to the hatred of those left behind. Nor must he drop so far behind as to place himself in a position where the others will be able to feel safe in despising him, because of the great lead they have. If that happens, the beaten rat drops into a lower league of the rat race, where again all the rats are more or less equal.

While a vicious circle is by definition self-perpetuating, it also has another aspect to which less attention is given, namely, that it can be broken at any point. And so, while it is true that the familiar wish to get out of the rat race cannot be achieved by winning it, it *is* possible to get out.

Breaking the vicious circle at *any* point means that immediately at that point a different kind of contact is made with people—they may still be in the rat race, and so may you, for that matter, but *in this instance* it becomes possible to establish contact between the parts of oneself and the other person that aren't in the rat race. *They* do not need to do you in first because *they* no longer feel threatened by your intention of doing them in before they can do it to you. When you are in the rat race, everybody is in it; but when you are not, you find that an amazing number of people are not. To those who have the capacity for sweetening the air, it does taste sweeter. The person who does not project a ruthless money jungle (but contains it, bears it, and by bearing it, modifies it) does not find himself living in such a world. He will take in a more benign external reality, which in turn will make his inner situation safer, which means his ruthlessness is more capable of being modified or restrained.

Of course, one unfortunate outcome can be a kind of ghastly goody-goodyness that is often observed in people who have rejected the values of the rat race. Where such a powerful human instinct as the one for self-aggrandizement is totally banished, or sublimated, it takes the bite out of life. Aggressiveness in its dynamic aspect is simply energy, and as such morally indefinable. It is necessary to have something of the hustler, of the go-getter, of the contender, the money-maker, in oneself, or one is merely passive.

In the past two decades it has become the norm for people on all levels to go into the marketplace and shout their wares. Nobody can afford to despise the process any longer; for with everyone else shouting, there is no other way of making yourself heard. Whatever you have to sell or offer now has to be pushed. It means that to a certain extent everybody is put in the position of having to hustle just in order to get by. Doctors, lawyers, authors, reformers, revolutionaries, religious leaders, moralists, prophets, scientists, academics, all have to hustle in the marketplace with the hookers and the pimps, the gamblers, wheeler-dealers, media men, ad men, car salesmen, politicos and abortionists. The person with no talent for attracting attention will simply be ignored. No use to keep your voice at a gentlemanly pitch; nobody will hear its mellifluous inflections.

One can see why this is so often the case. In a culture where there is an excess of most things, and markets are flooded with goods, whether cars, or records, or ideas, the public cannot try everything for itself in order to make up its own mind. There is just too much to try. And there is a lack of general expertise to enable people to decide between different car engines or refrigeration techniques, philosophical concepts or political solutions. The more there is to choose from, the less judgment can come into it. Even where judgment is still possible, in selecting a marriage partner, for example, it is simpler to take the best seller, the type that everyone else is going for this year, and about which there have been good reports. Even to work out one's own ideal is an arduous business; it's always less burdensome to take the generally accepted model. So on the whole, young men look for girls who correspond as nearly as possible to the most advertised image of desirability; the same goes for cars, dishwashers, morality, politics, religion. Anyone who has anything genuine to offer, and finding himself having to function within this context of a multiplicity of choices, knows he has to hustle at least part of the time. The alternative is impotence and silence.

It was this kind of problem that faced Norman Mailer in the fifties when he published two good novels, *The Barbary Shore* and *The Deer Park,* that almost everybody missed: either to accept the casual verdict, and allow his reputation and life to be determined by the exigencies of mood and opinion, or take the hustler's way of bending the moods and opinions of others to favor him. Mailer, perhaps because of his natural pugnacity, but also perhaps because he could see no other way, took the hustler's course, and boldly decided to advertise himself, something that he has been doing ever since. "The way to save your work and reach more readers," he wrote, "is to advertise yourself, steal your own favorite page out of Hemingway's unwritten Notes From Papa on How the Working Novelist Can Get Ahead . . ."[13]

But the techniques of hustling—however necessary and unavoidable—are not all lovely, and someone with something real to sell may feel demeaned at having to sell it *as if* it were kitsch. Mailer recalls having written to Hemingway to seek a selling quote for his novel *The Deer Park,* feeling that it would make the difference between a half-success and a breakthrough. But at the same time he was furious with himself for "stealing a trick from Hollywood." Perhaps because of his ambivalence he hustled rather ineffectively, by writing:

"—but if you do not answer, or if you answer with the kind of crap you use to answer unprofessional writers, sycophants, brown nosers, etc., then fuck you, and I will never attempt to communicate with you again.

"—and since I suspect that you are even more vain than I am, I might as well warn you that there is a reference to you on Page 353 which you may or may not like."

It was ineffectual because the tyro hustler couldn't resort to the kind of flattery and craftiness that were called for, couldn't humble himself enough, couldn't risk a rejection or an evasion, and so he bungled it. Ten days later his book came back, stamped Address Unknown—Return to Sender. His pride broken now, he sent off copies to a dozen other writers, including Graham Greene, Cyril Connolly and Alberto Moravia. Only Moravia, a personal acquaintance, answered, but because Mailer was reluctant to make use of someone he knew personally, he had written to Moravia that he didn't want his comment for advertising copy, and consequently he couldn't use what Moravia had to say. "So that particular effort to promote myself ended in fiasco," says Mailer. He then adds: "This confession off my liver forever, it occurs to me now that I must have carried the memory as a silent shame which helped to push me further and deeper into the next half year of bold assertions, half-done work, unbalanced heroics, and an odd notoriety of my own choice."[14]

If a hustler has not made it after a number of years, he becomes a caricature of the type: there he is, same as always, whispering in your ear of fortunes to be had, of connections, of deals, of ins with the high-ups, of formulas, dodges, devices. Some may even be workable. But like the boy who shouted "wolf," the man who has spent too long in hustling, in crying "Eureka!" when there was no jackpot, is not believed, and at best he spins out his days on his piece of somebody else's action. Or else he takes on one of the other positions open to him: he becomes a go-between, intermediary, agent, aide, yes-man to somebody who has made it. He becomes another man's instrument; he may have been smarter than the person by whom he is now manipulated, but probably he has lacked some touch of madness, or capacity for illusion that, ironically, turns out to have been more necessary than cleverness.

Or, if he *has* made it, his success often has a certain acrid taste to it. Why should this be? Why should he not be able to enjoy it wholeheartedly? Essentially it is because everything he has done has been built on the quicksand of his multifarious dealings, and only the speed with which he hops from one position to another disguises the fact that he is sinking.

He has abandoned his loves, whether they are people, things, principles, courses of action, or forms of enjoyment, for the sake of money. The penalty of his freedom of movement is that he never has a base. He tends to have little inner solidness, because being committed to nothing he has never stood his ground *anywhere*. The result is that his inner situation is a miasma of deals. His resources are split and scattered, and when it comes to a showdown he is like a mercenary with no country of his own to defend.

"The man who acts ruthlessly," says the psychoanalyst Dr. Eric Brenman, "introjects a ruthless superego, and is then at its mercy."[15] Whatever has needed to be done in the outside world is done again internally, with one's self as victim. The driving force to get on produces also the driven man.

A research project carried out at the Charing Cross Hospital in London arrived at the conclusion that some heart attacks are the result of "psychosis of work and tension addiction" on the part of individuals who are capable of destroying themselves little by little and insist on living in an environment that invites them to do so. The researchers concluded that the coronary patient suffered from a remarkable amount of hostility and aggression (though often repressed), and was very conscious of time pressure upon him. He regarded this as normal. He did not seem able to distinguish between doing and overdoing. He may, says the report, have preferred continued illness and the risk of sudden death to even a temporary modification in his way of living.

Such a picture is suggestive of the hustler type. In the case of the person who succumbs to the stress and strain of the rat race, there is good reason to think that what he is broken by is the unresolvable conflict between the demands of his greedy and self-aggrandizing nature on the one hand and the strict requirements of his superego on the other. This is what tears him apart. He is in the position of Claudius in *Hamlet,* who complains that his words fly up to heaven while his thoughts remain below.

> Offence's gilded hand may shove by justice;
> And oft 'tis seen the wicked prize itself
> Buys out the law: but 'tis not so above . . .

The reason why "stress" illnesses have become so widespread is not so much because the pace of life has quickened as because we live in a state of alienation from our conscience, acting and behaving in ways that we cannot reconcile with our sense of right. Like Claudius we wish to retain "the wicked prize" and to be pardoned. If we seek the path of virtue we are subjected to the derision of the trickster in us, who accuses us of being timid, gutless, afraid of dirtying our hands in the stuff of life, and holier than thou. If we go our own way not caring for others, we find our carelessness in external relationships duplicated inside us, so that we cannot care for ourselves—either in the sense of "like," or in the sense of "take care of"—with the sort of consequences we have been discussing.

Of course, it may be said that it is not always so, that some people do get away with it. There are plenty of rich wicked old men, while innocents also fall ill and die young. I am not suggesting that the money motive is more than a single strand in the motivational weave of the personality. What is clear is that it can in some cases become the predominant one, and that when this is so, everything, including the individual's health, is affected. There are enough variables, in personal circumstances, accidental happenings, constitutional factors, to account for individuals who apparently get away with it. But the overall picture, the sociological evidence, the historical perspective and the casebooks of psychiatry point to a connection between the obsessive pursuit of money and breakdown.

Some of those who escape are men whose businesses get bigger and bigger not because they want to make more money but because their capacities are enlarging and they need more to do, bigger things to run. These are cases of the individual's growth requiring external accommodation. And one would not expect this kind of man to fall victim to overwork or stress illnesses. For him it would not be overwork or stress. Others have recourse to psychological processes that obliterate all conscience, and so spare themselves.

9

The Double-Dealer

Of course we are *against* theft. If we are asked our views we say that the problem of crime must be tackled, the thief must be stopped. Harsher penalties, psychiatric treatment, social reform—whatever our pet solution, in principle we are in agreement: to steal is morally wrong and socially impermissible. Yet in a place of declared unreality like a movie house we will relax this moral posture sufficiently to allow ourselves to empathize with the robbers, to feel the excitement of the heist, the thrill of getting away with it, and take a gloating pleasure in the haul. Naturally, we would feel differently if it were our own money, but as it isn't, we can enjoy the story.

If we consider what we are so ingenuously enjoying, and why, we are bound to conclude that thieving is not as alien to our natures as our declared anti-crime attitudes suggest. It is true that the old Hollywood Code laid down that sympathy must never be aroused for the wrongdoer, and anyone who broke the law had to be shown getting his punishment, but this was always a formality, like the final clinch, and nowadays it is not bothered with too much. A film such as *The Godfather* makes no bones about asking us to identify with the criminals, and its enormous success is an indication of our readiness to do so. Of course, it's only a film, and we are not held accountable for what we feel when confronted with fictional events. Precisely for this reason we let them affect us without unduly censoring ourselves. We enjoy a good robbery on the screen and that's all there is to it. But is it? There is evidence that we do not confine the thief in us to our secret lives in the dark of the cinema; that, in fact, we take him out with us into our everyday world, let him indulge his larcenous appetites under the cover of bourgeois respectability.

Consider, for a start, the man who is seen everywhere and knows everybody. Observe him entering a smart restaurant, and watch how the headwaiter bows to him and the proprietor embraces him. The doorman has parked his car. The barman hovers, wondering about an apéritif to start with. The wine waiter waits patiently with his list. Our elegant diner imbibes the fashionable atmosphere as one to whom it is home. Exchanging greetings and pleasantries with other fashionable diners, he eases his elegantly clothed form into the depth of his chair, and considers the important question of what to start with. He tells his companions that he can recommend the oysters, escargots, giant Mediterranean prawns, the caviar. His manner is discreetly expansive, gently solicitous as to everybody else's gastronomic well-being; anyone observing him would conclude that he is a man with a position in the world, and the assured way he signs his bill at the end, adding 20 percent tip in writing, confirms the impression of a man of means, accustomed to spending. The last thing that anybody would take him for is a thief, and yet that is what he is. For the bill that he signs so grandly is not going to be paid.

In 1971, London's fashionable Aretusa Club wrote off £10,000 in bad debts,[1] and many restaurateurs have the same story to tell. A few of the customers who don't pay their bills have genuinely come upon hard times since their last supper, but others are the sort of people who just don't pay bills. Our elegant diner also hasn't paid his tailor. And if the tailor writes to him threatening legal action, he replies that the suits don't fit him; of all the tailors he has patronized none has made him such ill-fitting suits, and if the tailor genuinely valued his customer he would offer to replace these ill-fitting suits at his own expense rather than impertinently claim payment for shoddy work. Usually tailors don't sue customers when there is any chance of bad publicity; and restaurant bills are rarely large enough to justify legal action, considering the cost of that. So our elegant thief gets away with it in both cases, and next time he comes to the restaurant he is welcomed as effusively as before. The restaurateur Alvaro says, "Whatever has been going on between the office and a customer, when he arrives in the restaurant I know nothing about it. My manner is exactly the same. Am I going to have a different manner for all the people who owe me money? And how do I know which ones are just a little slow in paying, or forgetful, or have been abroad, and those who are the thieves and don't intend to pay. I don't know, so I have to treat them all the same."[2]

On this level of society, the rule is that such things as unpaid bills are not mentioned, and this, of course, enables some people to pile up quite enormous debts that are never paid. If they are not written off by those who have been swindled, the defaulters rather than pay up may choose to be made bankrupt. Of course, there are laws about bankruptcy, but if a man's home and its contents are in his wife's name, they cannot be touched. And in England if you have a private limited liability company, it is regarded in law as quite separate from its directors and shareholders. "You don't go bust, the company does," says the financial writer William Davis.

He adds, "Your creditors are entitled to your property—if any. But a really successful bankrupt will usually have ensured that it is out of reach."[3]

But do not weep too profusely over the plight of fashionable restaurateurs. Some of them more than compensate themselves for the anticipated bad debts by padding everybody's bills. This can result in the following kind of situation. A big spender had amassed a considerable bill at a particular night club. He was a man who never checked his bills, always signed them without hesitation. After repeated attempts to obtain payment, the owner of the night club finally confronted the big spender in his office, and flourished the sheaf of unpaid bills, amounting to over £1,000. "I tell you what," the big spender said, "I'll make you an offer—I'll give you £750." When the night-club proprietor protested that this was robbery, the big spender said, "Look, I'm only robbing you of what you cheated me by."

It is a system that prevails in other areas too. One kind of thief overcharges, another kind defaults on payment. In both cases respectability is maintained. The essence of all such transactions is their ambiguity. The man who steals a loaf of bread is beyond doubt a thief, but the man who either overcharges or underpays is operating in an area of uncertainty where individual acts cannot be accurately judged on the basis of the available evidence. It is necessary to see the total man, in all his dealings, to know if he is a thief or not, and very few people ever see the total man. Therefore, for the majority this type of person retains respectability, and only a few intimates really know what a crook he is. Where someone is said to have taken in everyone for years, it is not that he has necessarily resorted to such elaborate subterfuge, or that he has been so successful in concealing his true nature, or even that others have been so gullible; it is simply that stealing is tolerated as part of the system, as long as it is done in a sufficiently ambiguous way not to place anyone else in the embarrassing position of finding out. As long as what you do is *debatable,* nobody will regard you as a thief. They may call you that, but it is only a manner of speaking.

In the film business, for instance, it is thought of as "mildly crooked" but inevitable that theater owners will "understate" the amount they have taken at the box office (on which they have to pay percentages to the distributors) ; equally, the distributors' custom of charging to a particularly profitable film costs incurred on others, or even privately, is so well established as to be taken for granted. Telling someone to "Charge it to X" is a routine swindle perpetrated every day in most companies, without being thought about twice. One publicist says, "My God, the lunches and dinners and parties we had on ——," mentioning a highly successful film he had been handling. He had taken fifteen people to lunch at Maxim's in Paris, and charged it to this film. Who could ever prove that the purpose of this entertainment was to promote another film, or himself, or his girl friend? It is only from the fact that with big money-earning films large sums invariably "disappear," that such practices can be *known* to have taken place. To counteract this, some producers employ squads of accountants to go around the country and the world checking books and receipts, and the fact that the expenditure this involves is considered financially justifiable indicates the scale on which money was disappearing before.

Getting free trips out of rich companies, or having facilities placed at one's disposal, or being grandly entertained, or getting very favorable terms for buying the company's product—whether it's a car, or a house, or a color TV—or having various other of one's needs taken care of as part of an overall *service,* is regarded as the rightful due of someone in a position of influence or importance.

The Knapp commission, looking into police corruption in

New York, found that next to the Mafia, the largest source of bribery was "legitimate business seeking to ease its way through the maze of city ordinances and regulations." The report found that businessmen gave presents to the police in the hope that the police would give extra or better service and overlook minor illegal acts.

What happens with the police happens, with ramifications, wherever someone by virtue of his position is capable of being useful to someone else. Looking after a good connection is not quite the same as bribery, but it's close—as in the case of store buyers who regularly receive presents from sales representatives, as in the case of town hall officials who are sent gifts by businessmen in appreciation of past courtesies. On this level it is rarely a matter of someone's being offered a straight bribe in return for a particular "favor"; it is done neither so crudely, nor so explicitly, but in the guise of helpfulness. The person who has received generous treatment is "as helpful as he possibly can be" when he comes to have some hand in the affairs of the company that has been so adept and lavish in its "public relations" towards him. The essence of the transaction is concealed in well-chosen euphemisms. The network of business connections consists of dozens, even hundreds, of such relationships, in which one person is indebted to another and therefore "obliged" to be helpful when it is required of him.

Although it is never discussed in such a precise way, there is a definite correspondence between the degree of indebtedness that somebody has incurred by acceptance of largesse, and the size of the favor he may eventually be asked to perform, or the extent of the trouble that he may be asked to go to for his "friends." A few free meals and bottles of Scotch at Christmas involve a man in no more than courtesies in return; but as he starts to accept the richer pickings—the trips, the consulting fees, the half-price goods obtained through the trade

—he is all the time committing himself more and more to his benefactor.

In practice, there is so much of this going on all the time, varying from the automatic "servicing of contacts" to the rather more specific building up of a particular useful connection, that at any one time no individual recipient of such blandishments knows quite how deep he is in, and perhaps only when the pressure is put on him (on the lines of "Look, you can't let us down") does he realize to what extent he has forsaken his freedom of action and become somebody else's satellite. Even then it is unlikely that he will allow himself to pause and reflect on what he is doing. It would require a great disentangling of business relationships from private friendships, of genuine consideration for a generous friend's interests from bought loyalty, of the public interest from self-interest, in order to arrive at the truth, and most people in those circumstances don't bother. Only if something goes badly wrong are such connections and arrangements shown in the harsh light of disinterested inquiry, and then to everybody's horror they not only are but also look crooked.

What makes the system *look* perfectly respectable most of the time is that up to a point it *is* quite reasonable and justifiable and honest to cultivate connections, to engender a favorable climate for one's own activities, products, projects; when that point has been passed is often impossible to tell on a purely descriptive basis (When does a gift become a bribe?). ". . . there are no clear boundaries between propriety and impropriety in what one might loosely call the encouragement of a favourable market climate for a company's shares. At one end of the scale the process is downright fraudulent, but at the other it is legally permissible, generally accepted and, arguably, of benefit to the structure of industry and the economy," says a financial writer in the London *Times*.[4]

On Wall Street some of the most highly respected firms will

bring out a share issue in a company they know to be in a bad way. Financial advisers will cynically tell their clients of the alternative open to them: "Either you go bust, or you go public."

One of Britain's leading industrialists says: "Business is done in areas that may be defined as white, black and grey. The white area is one of indisputable honesty, and the black indisputably crooked, but a large amount of business is carried on in the gray area, where it could be either one or the other."

It is in this uncertain gray area that the respectable crook thrives. Everybody knows of permitted rackets inside his own line of business. Specialists working in National Health Service hospitals often lift expensive health service equipment and drugs for use on their private patients, whom, of course, they charge a fee. They would deeply resent being called thieves, and they are men of the utmost respectability. Waiters in restaurants by tradition take home a certain amount of drink and food. This kind of theft is in fact budgeted for: Alvaro says, "You always hope that the staff are honest. But, on the other hand, provided they rob a little you don't mind, it's when they rob too much that you step into it. Provided my percentage at the end of the week is correct, they can invite everybody. What I want is 30 percent. If they are able to make 35 percent and give the five away, or put it in their pocket, good luck to them. I don't mind. They can eat, they can drink what they like. But the figures have to come out right." If the drinks stock is down by £450, then there must be £1000 in cash or signed bills to cover it, because in the running of the restaurant it is calculated that the cost of drinks is 45 percent of takings. If in the weekly stocktaking these figures don't work out, it means that the staff have been putting too much in their own pockets, and the manager is told, "Sir, you need a change of air."[5]

In this sort of way thieving is kept within the bounds of respectability. Waiters are known to steal, and it is impossible for a man with several restaurants to keep a personal check on them. Therefore, what cannot be prevented is tolerated by tacit agreement.

The same kind of system applies with expense accounts. A certain level of expenses is considered appropriate to a particular job, and only when that level is exceeded are questions asked. Within the prescribed limits, falsification is tolerated. Periodically, company chiefs "tighten-up on expenses," and then accounts are more closely scrutinized, questions are asked, and everyone has to be more careful. But prosecutions for the falsification of expense accounts are virtually unknown, so much has the practice become part of the system.

The most distinguished precedents exist for this. When the Congress of the United States received George Washington's expenses[6] for winning the War of Independence it naturally enough did not question any of the details, though some were notably vague. The total came to £18,284, and this was at a time when a private in the Revolutionary Army got about 25 pence a month and major generals something less than £6.40, which suggests that Washington was not exactly depriving himself. On the first day, Washington put in for £329.42—or the equivalent of, say, hiring fifty major generals for a month. The entry in the general's neat and meticulous handwriting reads: "To Cash paid for saddlery, a Letter Case, Maps, Glasses &c, &c, &c." The "&c" is an extremely useful symbol in the lexicon of expense account writing, and Washington made ample use of it, supplementing it with such other favored categories as 'Sundry," "Reconnoitering" and "Secret Services." Other entries merely said "To Mr. Ritchie" and "To Mr. Van" without further explanation, though it transpires these payments were for Madeira wine. Congress, of course, paid its first President's expenses without question, and no company today that valued the services of its executives would be so vulgar as to question the "etceteras" or the "sundries" in their accounts.

Such matters are normally only raised by awkward radicals, who perhaps do not enjoy the facility of an expense account themselves. The convention is that on a certain level people's integrity is assumed to be beyond suspicion, and therefore there is no need to inquire into it. It is only when a scandal breaks, or a muckraking journalist makes some unsavory discovery, or private documents find their way into the offices of anti-Establishment journals, that it becomes clear how little justification there is for such blithe assumptions. In France it was discovered that the then Prime Minister M. Chaban-Delmas had paid no income tax from 1966 to 1969, and in 1968 had even had a tax refund. In the ensuing hullabaloo, his tax affairs were subjected to rigorous public scrutiny. No actual illegality on his part was discovered. Nonetheless, he shortly afterwards ceased to be Prime Minister.

What emerged from all the attention that the case received was a new awareness of how prominent and respectable French citizens could manipulate the tax system so that without actually breaking the law they could avoid paying tax. M. Chaban-Delmas, for example, was benefiting from a system that has operated in France whereby an individual receives a tax credit on his investment income. On the principle that company tax had already been paid, the investor could set a proportion of this income, 50 percent in some cases, against his own tax liability. In effect, anyone with sufficient resources could ensure he had enough credits to offset his entire tax liability.

Another expedient is to buy a building on the list of historic monuments and restore it; in that case, the state pays a subsidy of 50 percent of the cost of restoration, and allows another 50 percent of this cost to be deducted from taxes.

To say that such devices are perfectly legal is to be merely legalistic; one is meant to pay taxes if one's income is above a certain level (which a Prime Minister's certainly is), and to avoid doing so is, in effect, if not in law, robbing those others who *are* paying. But it is part of the system of the respectable thief that he does not look at it in this way. He is so deeply immersed in the intricacies of claims and allowances and write-offs and tax credits that he loses sight of what he is really doing, which is stealing, whatever the law says. If a Prime Minister avails himself of such opportunities, it may be assumed that many other eminent members of the community are doing likewise, and without considering themselves in the least dishonest.

In the United States, Western Union paid no tax for eight years despite profits in all of them. The company used the most profitable bookkeeping techniques "by accelerating its plant and equipment write-offs and treating interest charges as expenses for tax purposes though capitalising them in its financial accounts."[7] In Britain, the textile giant Courtaulds has taken full advantage of equivalent devices for avoiding tax; these include "turning all the freehold properties in the group into leaseholds and then passing the almost valueless reversionary interest on to a subsidiary thereby establishing a capital loss." This is in a year when profits rose from £42 million to £45.5 million. As one commentator put it, "What Courtaulds has proved is that there is a vast difference between the accounts a company draws up for tax purposes and what is on show for shareholders."[8]

Another time-honored system is to "live on expenses." There are people who pay for nothing. Everything is charged. One businessman said he could carry a £1 note in his pocket for two weeks without making any inroads upon it. His company paid him a modest salary of £3,000 a year, out of which he paid his tax, his rent, and for his breakfasts. Everything else was charged. He drove a company car. When he traveled abroad it was for the company; since he was in the leisure line the cost of almost anything he might want to do could be described as a business expense. As a restaurateur, his restaurant bills were expenses. He had to dine at his own restaurant to keep the staff on their toes and oversee everything. He had to dine at other restaurants to see what his rivals were doing. Naturally, he had to dress smartly; so his clothes were chargeable too, particularly as one of his companies ran a men's boutique.

A form of moneymaking revolting to conventional susceptibilities is to introduce girls to men, or men to girls, for their business and pleasure and your profit. It is called living off the earnings of prostitution, and the people who do this sort of thing are usually underworld figures, pimps. When, in the early sixties, a society osteopath, Dr. Stephen Ward, was found to have taken money from girls he had introduced to prominent aristocrats and politicians, with whom they later had sexual relations, for which they received payments, he was hounded down, and put on trial. In its day, it was a great scandal. Rather than face the disgrace of conviction on such an unsavory charge, Ward took his life.

In the climate of outraged bourgeois morality it was scarcely noted that the sums of money Ward had taken were trivial in the extreme, and that he was the sort of man who, always being hard up, would take money from anyone. He may have been a bit bohemian in his equal readiness to cadge off a prostitute or a Lord, but that is hardly the same as being a professional procurer. But the way it came out, it looked and sounded sordid.

Today computer dating does on a mass scale what Ward did occasionally, makes large sums of money out of it, advertises its services openly, and is considered respectable. The director of a computer dating agency is not regarded as a pimp, although one of the services he provides is to bring people together for the purpose of having sexual relations, and he takes money for this. But by operating in an area of ambiguity—it is not his concern what the parties with a mutual interest in sex actually do when the computer has brought them together —he is in the clear. The form of the advertisements, and the magazines in which they are placed, indicate the service being offered. But as long as such activities can be kept sufficiently ambiguous, they are acceptable.

The ethos that I have been describing is by no means confined to private acts; it has its most paradoxical and profitable flowering in large-scale business, corroborating the old Raleigh dictum that taking millions is never regarded as a crime. There is a whole series of offenses, some of which are technically criminal, which do not reflect adversely upon those who commit them. The establishment of monopolies is the most obvious one. It may be illegal, but in a bourgeois society nobody will recoil in horror from you, or refuse to have you in his house, because you are a monopolist.

On the one hand the U.S. Department of Justice charged the gigantic IBM corporation with wielding illegal monopoly power. On the other hand, one of its principals, Arthur Watson, was appointed the United States Ambassador in Paris.

The reason that monopolies are not permitted in most societies is because they *are* a means of robbing people, in the way that the "robber barons" did. But there is no social stigma attached to this kind of robbery. There is a long catalogue of business crimes that are similarly exempted from moral censure. While it is not my object to associate any particular company with a particular crime, most of the offenses that appear below are sufficiently widespread to be regarded as normal business practice. They include tendentious double-entry bookkeeping, designed to tell one story to the tax inspector and quite another to the investor; misrepresentation in advertising; giving short measure by means of packaging that creates the impression you are giving people more for their money than they are in fact getting; the creation of a favorable market feeling for shaky companies; using substandard materials; catch clauses in contracts whose true import only becomes apparent later; industrial espionage; labeling or describing products incorrectly; cutting costs by reducing safety margins; price-fixing; large-scale political bribery by means of contributions to party funds or projects; the manipulation of privileged charitable foundations to further one's business aims or to hinder those of a rival; the stealing of industrial processes and formulas; pollution; over-exploitation of natural resources; making commodities that are unsafe; making weapons of aggression, torture and oppression; subjecting workers to harmful conditions. All of these are crimes sometimes, and in certain circumstances prosecutions do take place, convictions are obtained, fines imposed. But there is no real loss of social standing in being found guilty of such offenses.

The sort of moral contortionism in which "decent" people indulge where moneymaking is concerned was illustrated by the thalidomide case. The original manufacturers of the drug contravened or ignored many safety considerations in promoting this calamitous tranquilizer. In their determination to capture a profitable market, they concealed or refuted counterindications that came to light. It is an almost unbelievable story of men abandoning human considerations and standards of scrupulousness in the grip of the money motive. But the men who did this were not monsters or criminals, in the accepted sense; they were all respectable people: businessmen, doctors, chemists. At their trial[9] in Germany, *the prosecutor* made the case in mitigation on their behalf. The accused, he said, belonged to a group "which as a collectivity of persons is open to the charge of accepting an improper division of risks between the justified interests of the consumers and the commercial interests of the company." But "The individuals accused as members of the said collectivity were victims of the existing group pressure." The prosecutor said that it had to be borne in mind that the accused had undergone much personal suffering since the opening of the criminal investigations in 1962, and that in doing what they did "they were impeded by the social structure characteristic of modern industrial society." The prosecution went on to say: "But the individual who belongs to a group is also in danger, since it is difficult for him to exempt himself from the rules of its particular game, which are not always compatible with the requirements of the law. The individual often stands alone against the interests of the group, which are partly explicit and partly carefully hidden in small print. He is in many cases left to his own resources when the economically stronger party—individual or group—can also rely on the support of influential figures or institutions, for whom our social order makes it quite possible not merely to conceal mistakes from the public but even, in extreme cases, to declare them legitimate practice."

It was decided by the court and the prosecution that in view of all the factors it was not in the general interest to continue the trial, and it was therefore suspended. In effect, the court was recognizing that the particular men before them had been acting in accordance with an ethos that was general, that what they had done was the prevailing practice.

Nothing could illustrate more clearly, or more tragically, how the ruthless moneymaker functions in alienation from human decency, and how when things go badly wrong society exonerates such behavior by saying he is no worse than any other, a truly stupendous piece of rationalization.

The thief is not confined to the underworld, or any particular class or condition of people; he exists on all levels of society, though on some levels he can throw up a smoke screen of self-justification which conceals from himself and others the true nature of his acts.

In the case of "the criminal classes," all sorts of reasons could be found for their antisocial behavior, ranging from dire need and bad upbringing to inherent viciousness, psychopathology and not knowing any better. But why does the affluent, well brought up, well-educated, respectable citizen steal? How does it come about that the desire for money (even when people have no pressing need of it—that is, are not going short of anything essential to their well-being) can make cultivated men act with the indifference to human consequences of the original thalidomide-makers in West Germany?

The sense of shock and shame and fascination that crime can arouse in "decent people" is largely a matter of its ambience, and its usually overtly violent methods. The robber is equated with the ruffian. Robbery is thought of as a violent deprivation. In its most primitive form it consists of physically taking something from somebody else by force. But physical robbery, as we see, is by no means the only kind, or even the most practiced today. Reworked, the basic impulse to rob finds its expression in many socially sanctioned activities. The fact that these may appear to be nonviolent, even gentlemanly, in execution does not mean that the essential violence of robbery has been disposed of; it means only that the violence is much more hidden, and not acknowledged.

The person who evades taxes would not regard himself as

doing anything violent. But looking closely into the emotions of the large-scale and systematic evader, one usually finds in him a triumphant feeling of "having got away with it," a gloating pleasure in his hoard. This differs very little, emotionally, from the robber's satisfaction with his haul. Only their methods differ. And when one goes further and asks what is the source of this pleasure in the illicit pile, one has to conclude that it depends on others *not* having it. Those who pay up are thought of as fools. It is not without meaning that the more outspoken of those who get away with it often speak of those who do not as poor buggers, sods and suckers. In this terminology of contempt one can see the sadistic triumph over others that the respectable thief just as much as the violent criminal feels in his heart. And this is not merely his fantasy, because, of course, ultimately the income tax evader, just as much as the robber, *is* depriving others of things that are theirs, and on the deepest levels of the mind the difference of *method* does not change the basic meaning of the act.

When we say about somebody, "Oh, he's a thief," we are perhaps giving a truer estimate of his nature than we realize at the time. And when we are so exultant about getting some bargain that we describe it as "a steal," we are probably expressing a momentary insight into our own motives.

If we wish to penetrate our cover of respectability, and face the truth of our motives, we need to look not so much at the strict legalities of a particular transaction as at its emotional background.

We want *more* than we are entitled to. We could, and sometimes do, resolve our problem by reducing our desires, as Zen Buddhism urges. But this is the hard way in our society, which does not readily allow us to want less. The other way is to *pay* more—in effort, in struggle, in toil, in responsibility—so that the desired "more" shall have been earned.

Some are able to take this course. But for many it is impossible to pay more; they lack the strength, or some deep-rooted meanness prevents them from paying the true worth of anything; they must hang on to their valuables. And such people, caught between their overstimulated desires and their underdeveloped capacity for payment, resort to theft, of one kind or another.

It is not only money and possessions that are acquired in this illicit way, but also standing, reputation, honor, respect, position—all these are cashable, since there is a direct relationship between such attributes and monetary reward. The thief does not have to steal money in the first place; he can steal another's eminence, and it is as good as money. Here again there is a purely formal distinction between the respectable thief and the underworld criminal: it is the difference between appropriating somebody else's ideas, say, and robbing a bank. Descriptively, the latter may *look* much more like stealing than the former, but in motivational terms they can be very alike, and in cash terms they may well amount to the same thing. But plagiarism does not have the same connotation of *crime* as putting your hand in the till, or shoplifting, or burning your house down for the insurance.

The point at which the double-dealer reveals himself is when, under the pressure of impulses that he does not understand, he resorts to an unequivocal crime. There are well-off people—daughters of millionaires—who are caught shoplifting. There was a case in England not long ago of a *magistrate* caught shoplifting. He told the court that so many people had appeared before him on this charge, he had decided to test for himself whether it was true that someone might be caught absent-mindedly putting in his pocket something that he had no intention of stealing. He admitted to the foolishness of his experiment, of which he had not told anyone else in advance, and that he had been under mental strain.

The recurring cry in such cases is "I don't know what came over me" and "I can't think why I did it." Why would a rich man's daughter or a rich man suddenly give way to an impulse to steal? Certainly, it is unlikely that such a person has suddenly given way to an *alien* impulse. It is more likely that at this particular moment the thief, who had long been stuffing his pockets in respectable ways, came into the open, perhaps with the desire to be caught and punished for his previous offenses. It is the whole system of respectable thieving by which we live that such a person wishes to have taken into account when in a moment of confused "owning up" he resorts to some clear and unmistakable theft.

If we dismiss the sophistry that it's all right because everybody does it, and accept that we are dealing with a widespread criminal impulse, the question arises: How does it come about?

The case of a highly respected London businessman provides a useful illustration.[10] David (which is not his real name) comes from a middle-class background; his father had a small business, and there was never any shortage of money. As a young man he ran away from home, and took on various laboring jobs. He found them very satisfying because of the sense of freedom that he got from going right outside the middle-class milieu that he was accustomed to, and from being able to hold down a job that consisted of hard manual work. At the same time he started to go in for what he calls "elaborately literary sort of offenses." At one time while he was working in a hotel, he would make extra money by pimping— "I'd sell the hotel waitresses to the hotel clients." Later, in the course of his drifting through different countries, he started snatching handbags from women. He says, "It was far more exciting to steal the money than to make it. In grabbing a handbag or introducing a girl to a client there was a lovely feeling of breaking the pattern of behavior, a liberating thing. The little feelings of guilt were usually pleasurable. Basically there was a sour feeling at the end, but it is a pleasant thing to have done in the past. When I stole, it was to drink in a pub, it was to blow the money in some way: money earned by working one spends in a more sensible and controlled way."

Some of David's bitterest memories of his home life are of the way his father used to take out "dirty great wads of pound notes," and peel off a few to give out to members of his family. David hated the philistinism, the lack of books and music, the absence of any works of art, the reproduction furniture, the sticky sweet cherry brandy drunk out of tiny liqueur glasses.

David's case illustrates a key factor in the make-up of the respectable thief—the exhilaration afforded by the token overthrow of oppressive parental authority. A leading English psychoanalyst, Dr. Eric Brenman, says, "Most people want more than their entitlement. In the ideal relationship the desire to take would be modified by some regard for the person from whom one takes; out of this consideration, modification of greedy wants takes place. But most people instead of facing up to the conflict between what they want and what the other person can give, deal with their inordinate desires by means of inhibition. In other words by means of a strict and repressive super-ego, or by submitting to the super-ego imposed by society in the forms of laws and regulations. In this way, they suppress a part of themselves. Therefore there is always a suppressed part of themselves that wants to steal, wants to take. If the suppression has been accomplished mainly by means of fear, through a persecutory super-ego, rather than out of concern for the other person, then there is a sense of timidity and cowardice about not permitting one's desires."[11]

Breaking out, transgressing against these prohibitions, by

snatching handbags or by shoplifting, affords the kind of liberating excitement that David spoke of, and that is clearly a factor in "white-collar crimes," that are done for the thrill. The sense of liberation obtained is liberation from the dictates of superego—the internal representative of parental authority and moral law. It follows that if people accept standards of conduct because they are forced to, however much they may pay lip service to a prevailing system, they will entertain a secret resentment at having had their instinctual desires brutally curbed. In these circumstances the bourgeois morality to which they conform will in a part of them always seem like a cruel dictatorship—an unjustifiable limitation of their wants.

The kind of society that forms its standards of behavior not on the basis of compassion, but in response to the dictates of a tyrannical superego must secretly admire the criminal for having the guts not to submit to such an oppressive system. And it will contrive to find ways of doing what the criminal does without incurring the moral disapproval that the criminal has to face. It does this by accommodating its stealing impulses within a socially sanctioned system.

The individual once caught up in such a larcenous system, can't get out. The prosecutor in the thalidomide case said that it was difficult for the individual to exempt himself from the rules of the game as it is played by the group. This means that because people are robbing you, you rob them. It's the way things are. Since everybody else is a thief, not to be one is to be a sucker, a mug, soft. The man who scrupulously pays his taxes is a fool. The person who never bumps up his expenses is cheating himself; after all, his employers expect him to bump up his expenses, and pay him in accordance with that expectation. The waiter who doesn't put a bottle of whiskey under his jacket is just letting somebody else take two. As for paying one's bills, do not tradesmen allow for bad debts in their profit margins, and still make a handsome profit? In not paying bills one is simply compensating oneself for the excessive prices that are charged. And so on. Locked into such a system, everybody can justify his own position somehow. Bernie Cornfeld says he can explain everything. The game is: You steal from me, I steal from you, and it's all right as long as nobody steals too much, or more than anybody else. In the end, it more or less balances out, except for a few suckers and some excessively greedy thieves, so what is the harm?

The tacit acceptance of a system of respectable thieving has to be seen in the context of an overall change in money morality. Gradually, the old concept of selling out has been replaced by the more cosmetic and positive-thinking one of cashing in.

Positions and attributes not in themselves profitable may have cash-in value: a great name, for example. When James Roosevelt, son of F.D.R., left Harvard he was offered a job in the insurance business at $15,000 a year, which was handsome pay in 1931. Apparently the work was not excessive. In an interview, he told *Collier's* magazine: "I knew perfectly well that they were paying me for the name . . . I was newly married, and I needed the money." Later in life, after having been U.S. Ambassador to the United Nations Economic and Social Council, he joined Bernie Cornfeld at IOS. His salary was "splendid," and he was given the benefit of the stock option plan.[12]

Cultural prestige, too, has cash-in value. Kenneth Tynan's position as literary manager of the National Theatre in Britain and his reputation as a critic made *Oh! Calcutta!* (which he conceived) acceptable fare to the sort of theatergoers who would have felt they could not be seen going to a strip show. By lending his name to the production, Tynan made the show *respectably* scandalous. It is said to have made him a fortune.

The conversion of fame into cash is now a regular business. The endorsement of sports clothes and sports equipment by golfers, tennis players, swimmers, can make top sportsmen into millionaires. After winning all those gold medals at the Munich Olympics, the swimmer Mark Spitz, twenty-three years old, signed advertising contracts worth $5,000,000, according to *Time* magazine. And the business is growing. The older morality which insists that athletes should be amateurs, i.e., unpaid, has little chance of surviving in a world system in which every other accomplishment is monetized.

Until recently there was not a great deal of money in being a chess Grand Master. But Bobby Fischer changed that. Not only did he get the prize money increased by $125,000 (it was put up by financier Jim Slater to get Fischer to the table when he was dilly-dallying), but when he had won the world championship he received commercial offers worth $1,000,-000. Nowadays no acknowledged genius needs to starve in a garret, or write begging letters from his deathbed as Beethoven had to do. Even if his work does not bring him a great deal of money, he can cash in on his reputation by going on lecture tours, as Dylan Thomas and Brendan Behan did, to their immediate profit and eventual cost.

The way cash-in value works is illustrated by the case of the TV critic Peter Black, who aroused controversy by appearing in a commercial advertising a certain TV rental company.

In an openly ambivalent apologia,[13] Black wrote that it had taken him three years of his spare time to write a book about television, *The Mirror in the Corner,* for which he received exactly the same amount of money as he was offered for one day's work making the TV commercial. Of course, he realized he was not being paid as an actor but for his standing as a critic. In effect, he was realizing the cash-in value of his reputation.

Although Black later had doubts about what he had done, and said he wouldn't do it again, the fact that he did it in the first place is an indication of how money morality has changed. At one time it would have been beyond question that the opinions of somebody in the business of offering independent judgments should not be for sale. But nowadays the argument runs that since everybody knows that a commercial is a paid testimonial, where is the deception? (It is in the implicit message that a particular advertisement is truer than others because of who is doing it.)

Black had misgivings. But, in fact, the new money morality does not condemn what he did. It merely argues the pros and cons, discusses where the line ought to be drawn, and quietly acknowledges the precedent. Black's reply to his fellow-journalists who had criticized him was: What about the free trips, and the lunches at the Savoy, and the Christmas drinks? Were these not ways of buying, or at least influencing a journalist's views? And didn't everybody accept such blandishments?

The answer is that they didn't always. In some newspapers it used to be the rule that all hospitality had to be returned, that no journalist should put himself in the position of being indebted to someone about whom he was writing. Such rules are no longer widely applied.

Journalists say that their views are not affected by drinks and lunches, trips and token gifts. If this is so, one would have to wonder why the public relations industry continues to spend large sums of money on such entertainment.

In the end, the new morality cuts through all the tortuous ethical considerations and simply asks: Is it done? Tautologically it concludes that if it is, it must be all right.

What harm can there be in something that everybody is

doing and seems to enjoy? Bernard Shaw depicted hell in *Man and Superman* not as a place of torment and torture, but as an endless round of pleasure and falsehood—*there,* anything one wished was so. And, of course, all the best people were there. Its only drawback was its unreality. Heaven, by contrast, was the place of ultimate reality, in which the inmates of the lower place saw absolutely no advantage. Our new money morality is somewhat like the system of Shaw's hell: It is subscribed to by the best people, it is amusing, it ensures the continuing pleasures of endless consumption. Only its unreality, its underlying falsehoods are to be held against it. Dr. Albert Mason, an American psychoanalyst, says, "The best place for a mad person to feel sane is in a lunatic asylum, because there everybody else is as mad as him and will therefore support his delusion."[14] Likewise, the best place for a dishonest person to feel honest is in a larcenous system, because everybody else is just as dishonest as he. But it is the solution of the madhouse.

10
The Criminal

If the respectable thief is forced into forms of behavior that he can no longer justify to himself, he breaks down, or brings about his own downfall. If the romantic loses his belief in El Dorado, he comes to realize that what he is doing amounts to plundering. If the "numbers" man ceases to see beauty in the symbols of acquisition, his lexicon becomes a meaningless jumble, and he declines into misanthropy. And if the hustler finds himself in the sort of situation where he is not confirmed in his belief that everybody is taking him for as much as he is taking them, he loses his touch, becomes unable to act. In all of these instances the individual's conscience, which has been kept in abeyance by one device or another, begins powerfully to reassert itself at a certain point. As a result, we get the familiar pattern of the ruthless moneymaker paying out conscience money. But there is one type of person who apparently suffers no retribution for his actions, for whom the sense of guilt simply does not exist.

D——,[1] all-round villain and gangster, says, "I wouldn't ever kill anyone intentional, but if I ever hit anyone and they have a thin head, that's different. Usually I don't need to do much, because they all think I'm a right gangster. People think I carry a gun because I was done for attempted murder. I don't. I don't need to. They think I do and they're so scared you're going to shoot them I don't have to take my hand out of my pocket."

This is said, if that can be imagined, quite unmenacingly, in an amiable, matter-of-fact sort of way by a young man with white flashing teeth, long sideburns, wearing a three-piece custom-made suit, handmade shirt, shiny shoes; he's a villain, all right, and not one of your clerk-type criminals who does it all in the head. D—— is what is called a hood or a thug. He is available for hire in the underworld to beat up people and make them cough up. He was once charged with attempted murder. The gang bosses had sent him to do at least one other murder. He says he refused because the man they wanted rubbed out hadn't done anybody any harm. The way he tells it, D—— went in search of his man, found him, and then the gun didn't work. "I pulled the trigger twice, nothing happened. I was doing it so they'd think I'd done it like they wanted, but the fucking gun didn't work. They kept asking me, why isn't it in the papers?"

D—— is in this line of work "for the money and the adventure." He wouldn't want to do anything else, except "be a painter like Constable." "If you've got enough money," he says, "everything's within your reach. Lots of people say money isn't everything. I think it is. It will buy you anything, definitely." His rate of pay varies. He has got $1,200 for beating up somebody for his gang. He had to threaten a boxer once; he got $500 for telling him, "You're going to go for a walk." For bodyguard work, he picks up $100 for an evening.

He has a restaurant that pays him $50 protection money whenever he drops in. If they didn't pay up? Well, he'd just smash up the place, wouldn't he?

In talking of his life, which he doesn't expect to be long ("somebody's going to get me sooner or later"), he displays no sign of any compunction about the things he does. It's his line.

Every day, newspapers contain stories of criminals who, similarly, have no conscience about what they do, be it violent robbery, murder, kidnaping, extortion, blackmail. In them the money motive is supreme, and the most striking characteristic of the type is apparent lack of all conscience. How does this state come about? Melanie Klein says: ". . . it is the excessive severity and overpowering cruelty of the super-ego, not the weakness or want of it, as is usually supposed, which is responsible for the behaviour of asocial and criminal persons."[2]

This theory provides a new insight into the functioning of the criminal's psyche. In Freud's scheme of the mind the conscience is part of the superego, which has been formed out of the imagos of the parental figures, and thus embodies their authority, restraints, restrictions and exhortations to betterment. Now, what Melanie Klein is saying is that if the superego is excessively severe—is experienced as an intolerable inner persecutor—then it will be thrown out *in toto,* and with it conscience, and all sense of guilt. Some people find their sexuality unbearable, perhaps because the conflict it produces makes them too anxious, perhaps because they fear retribution, and so they renounce it entirely, become sexless. They become frigid, or impotent, or go to a nunnery. In this kind of way, the criminal robber becomes conscienceless so that he will not have to contend with his own guilt. He becomes morally impotent.

Such a person lives in a curiously flat emotional landscape

of largely undifferentiated feelings. Everything is pretty much the same for him, since he has thrown out the part of himself that is capable of giving definition and meaning to his acts. He takes what he wants, because why shouldn't he? This kind of man was portrayed in Jean-Luc Godard's film *A Bout de Souffle*. The small-time gangster played by Jean-Paul Belmondo takes a very matter-of-fact view of everything. When his girl wants to go for a drive, he goes around the corner and steals a car. When she wants to be taken to dinner, he goes into the washroom of a night club, knocks out the only occupant, and makes off with his money.

The life of D—— follows this kind of pattern. He gets up late, usually around noon, and after his daily workout at a gym—he has to keep fit in his line—meets his pals in a bar, and later in the day drifts around to see what's doing. He'll drop in at various bars and night clubs. Or he may call on a girl friend of his, a prostitute. He looks after her, in the sense that "if she ever has any aggravation with customers I tell them to leave her alone, and they do." Sometimes he'll drop in at a discotheque that is frequented by middle-aged women on the lookout for young men. If he's short of money, he'll visit one or other of the places that he "protects."

If he's got a job on, it will be something like putting the squeeze on somebody who hasn't paid out "pension money," or he'll beat up somebody. He's very expert at this. He can do a job that will give a bloody nose, and he can do a job that will need stitches. He lives with his parents (though after a job he always stays away for a while, doesn't believe in bringing trouble home) and can't imagine any other kind of life. Once he wanted to be an artist, and he still draws and paints a little. But he wasn't good enough, or did not try hard enough. "If I could paint like Constable, villainy wouldn't enter me head, would it?" he tells you.

Still, he is not discontent with his life, and he lives it without guilt or remorse, even with pride. When he walks into a room, people are scared of him. This makes him somebody, because people are not scared of nothing. Their fear gives him a sense of himself. And in taking their money he takes their fearful tribute to his being.

This type of criminal may have eliminated his bourgeois conscience, but he retains an absolute belief in the bourgeois symbol of potency, effectiveness, love, worthiness, power: money. And by stealing the symbol, he believes he has become potent, effective, lovable, worthy, powerful. Psychoanalyst Dr. Albert Mason says, "It's like somebody stealing a room full of Rembrandts, sticking them up on his walls and saying, 'Look, what I've done,' *as if he'd painted them.* The criminal steals the money that others have had to work for and produce by their real potency, and then says, 'I've got all this money, doesn't that make me potent!' And a lot of people would agree with him that it does. It buys the same things as the potent man's money. How do you tell the difference between a criminal and a successful man from their possessions?"[3]

Behind the criminal's desire for money is desire for respect, which is a form of love. D—— gives waiters large tips "because people think that being a villain you're a right no good bastard, and you want to show them that you're okay, so they'll treat you with respect." The gang's bosses used to send money to charities—some of which returned it; they also bought a vicar a new roof for his church. Some of the people D—— had to beat up had committed the unpardonable offense of not showing proper respect, of being too familiar, of cuddling the gang bosses in public and therefore making out they were more intimate with them—the kings—than they actually were. Such offenders had to be "shown up" in front of their friends.

This respect—the visible sign of love—is also what the American mafioso is so obsessively concerned with. The vows, the expected loyalty, the tradition of *omerta,* the revenging of one slaying with another—these are all forms of showing respect and love. It is, of course, an extorted respect/love, obtained by means of money. Money—the size of the racket—is what makes a man boss and enables him to pay for the rubbing out of anyone disrespectful.

The awed respect accorded to the bosses of the Mafia, nowadays even by the straight world—the movie companies, authors, commentators—is directly related to their financial power. In America it has been said that organized crime probably nets more profit each year than the combined earnings of United States Steel, ATT, General Motors, Standard Oil of New Jersey, General Electric, Ford, IBM, Chrysler and RCA. Earnings of between $10 billion and $40 billion annually are attributed to the gangs. The Mafia is said to have a finger in everything. In 1965 United States Attorney Robert M. Morgenthau told newspaper reporters that his office had information that Mafia groups owned the property on which *The Wall Street Journal* was published, and even the building where the FBI had its headquarters. Judges, politicians, banks, administrations, unions, police forces and Congressmen are controlled, sweetened or paid off by Mafia money. And so the confusion of potency with the symbol of potency becomes total. If money *is* able to exert such enormous power on all levels of society, and buy respect and compliance, then those who wield it *are* ipso facto powerful men, and absurd as this may be, lovable too.

The actual end product of this whole process is always more money. Since it has no practical value or use once a certain number of shirts and cars and judges have been bought with it, the millions said to be possessed by individual mafiosi must buy them something else. What it buys them is power, standing, respect, position, fame—the very things which are normally *rewarded* by money but which they, inverting the whole process, obtain by means of it.

The "respect" that they so deeply desire, and will kill to get, is a kind of black-comedy caricature of the respectability that the bourgeois citizen seeks. Except for some differences of approach, the underworld apes the world above, and in doing so gives us a mordant parody of our normality.

Bill Bonanno, son of one of the top bosses of the American Mafia, contends that the mafiosi are really servants in a hypocritical society; they are the middlemen who provide those illegal commodities of pleasure and escape that the public demands and the law forbids. As he sees it, the gangs fill a gap in the entrepreneurial system. During prohibition, they provided people with the liquor they wanted. To the poor with no credit rating, they provide loans at 20-percent interest without security, relying on strong-arm tactics to collect. Where betting is desired and is illegal, they run the numbers rackets. They provide prostitutes or drugs. They are just businessmen operating on the wrong side of the law, according to Bonanno.[4] They have to make their own laws, and where these are disputed, or contravened, there are beatings and killings. It is in some ways a persuasive case, and is in accord with the basic business ethos articulated by the head of a giant British company, namely that "the purpose of business activity is to satisfy wants at a value to the consumer greater than the cost to the producer."[5] With this principle the Mafia complies.

But whereas the corporation chief can claim that his *purpose* is making cars or refrigerators or washing machines, not money, that the money is just the symbolic expression of his successfulness, the mafioso has to say that his whole purpose is the money, since he will, if need be, get it out of businesses by ruining them, by robbing them from inside. He is someone who has become so attached to the money symbol that he has lost sight of what it symbolizes. His money is symbol divorced from meaning.

In this respect money is rather like the totems of primitive tribes. Because of past associations (now lost) certain animals, or plants, or an act of nature like thunder or rain, came to stand for power or potency, and elaborate rules of respect were devised which determined how the totem was to be treated by members of the tribe. To the observer the awe in which a plant, a bird, a snake, a lizard, or even a mouse may be held by a particular tribe seems ludicrous, because the original meaning has been lost and only the symbol is left. If we take money as being in this sense totemic, this does not mean it is without power. The totem has great power *insofar as the tribesmen endow it with that power;* the witch doctor who controls the totem and decides how it is to be approached is next to the chief the most powerful man in the tribe. If we regard money in this light, we see that what the robber does is to steal the totemic symbol of power, and his motive for doing so must be to obtain the esteem and respect that possession of the totem bestows on the possessor.

In the thief's motivational spectrum the element of sheer excitement also has a place. To D—— the criminal life is the only life, and even if he were to pull off the big heist and get away with enough to retire on, he wouldn't want to. He'd have his villa in Portugal, and his Mercedes, but he'd keep his hand in. He'd still be available if a job needed doing.

There is a kind of glamor to his line of work that he, in common with other criminals, evidently craves. You get this feeling when he says, "I'm known as one of the top notchers. When somebody wants somebody hurt, they call me, because they know I do a professional job. If somebody hasn't paid their pension or something, I just say to them, 'You know what you're going to get, and you know what it's for,' and I give it to them." He adds with a disarming air, "I never hurt anyone that didn't have it coming."

There is also for some a quasi-sexual excitement in the act

of stealing, and this points to another aspect of the criminal's money motive. The eroticism of thieving is proclaimed by Jean Genêt in his autobiographical book *The Thief's Journal.* In one part he describes how he seduced a handsome twenty-year-old guitarist, called Michaelis, who had been making himself available to the city's rich queers: ". . . I pointed out to him that theft would be more beautiful than prostitution . . . I told him about a few thefts and that I had been in prison; he admired me for this. In a few days, with the help of my clothes, I became a glamorous figure to him. We pulled off a few jobs and I became his master."

Throughout the book, theft is endowed with beauty and erotic meaning; it becomes a kind of orgastic act for Genêt. "Repudiating the virtues of your world," he writes, "criminals hopelessly agree to organize a forbidden universe." The thief is romanticized, glorified. "I prepared for my adventure," says Genêt, "as one arranges a couch or a room for love; I was *hot* for crime."

This sexual element in theft is borne out by the findings of psychoanalysis. Ernest Jones thought that stealing from a woman could have the meaning of having a baby by her. And Melanie Klein discovered in her treatment of a child thief that his breaking open of the school cupboard, and the taking out of articles from it, had the same unconscious cause and meaning as his sexual assaults on little girls, to which he was also prone.[6]

That there should be this element to theft becomes more understandable if we take into account that the first source of riches, and therefore of envy, is the mother's body, which not only contains valuable milk, but also is full of other treasures, i.e., babies. The first form of robbery is a fantasy of robbing the mother's body. In this there is a good deal of sadism too. The fantasy is of getting inside and scooping out all the valuables. But the inside of the mother's body is both an exotic and a dangerous place, Aladdin's cave and a den of thieves. There is the fear of not being able to get out. There is also the fear of meeting the father's angry penis, the rightful inhabitant of the inside of Mother's body, and the guardian and protector of the treasures. Thus robbery can be a fantasy heroic adventure.

The etiological factors that lead a person to express his inner condition by becoming a thief are obviously varied and complex. But there is one main element that can be isolated. The thief has a grievance. Life has not been fair to him. *He* has to steal what others get by right. In this respect, he has a very particular sense of cosmic justice: he believes that there are possessions to which he is *entitled,* because others have them. Since he lacks these things, something clearly has gone wrong. This feeling of *lacking something* is *permanent* and never goes, however much loot he accumulates.

What is the great injustice under which he labors? His size. He is so small, and Daddy is so big. That is the original unfair situation; the spur to all development—but something that in the criminal sends him along a prohibited route. He cannot tolerate dependence, subservience and inferiority: the lot of childhood. For him these conditions are unbearable because of the deep anxieties they arouse. He compensates for his littleness by stealing. In this sense, all robbers are Robin Hoods: they rob from the rich (Daddy) to give to the poor (their child-selves) .

The robber must always have been a desperate child, believing that there was no other way open to him. He must have had very little belief in the kind of love that ensures that children are fed, cared for. For such internal pessimism to create an out-and-out criminal it probably needs to find confirmation in external reality; in this way bad environment and bad parents *prove* to the budding criminal that his version of life is right: to get by—to survive—you have to steal. Therefore, while the criminal tendency is rooted in a psychological condition (as prevalent among the children of the wealthy as among those living in slums), it is when life seems to bear out the dismal false alternative, steal or die, that the robber becomes established. And obviously this tends to happen most often where external circumstances are in fact bad.

Paradoxically, an overindulged childhood can also be a factor in the etiology of the robber. His majesty the baby takes the view that he owns his objects, that they are his by divine right, and must serve him forever. With the onset of reality, life becomes a grievous disappointment. Dr. Eric Brenman says, "The spoilt child actually thinks he owns the world. It's mine, it's mine, he says. And when the reality principle tells him that it isn't, he is outraged. He feels it's a bloody cheek. I quite clearly recall, he says, that Mummy told me again and again that I am the whole world, and now you tell me I'm not."[7] For the robber, the money that he has stolen is the tribute to his greatness that his Mummy promised him as a child, and on which the world has defaulted.

There is also the type of person who cannot bear that somebody else has something that he wants and does not have. He cannot bear his own envy. For him robbery is a way of getting rid of his envy; if he can simply take whatever he wants, he need never feel envious. Then he need never be put in the painful position of wanting what he cannot have, since he has found the perfect solution, which is to steal what he wants.

Although the robber does not need the esteem or approval of the straight world, he cannot exist in a state of self-acknowledged worthlessness. This is why he lives in the underworld, among people like himself, who subscribe to the same system and standards as he does and will give him support. D—— thinks of himself as "a sort of underworld cop" who dishes it out "to those who have got it coming." The villain rationalizes his villainy. Brenman explains, "You can call yourself a hero, and if everybody else in your world agrees with you, you will be supported, and you will become a venerable hero. As long as the system doesn't break down and you do not pause to reflect—do not deeply examine yourself—you can live out your life without ever discovering what a travesty it has been."[8]

It is evident that a man like Meyer Lansky, the American gangster who was not allowed to settle in Israel at the end of his life, felt self-righteously aggrieved at this denial of his right of return. This kind of man can justify his life to himself by saying that anybody he has rubbed out or double-crossed deserved it; it's a jungle world, and in a jungle, better be a wolf than a sheep, and so on. How can he now be denied, in his old age, the right to live out his remaining years in his homeland?

Such a person seems to have got rid of all conscience and sense of guilt, by the methods described at the beginning of this chapter. Hence he is innocent. But there are consequences inherent in recourse to such a mechanism. He has not really got rid of his superego; what he has done is *project* it. It becomes identified with outside forces—the cops, the system, the screws, the law, the authorities—who can all be more safely hated, attacked, eluded, evaded, than something within himself. The result is that he lives his life in hiding from himself, which takes the form of hiding from others. Life is lived in a state of siege. But eventually "somebody must get him," as D—— put it, because his suppressed guilt requires it, and in the end he probably chooses his own retribution.

11

The Gambler and the Loser

The gambler needs to be distinguished from the person who sometimes (or even regularly) has a bet. Everybody, at some time, has wanted to win—held his breath and prayed for fate's favoritism just this once! It is a universal longing. And it is what makes bookmakers, casino owners and numbers-game operators rich, and why in some countries the State itself runs lotteries of one sort or another. When somebody wins a large sum of money, it lets others dream. That is the purpose of such betting; the real return sought is in fantasy. With chances in the one-in-a-million category, nobody really expects to win. The type of person who dreams of money in this way has already been described in the first chapter of this book.

The gambler is something else. He has a real expectation of winning. In his case, he does not risk a mere token sum, but an amount the loss of which will hurt him. He has a system. At roulette—let us say—he plays red and doubles up when he loses. According to the laws of mathematical probability, every time you play red your chance of winning is exactly fifty-fifty, no matter how many times black has come up before. But the gambler feels that if black has come up several times in a row, the chance of red coming up next increases proportionally with every successive turn of the wheel. Even though this is not mathematically true, the feeling that now red is bound to come up—it must come up next, and if not this time, then all the more certainly the next time —grows in the gambler to an absolute conviction. He can actually *see* it. He backs his inner certainty, and wins. This confirms his belief that he was bound to win, that he *knew* he was going to, although the truth is that the odds were always the same: fifty-fifty.

We may define the gambler-who-wins as someone whose delusional sense of knowing is confirmed by chance. If chance consistently confirms his hunches and his foreknowledge—and statistically there are bound to be some people so favored— then it produces in such a person the feeling that he "can't lose." In reality, he has just been lucky, but his luck has happened to coincide with an inner certainty that he was going to be lucky, which easily extends to believing in his luck as a sort of special gift, given to him as a chosen individual. Being, as he believes, fated to win, his winnings take on the meaning of a tribute from destiny. What this kind of gambler craves, and sometimes gets, is the sense of being "hot." He wants to discover that the odds of life are in his favor. Why else do rich old ladies spend night after night at the gaming tables of the casinos? They are having their fortune told in money. The ancient role of cards and numbers and dice in the rituals of fortunetelling, magic and astrology points to this connection.

But the gambler does not just accept what the cards foretell. He will also seek to extort his win from an uncompliant chance. When his numbers aren't coming up, something drives him on, he doubles up, he keeps raising the ante. In his daring, or desperation, he will redeem all his losses at one stroke. In this type of behavior the gambler is seen as someone who deludes himself that he must win, while acting out his inexorable losing pattern.

Nick the Greek (Nicholas Dandolos) was perhaps the world's greatest gambler; he regarded himself as an artist who worked not in stone or marble but in money. Between 1928 and 1949 he won and lost more than $50 million, and he died like many an artist—poor. There is a saying among inveterate gamblers that if to gamble and win is the greatest thrill anyone can have, to gamble and lose is the second greatest. According to the Kefauver Committee of 1951, Americans pay out $20,000,000,000 a year for the second greatest thrill.

One theory, advanced by Albert Lauterbach, is that gambling thrives wherever rational action appears to offer little hope. "To assert one's 'luck,' *corriger la fortune,* then helps to preserve one's self-esteem, and the drive to do so becomes more powerful as the gambler wins and irresistible as he loses."[1] On the other hand, psychiatrists and sociologists have long recognized, on the basis of the empirical evidence, that many addictive gamblers unconsciously *want* to lose.

That such a compulsion exists was borne out by a survey of betting shops conducted by the University of London under the sociologist Otto Newman. He found that particular places attracted a particular clientele with certain common characteristics. There was, for instance, an anti-favorite shop, where social misfits, prostitutes, tramps and small-time criminals tended to gather. In their betting patterns it was seen that they never followed form, but would bet on horses on the basis of rumor or hunch. Betting here was invariably emotional, chaotic—*and unsuccessful.* Other betting shops, Newman found, had the sort of clientele that operated on a different basis; they backed favorites, or they studied the way the odds varied, and they were generally much more successful.

It can be seen from such a survey that to some extent the chance that attends upon people is of their own making. Of course, the losers in the anti-favorite betting shop would not admit that they set out to lose, but it is a conclusion that the empirical evidence suggests. And it indicates, too, that it is precisely the sort of people who believe, against all the evidence, in their luck—in hunches, in tips, in the pin that is going to pick out the winner for them—who are, in fact, in the grip of their losing pattern.

What must be regarded, then, as *the impulse to lose* is not confined to the already defeated people of the anti-favorite betting shops—they are gathering there in the final phase of their losing life pattern—but exists on all levels. It was seen—in one of its most dramatic forms—in the case of the Polish beauty, film star and mistress of Darryl F. Zanuck, Bella Darvi. In the grip of her gambling mania, when she had lost everything else, she would strip her rings and jewelry off and throw them down on the table to call a bet. She ended up so deeply in debt to the casinos in France that the French government seized her passport. Zanuck got her out of trouble up to a certain time by paying her gambling debts. But, finally, there was nobody to make good her ever-mounting losses, and she committed suicide.

Nor is the gambling mania to be accounted for solely by a desperate need for money. A multimillionaire art collector recalls that at one period of his life when he was acutely unhappy, a time when his first marriage had broken up, he handled money very irresponsibly, gambled, lost, spent recklessly. He has no doubt that this was an expression of his state of mind at the time, and that his *intention* was dissipation. "The only excitement of gambling is risking more than you can afford; the only point of it is to do it to excess,"[2] he says.

Whether it is the man with millions gambling to excess, or a clerk blowing his week's wages at the racetrack, the underlying compulsion is to lose. Herman Mankiewicz, the Hollywood screenwriter of *Citizen Kane* (for which loser-style he got little credit until after his death) typified this kind of gambler. He once explained, "It's no fun gambling if I lose $2,000 and just write a check for it. What is thrilling is to make out a check for $15,000 knowing there's not a penny in the bank."[3] He was such a compulsive gambler and borrower that his colleagues at Paramount used to line up with him on payday as the only way of getting back some of the money he had borrowed from them during the week. On one occasion, Louis B. Mayer, to get Mankiewicz out of financial trouble agreed to advance him $30,000 on a new contract, if he would take a solemn vow never to gamble again. Mankiewicz gave his sacred word. The next day Mayer found him in a poker game, on the point of raising the stake to $10,000.[4] This ensured that he left the MGM lot fast and never set foot there again.

Perhaps the classic example of this kind of gambler was Dostoevsky. His papers published after his death, and his wife's diaries, provide ample documentation of his passion, and in this material the character make-up of a gambler is vividly conveyed.

Dostoevsky's worst phase was in Germany, in Baden-Baden. He rationalized what he was doing by saying that he was trying to win enough to be able to return to Russia, without being arrested for debt. But he was himself aware that this was no more than a pretext; his chief pleasure, he said, was *"le jeu pour le jeu."* In a letter he wrote: "The main thing is the play itself. I swear that greed for money has nothing to do with it, although Heaven knows I am sorely in need of money." His passion for play was such that he would remain at the gaming tables until he had lost everything and was "totally ruined." Only then was he rid of his demon. Time and again he promised his young wife never to return to the tables, but he always broke his promise. He stole her wedding ring and gambled that away. Thereupon his self-accusations became even more extreme, he called himself every name he could think of, he abused himself before her, he said he was undeserving of her love, that he was useless, despicable, vile. If only, despite all his vileness, she would forgive him, he swore by all he held dear that never, never again would he give way to his terrible passion. And of course did so immediately, as soon as he had got his hands on money or jewelry meant to pay for food and clothing.[5]

In this kind of behavior the "repetition compulsion" to keep on losing is very striking, and since the game of chance is merely a formalized setting for the working out of such a pattern, we would expect it to manifest itself equally in the conduct of life. Common observation shows that this is indeed so. There are certain people who do seem to be "losers," for whom things always go wrong, almost as if it were planned that way. The most obvious expression of this trait is to actually lose money: to leave purse, handbag, wallet, valuables, in buses, trains, shops, public lavatories. There are people who "are always losing things," and such a pattern seen over a period of time must rule out simple absent-mindedness or accident.

Then there are all those people who, though they may not lose cash by leaving it somewhere, do what amounts almost to the same thing. They consistently misjudge situations, buying just before the market starts to fall, selling just before it has begun to rise, putting their money into dud companies. It is said of them that they can't handle money. They have "the dead hand," or some other blight that seems to ensure that whatever they touch turns out profitless for them. This sort of person is forever seeing his schemes fall through, having victory snatched from his grasp. It is very mysterious the way it keeps happening. Always at the last minute something goes wrong. The "loser" is a master at booby-trapping everything he undertakes so that the misfortune that he brings upon himself will always seem to be somebody else's doing. He can prove it. His main customer went bankrupt. How could he have known that would happen? His suppliers had a strike. Nothing to do with him. His partner turned out to be a crook. Who could have foreseen such a thing?

In many cases, it is difficult to distinguish between somebody who is "a dead loss" (i.e., innately incapable) from the true "loser," who is essentially an able person, perhaps even brilliant, who conspires at his own downfall. The type is most strikingly revealed in the case of the person who has at one time excelled at something, and then inexplicably—as it seems—loses everything. Show business, with its built-in ups and downs to act as a cover for such a self-imposed pattern, produces many examples of this kind of reversal. The popular composer Lionel Bart (*Oliver, Blitz, Maggie May,* etc.) made millions and lost everything. He had a castle in Morocco, and a house in London that cost him £165,000, and it all went. He says, "I had this desperate need to be loved, you see; and people I considered my friends could get the world out of me. Money was no object. I used to think that giving somebody an expensive gift was a foolproof way of buying their admiration . . ."[6]

Another case is the British disk jockey and TV chat show host Simon Dee.[7] His story provides some insight into the actual mechanics of the downfall, and for this reason I will treat it in some detail.

Dee made his name on the pirate station Radio Caroline, and when he left, he found himself in demand. He was offered a great many shows on radio and television and rapidly became a star of that chancy firmament. He had been unemployed, a drama student, then a vacuum cleaner salesman and a number of other things, but suddenly he was making £400 to £500 a week, more some weeks. He was in the money, and very soon was, as he put it, "riding the wild horse of success." He got his own TV chat show, the sort of spot that made David Frost and set up Frost as a millionaire. Dee's ratings were good, he was getting audiences of ten to twelve million, and there seemed no reason why he should not continue to do well. And yet it all faded out, his contract was dropped, and six months later, with no reserves to fall back on after the years of success, he was on relief, collecting £6.90 a week, and finding himself in what he called the unique position of "not being able to get a job inside show business and not being able to get a job outside show business."

It is true that the slender art of disk-jockeying is not exactly a trade in the hand of the kind that mothers want for their sons, but it is clear that Dee had as much flair and professional expertise as any of those currently prospering in this line. Why could he not get work? Even when he applied for a job as a salesman or a copywriter in an advertising agency he did not get it. It was thought that either he wasn't serious, or that his face would be too famous, that "it would be rather like David Frost serving somebody with groceries." Soon he was penniless, and supporting his wife and two children by selling one by one the remnants of his success—a Bentley car, an organ, and other such acquisitions.

On the face of it, such a sudden fall coming after such a sudden rise may seem like something that was only to be expected in so insecure a line of work as chatting up celebrities and spinning records. But the point is that he had made a lot of money, and you would have thought he'd have had enough assets to see him through a few months of bad times. The fact that he didn't, of course, compounded his difficulties, in that it forced him to go on relief, with all the attendant publicity, which can't have helped his image as an in-demand TV personality. Considering that at the time he was paying about £1,000 a year in school fees for one son to attend boarding school, drawing £6.90 on relief would seem to have been less than the absolute necessity he claims it was. He was, in fact, advertising his losing position to the world at a time when he should have shown himself in a winning aspect in order to reestablish himself. But this particular piece of miscalculation was only the final one, and like all the other mistakes, it was of course, "unavoidable."

Dee says: "I didn't invest any money, I never invest money. If you invest money you invest in other people's decisions. I do not play the stock exchange because I believe that whole thing is a fallacy anyway. I didn't have any insurance policy because I don't believe in insurance either. I don't have any life insurance at all. The logical argument is what happens if you get run over by a bus, what happens to your wife and children? Well, first of all, I'm not going to get run over by a bus. I take every precaution to make sure I am not killed. I maintain there are only acts of God and acts of man on the face of this earth, and you can avoid acts of man, you can't avoid acts of God, and anyway you can't insure against acts of God, so the real insurance you can't get. Anyway, I don't like it, it helps build these incredible financial empires that are hopelessly out of control, that are distorting our way of life. You know, all the big buildings in all the big cities belong to the insurance houses, which is ludicrous. I went into the possibility of owning a house, and then I realized that if you take a mortgage on a £10,000 house it means you end up paying £40,000 over twenty years, that to me was just not on, folks. Just purely illogical. How can you possibly buy a £10,000 house and spend forty grand on it? By the time you've paid back your money to the insurance company, if you add it up over the years, you pay four times—five, six,

God knows what, times—the cost of the house. To me now, basically, I will not accept it. And I will never buy anything unless I pay full cash for it."

The actual fall came in the following way: "They paid me off and I fell from television. The immediate cause of that was—well, I suppose, personality clash, you know they really think that the person who runs a live television show is the same as everybody else and should be treated the same as anybody else, only we're not the same. We're neurotic, highly keyed, very alert, very aware human beings. Stella Richman said, 'We can't go on like this,' so I said, 'No, we'd better forget it,' and they did. Oh, there were rows, because I wasn't allowed to have people on that I wanted, they called the show *The Simon Dee Show* but the last person who was allowed on was any of my friends."

What is revealed by such a tale is not just ignorance of the handling of money—after all, anyone can obtain professional advice on this, at least to the extent of having the advantages of buying a house explained—but a deep-rooted emotional attitude of suspicion and resentment of money power, leading to the inevitable loss of it.

The "loser" is not an unlikeable person, indeed there is often something rather touching about his eagerness to lay his head on the chopping block. Often people try to stop him —but no, no, he will not heed their advice.

Since this kind of "loser" often possesses real ability, he tends to rise again from his fallen position—he is forever making comebacks. Being down does not destroy him as it might others. His "down" phase is the prerequisite for his next "up" phase. Sir Walter Raleigh—who, as well as being a romantic, had many elements of the "loser" in him—spent thirteen years imprisoned in the Tower in one of his "down" phases. At the end of it he was still undaunted. At the age of sixty-four, he was as sure of finding the Guiana gold [El Dorado] as ". . . of not missing his way from his dining room to his bedchamber." What was the basis for his great certainty? His first expedition twenty years earlier had failed. By the time he set out on his second expedition, nearly everybody else had given up looking. But Raleigh was sure he would succeed—he sold his own and his wife's property for £10,500, and set off. He remembered a vision of twenty years before of "a mountaine of Christall that was like a white church tower of exceeding height over which poured a great river that did not touch any part of the mountain." Beyond it, he was sure, lay the high, cold, unviolated city, with its golden eagles and jackals, and its roofs and walls of precious stones. In a hundred years of searching, all the other expeditions had failed, but during his long imprisonment Raleigh had mapped it all out in his mind: the high pass, the access to it from the Orinoco river—he could *see* it. This was his chance to redeem his fortune. This is exactly the gambler's passion; whipping himself up into a state of hallucinatory *knowing*, whereby he can actually see the numbers that will come up. To speak of overconfidence or overoptimism does not really explain it. One is bound to see in such ill-judged ventures—that so patently go against all the laws of probability, and yet are attended by the certitude of success—the workings of the losing drive. Raleigh on this expedition lost all his money, his health, his son's life, and on his return to England, his head.

How are we to account for somebody's bringing such things upon himself? What are these various "losers" seeking? Consider what they get: humiliation, recrimination, hardship, confinement, poverty. Can such consequences actually be desired? To answer this we must look into the "loser's" life and see what it really involves.

There is obviously something quite satisfying about the

"exercise in survival," the sense of being up against it and managing. At such times people turn their home and family into a fortress against the world, and this probably results in a corresponding closening of relationships and tightening of bonds within the unit. "We got our priorities right," says Dee. "I'm glad it [his success] stopped because I was able to determine what I knew and what I didn't know, what was important and what wasn't. And what was important was reality, the truth, my two children, my wife, and what really was valuable, and so in a funny way the first reaction was one of happiness—total shock and horror—but by the same maxim happiness, a different kind of happiness to the one I'd known before, which was sponsored by money; this was sponsored by life."

From the popularity of the Robinson Crusoe story and its many variants, it is obvious that the game of survival has its appeal. It's something that middle-class, comfortably off people indulge in for a couple of weeks a year when they go camping and "live hard" in a place devoid of the comforts of civilization. It's a mild testing of one's own resources, and it is amazing the sense of hardiness that a small amount of deprivation can engender. But although being broke does play on this fantasy of living simply and making do on very little, this is hardly a sufficiently compelling need to account for anyone's going to the lengths of actually ruining himself in order to enjoy the challenge of being up against it.

The "loser's" life really is uncomfortable in a way that playing at doing without certain comforts for a few weeks is not. There are sheriffs who come to take his property, evict him from his home. There is the endless waiting. Waiting for the telephone to ring (if it has not been cut off) . Waiting for something to turn up. There is the bitterness of seeing others less deserving, less able, being rewarded, and thriving. It is boring. Suddenly, you have to think about the cost of a bus ride; a visit to the cinema is beyond your means. It is impossible to invite people over. Wherever you go, you are the one who is kept waiting, hanging about, told to go here, and then to go there, fill this out, try that address, wait, come back; the social system leaves little doubt as to how it regards the individual without money or means: he is the lowest form of life. And at every encounter, his impecunious circumstances serve to militate against him. People's attitudes change when they are dealing with an obvious "loser"; they are perfunctory, they order him around, they do not bother to conceal their own feelings of superiority. Friends lecture him. You should do this. Or that. Get on with it. Buck up your thinking.

The "loser" lives in a world where others are winning; he is locked into the system of the invidious comparison. His defining condition is that others have more than he does. In effect, this means more money. And since he lives in a society that has elevated this "more" to the level of the life goal, not being within reach of it demeans him, makes him worthless, a *nobody*. The particular painfulness and humiliation of losing can only be understood in the context of the tacit assumption that the meaning of life is *winning*.

To have fallen so far behind as to no longer be a contender is to be left out, ignored, belittled, ground down. The fact that he still is better off than many others is no consolation to him. As Mother Teresa of Calcutta has observed, the fact that the poorest Englishman is rich by comparison with the average Indian, say, doesn't make the Englishman feel any less poor. People's sense of impoverishment is in relation to their own time and place. One can, in practice, be quite wealthy, and feel poor. This is the common experience of those who live above their means. They are desperately hard up on $20,000 a year, and it is not an act: they are. In the milieu in which they move, what they earn is not enough to pay for what they have come to regard as their needs. It is even possible to be a millionaire and broke, if your tastes are in proportion to the means of a multimillionaire.

The great pain that the "loser" suffers is to see those in his immediate circle possessing more than he. There are several basic ways of dealing with this pain. One is to pretend to have as much as the others—this is the method of the *Hochstapler,* the person who lives out his pretenses by a mixture of bluffs and boasts and airs; he maintains himself in his position by means of petty deceptions, and finally is driven to crime to keep up appearances.

The other anodyne for the pain of losing is to make a life among those even less successful. In this way the "loser" is not constantly reminded of the way he has been defeated. At one time the failed sons of the English upper classes were sent off to the colonies, where they could lord it over the natives. Failed artists often create little colonies in countries where the standard of living is very low, and where they can feel better off than the inhabitants. Hence, too, the coziness of slums, and the conviviality of the hangouts of deadbeats and failures. There are, of course, other aspects, real hardship and real deprivation of essentials, to be borne; but the pain of losing out is mitigated. Everybody is equal in failure; indeed there is something comforting about a milieu, even if it is *the lower depths,* where competitive standards no longer apply.

There is also the defense of apathy, the beachcomber life; the person who resorts to this says he does not want anything. Indolence is also a way of avoiding the pain of having lost. The person who does the absolute minimum work he can get away with and puts his feet up at the end of the day—"Catch me killing myself for anybody"—is rationalizing having lost.

The "loser" becomes a piece of flotsam, carried this way and that, powerless to control his own movements. He becomes totally dependent on the whims and decisions of others, and therefore in a sense totally passive. The person with no money in hand can undertake nothing on his own account. He becomes aware of how fundamental money is in securing even the most elementary freedoms. Without it, he is a slave to his most pressing needs. And, of course, it gets worse. As the shadow of total destitution hovers, the "loser" experiences panic. With real anxiety about food and shelter hanging over people, the unity of the fortress-home breaks up, and the mutual accusations and reproaches become ever more savage. Somebody has to be blamed for such an intolerable situation, and the "loser" is clearly the one. The money quarrels of families where there is real deprivation, where the father's pint of beer deprives a child of food, are among the most terrible exposures of basic human nature that are encountered in a social situation.

What makes the plight of such people particularly acute is that all sorts of other secret terrors are lumped together and attributed to the one great ogre of poverty, and they become persecuted by their lack of money. Their debts appear irredeemable. And under the stress of this kind of grinding, degrading money shortage, rapid character deterioration sets in; people draw back into the basic animal postures of self-survival.

Is it conceivable that anyone would actually seek such conditions for himself?

The psychoanalyst Beryl Sandford tells the case history of a man who "had to be kept."[8] He could not earn money. He lived on sickness benefit and on what his brother gave him. His illness, he claimed, prevented him from doing work. And yet he was perfectly capable of doing *unpaid* work for a political association for which he canvassed, made speeches and acted as honorary treasurer. At a time when he was suffering from a whole range of crippling neurotic symptoms—he could not go out of the house alone—he was able to do extremely useful work, *as long as he was not rewarded for it.* When the chairman complimented him on a long report that he had written on the organization of a fund-raising fete, the "loser's" terror of success at once asserted itself. Sandford observes that from that moment her patient "began unconsciously to arrange things in such a way that, in the end, he would get no kudos for the success of the enterprise." He told his analyst that he would resign from the association when the fete was successfully over. "I shall just pack up and fade out."

This fading out at the prospect of success went back as far as his childhood. At school he had once set out to win the first prize in a sports competition. He won every event outright until the finals of the high jump. "He then did a five-foot jump which made him equal with another competitor, and although he had often jumped higher than that without any strain, he collapsed on landing and lay quite unable to move. He has no memory of feeling at all ill; he remembers thinking to himself that he must 'fade out' for a bit." In this particular event he had tied with the other boy, but he had won enough of the preceding events to gain the first prize. But instead of permitting his schoolfellows to carry him off in triumph, he crept away to his mother and, in his own words, "I buried my head in her; I just blotted myself out and clung to her with my eyes shut all the way home." The sight of the cheering schoolboys was deeply disturbing to him.

This is a case where the need to lose resulted in an acute aversion to any form of moneymaking. This patient only felt safe when in a losing position, and anything that smacked of success overwhelmed him with anxieties.

Equally striking as an instance of the "loser's" life being sought out was George Orwell's descent into the world of the down-and-outs of Paris. After an education at Eton, and service in the Indian Imperial Police, his reduction to the state of impoverishment cannot be explained solely in terms of hard times in a writer's life. Reading his classic account of those days, *Down and Out in Paris and London,* one senses an almost sensual attachment to his lowly position. He discovered that:

> Within certain limits, it is actually true that the less money you have, the less you worry. When you have a hundred francs in the world you are liable to the most craven panics. When you have only three francs you are quite indifferent; for three francs will feed you until to-morrow, and you cannot think further than that. You are bored, but you are not afraid. You think vaguely, "I shall be starving in a day or two—shocking, isn't it?" And then the mind wanders to other topics. A bread and margarine diet does, to some extent, provide its own anodyne.
>
> And there is another feeling that is a great consolation in poverty. I believe everyone who has been hard up has experienced it. It is a feeling of relief, almost of pleasure, at knowing yourself at last genuinely down and out. You have talked so often of going to the dogs—and well, here are the dogs, and you have reached them, and you can stand it. It takes off a lot of anxiety.

Here, then, is an indication of what the "loser" may actually be seeking: relief from anxiety, and he finds it, mysteriously, in a condition of punishing poverty. At one point in his book Orwell describes how he begins on the life of a tramp in London. To raise a little money he decides to sell his clothes, which are good and clean. He asks, in exchange, to be given some older clothes and as much money as the shopkeeper can spare. He is given some dirty-looking rags and a shilling. "I was going to argue," says Orwell, "but as I opened my mouth he reached out as though to take up the shilling again; I saw that I was helpless." He goes on to describe the real ghastliness of his new clothes with a positive relish for their "patina of antique filth," their gracelessness, their shapelessness; their condition far exceeded mere shabbiness. In these rags he noticed how women shuddered away from a badly dressed man with a quite frank movement of disgust. "Dressed in a tramp's clothes," he found, "it is very difficult, at any rate for the first day, not to feel you are genuinely degraded."

Rarely have the "loser's" world and feelings been so accurately and brilliantly chronicled as in this narrative. There is a similarity between the conditions that Orwell created for himself—how he actually got into these states of utter impoverishment is not made clear—and Dostoevsky's perpetual self-impoverishment through gambling. The gambler, with his addiction to a losing game, illuminates the motivation of other "losers." The key discovery was made by Dostoevsky's wife when she noted in her diary that at no time did her husband's writing go better than after one of his terrible losing bouts at the casino.

Freud comes to the conclusion that what Dostoevsky was doing in ruining himself at the tables was something that many neurotics and compulsive gamblers do: *He was turning his burden of guilt into a burden of debt.*[9] He postulates that Dostoevsky's gambling was an aspect of his self-punishing nature, which also revealed itself in the fact that he passed unbroken through the years of humiliation and imprisonment as a political prisoner in Siberia. The need for punishment enables people to embrace conditions that destroy others. Their mental economy is such that it requires degradation and humiliation as a means of "balancing the books." Without such self-imposed retribution, the unexpiated guilt becomes unbearable.

What is the nature of this guilt that has to be discharged in such losing rituals? There are of course many sources of guilt, but Freud believed that there is universal guilt arising out of the Oedipus complex. In Dostoevsky's case, this Oedipal guilt was particularly acute. His own father had actually been murdered. His preoccupation with this crime, and the burden of it upon him, is made very clear in *The Brothers Karamazov.*

But there is also another aspect to the "loser's" impulse. In *Mourning and Melancholia,* Freud writes: "The self-torments of melancholiacs, which are without doubt pleasurable, signify, . . . a gratification of sadistic tendencies and of hate, both of which relate to an object and have both been turned round upon the self. . . . the sufferers usually succeed in the end in taking revenge, by the circuitous path of self-punishment, on the original objects, and in tormenting them by means of the illness, having developed the latter so as to avoid the necessity of openly expressing hostility against the loved ones. After all, the person who has occasioned the injury to the patient's feelings, and against whom his illness is aimed, is usually to be found among those in his near neighbourhood."[10]

In other words, it is not only self-punishment that the "loser" seeks as a way of expiating guilt, but also the covert punishment of those nearest and dearest ones whom he cannot openly admit wishing to attack, and against whom he bears grudges of such ancient origin that he is by no means aware of their nature. Losing, then, becomes a means of attacking loved ones. It affords that perverse satisfaction of dragging others down with oneself.

Another motivational strand in the "loser's" behavior is revealed in Sandford's case of "the man who had to be kept." Here there is a real fear of winning. The man went in dread of having anything better, bigger, stronger or more powerful than what others have, because of the retaliation that he felt such superiority was bound to arouse. He therefore put himself in the position of a "loser," a nothing, a nobody, so that he would not arouse anybody's envious attacks. This is the reasoning behind the expression "Don't give people big eyes," which means don't show how much you've got, because if you do they'll get envious and greedy and want to take it away from you. Rather make out you've got less.

The "loser" is someone who finds it much too dangerous to win, because for him winning has all sorts of terrible and exciting meanings. It means being bigger than. It means having more of. It means beating the other person. It means the realization of all sorts of secret fantasies, of smashing, annihilating, finishing off the rival. If I do that to him, what is he going to do to me? So the "loser" chooses the defense of appeasement, and his method of appeasing is to show his littleness, his nothingness. The story of how Scott Fitzgerald displayed his somewhat below average-size penis to his big virile friend Ernest Hemingway, ostensibly to seek reassurance about it, is surely an example of compulsive appeasement. Loser-style, Fitzgerald had to show that his was smaller.

"The man who had to be kept" appeased his brother, the original rival, by placing himself permanently in the subservient position of somebody who had to be supported by him. Professor Ivor Mills of Cambridge reports the case of a district manager overburdened with work who was told by his firm to take on a deputy, and decided to take the lower job himself and give his own job to the new man. Such people find the exercise of superiority fraught with fears of the inferior's revenge.

Insofar as money is both the symbol and the instrument of power in society, some people are compelled to rid themselves of it; they will be found among the ranks of the "losers."

12

The Non-Player

There is a final money type: the non-player. He may be a temperamental dropout, or an active exponent of the counter-culture, or he may have taken a vow of poverty out of religious conviction, or he may not believe in possessions, or he may be one of nature's kibbutzniks. What these different types have in common is their refusal to play the money game. On the most elevated level, the rejection of money and of the pursuit of personal profit can be an assertion of superior values of one sort or another. In this respect, Jesus Christ, Jean-Paul Sartre, Albert Schweitzer, Mother Teresa of Calcutta, and St. Francis of Assisi are all linked. Sartre refused the Nobel Prize for Literature (worth about $100,000 then) because it went against his principles to accept it; he lives in a one-room apartment in Montparnasse, collecting no possessions except books, and most of his very considerable income is given away to struggling left-wing writers and to the leftist press.

As an antidote to the soft life and personal compromises

dictated by a money culture, this way of living has considerable attraction for the idealistic young, especially in the
United States. There, many middle-class children born with
the bad taste of money in their mouths rejected the material-
istic values of their parents and tried to find a more valid
alternative for themselves. Some of them, seeing how their
dads killed themselves in the rat race, and their moms suffo-
cated with boredom, took the road to Katmandu, and though
they picked up their remittances at Poste Restantes on the
way, felt for a while the purifying sensation of being free of
monetary worries and obligations.

Among the dropout generation a few years ago, the slogan
went:

> Make what you want
> Take what you need
> There is plenty to go around
> Everything is free

The aim was to abolish the source of all evil, and thereby
improve the quality of life. How did they go about achieving
this? *Some* money was, of course, needed even by them, but
as long as this was obtained outside, or in defiance of, the
system, and no wage-slavery or exploitation of others was involved, it was all right. They therefore set out to create a
moneyless mode of living by becoming urban Robinson
Crusoes who simply took what they needed. How this worked
out in practice may be surmised from a detailed guide that
circulated among dropouts, giving them free advice on how to
live for free.

It was a fairly comprehensive document, from which I shall
quote a few of the more original expedients advocated.

Dropouts in need of a rest were advised to get themselves a
psychiatric condition and obtain admission "as a voluntary

in-patient to a luxury mental hospital." (Obviously, this would only work in countries like Britain with a free National Health Service.) Alternatively, they were told to sleep in the carpeted corridors of luxury apartment buildings. This could be done by pressing one of the entryphone bells and telling whoever answered that they had pressed the wrong bell by mistake; they actually wanted Mr. X next door. Sooner or later somebody would press the door-release button and let them in instead of telling them to try ringing the right bell.

Bankruptcy was advocated as a means of obtaining essential possessions. "Order something," was the advice, "then let them repossess it; keep being out, and they can't break in; keep moving, you don't have to tell them." To carpet a room, if they wished to go in for such bourgeois affectation, drop-outs were told to go from store to store asking for carpet samples. (They would still have to sew all the samples together, of course.) Free clothing could be obtained by going to organizations that specialized in the aftercare of released convicts and pretending you had just come out of jail. Free food could be obtained in Amsterdam. Every night after one A.M. trucks unloaded deliveries of milk, yogurt (plain and fruit), chocolate and vanilla pudding, outside dairy shops, and left them there until the shops opened next morning. To get drunk you only had to find out when a private viewing of a new art exhibition was being held, and crash the cocktail party. Supermarkets in the States were highly recommended. The trick was to pick up the food and eat it before you left the store. This method was a lot safer than the more usual form of shoplifting because in order to be prosecuted you had to leave the store with the goods. "If you have eaten it," the dropout's guide counseled, "there is no evidence to be used against you." It was also useful to bear in mind that in the States you could sell your body for research to the universities and get an advance of between $150 and $600. Gas could be obtained by syphoning it out of somebody else's tank.

Richard Neville, one-time editor of the underground paper *Oz,* added this personal advice in his notes for survival on the road to Katmandu:[1]

"Begging works in the outer city areas, and especially in countries where Europeans are considered a novelty . . .

"In emergencies girls can fuck repressed Moslems for a fortune. Couples can make money by letting them 'just lookee.' Throughout the Arab world the youthful male is regarded as having charms quite equal to those of your over-worked girl friend . . ."

And he went on with mounting passion for the free life:

"Your blood value varies from £3.10.0 a pint in Turkey to £28 in Kuwait . . .

"A factory in Lahore makes firearms to any specification for the price of toy ones, and many a flower child has kept alive by gun-running . . .

"Men in tight, checked-suits and horn rimmed glasses will offer you small black cases to deliver in Copenhagen in return for a free air ticket to anywhere in the world, but don't . . .

"Once you could make 500 per cent profit bringing back sheepskin jackets from Kabul, and you can still triple your money with antique robes."

The aim was to live without families, nationalities, money or status, but it sounds pretty desperate. Before Mr. Neville's book—it was called *Playpower*—was in paperback, he had become disillusioned and was complaining in his magazine about hippies who gave him bad checks and stole his possessions after using his house as a crash-pad. Though in his book he had approvingly quoted a *Fortune* story that claimed that 40 percent of college students showed a lack of concern about making money and that the most intelligent young were dropping out and ignoring the contracts proffered by big business, Neville himself stepped straight out of the dock (after being tried for obscenity and acquitted) and into the London *Evening Standard,* which gave him a star column.

It shows how hard it is to live without money, even if you want to. The poet Laurie Lee once said: "The way to exist as a poet is to *enjoy* a low standard of living." But it is no longer that simple. Ernest Hemingway could write about his lean years in Paris that "all the paintings were sharpened and clearer and more beautiful if you were belly-empty, hollow hungry,"[2] but in those days the rate of exchange for the dollar enabled you to have a plate of *pommes à l'huile* at the Brasserie Lipp and to go off to see the bullfights in Spain even when your stories were not selling.

The times when it was still possible to live decently as a poor artist have gone. D. H. Lawrence was always desperately hard up—a £50 advance from his London publisher for *Sons and Lovers* had to keep him and Frieda for seven months or more. But even so, they were able to rent a garden apartment in the Villa Igéa in Gargnano on the Lake of Garda. The lake was fifty yards away, there were vineyards at the back, the rooms were large, furnished—a pleasant dining room, kitchen, and two bedrooms. There was a garden with peaches and bamboos. The rent was 80 lire a month, which was just over $7.50. A liter of wine was 60 centesimi (about 6 cents), and Lawrence spoke of getting "a huge lot of figs" for what would now be 2½ cents. A village woman to do the cleaning could be got for 25 lire a month (63 cents a week).[3]

Now the places that Lawrence and other impoverished writers lived in have become the rustic retreats of rich industrialists who pay a fortune to have the experience of struggling to cook their T-bone steaks over the glowing charcoal of a *fornello.*

The truth is that doing without money depends on the existence of congenial countries with an extremely low standard of living. As their standard of living rises, the would-be lotus-eater finds the rate of exchange for his foreign currency turning against him, and then he has to again engage in moneymaking to survive. This is the discovery of those who seek to remove themselves physically from the society whose money values they despise.

Others attempt to remove themselves from the money system while remaining inside their society. They engage in activities that are not designed to make money. Usually, the only way they can do this is by obtaining state subsidies or foundation grants. In this way scientists, researchers, theater directors, sociologists, artists and others, are able to exist without being subject to commercial pressures. The only trouble is that nowadays the competition for the grants, the subsidies and the handouts has become almost as much of a rat race as making the money, and some people, having been hat in hand around the foundations, find they prefer the workings of the open market to the intrigues of philanthropy. Even when the grants come easily and without strings, as they sometimes do, it has to be borne in mind that they are the means whereby the foundations justify their existence and their tax exemptions. The big American foundations only distribute about half of their income; the rest goes in building up their future resources by means of investments and playing the markets. Thus even the recipient of this kind of grant is participating in the capitalist system.

While it is virtually impossible for people to opt out of the system completely (even the kibbutzim now have to take on paid hands to supplement their labor force in manufacturing), there are people who genuinely manage to be indifferent to money. They are very few, and usually have some greater passion to occupy them. Albert Einstein, for example, was asked to name his salary when the Institute of Advanced Study at Princeton, New Jersey, asked him to join their staff just before the outbreak of World War II. In a state of "flame and fire" to get started, Einstein asked for $3,000 a year. Even for those days, that was a meager salary. The Institute said nothing, and paid him $16,000.[4]

Such people are rare, but they exist. They have no need of monetary riches because their lives are so rich in other respects.

PART THREE

Money Relationships

13
Money and Sex

Some of our most intimate relationships are determined, or affected, by money, though this is often denied. The sort of girl of whom it is said that she will undoubtedly marry a rich man—and then she does—may say she did not marry him *for* his money; it just happened that he was rich. In a sense she is speaking the truth. In her the money motive has become so interwoven with the sexual and the emotional that in her own mind it is impossible to tell them apart. She falls in love only with rich men, the way other women fall in love only with brainy men, or older men, or tall, dark and handsome men. It is happening on a deeper level than mercenary calculation. For her, money has become sexualized—it has become, if you like, a mating call, and she responds to it, emotionally and physiologically, the way the stickleback responds to the red markings of the male. Zsa Zsa Gabor says that the only man she married for his money was Conrad Hilton;[1] nonetheless the statistical evidence suggests that the number of very rich men in her life cannot be accounted for solely in terms of serendipity. This does not mean that Zsa Zsa Gabor is a gold digger; it means that like many other women she seems to be excited by money, that it is almost aphrodisiac to her.

That most philandering of the gods, Zeus, knew his phallic symbols when he turned himself into a swan for the conquest of Leda, a bull for the ravishment of Europa, and a shower of gold for the seduction of Danaë, the last being perhaps the cleverest of his disguises, in contemporary terms. For the money dance is recognized as part of the ritual of arousal, whether it's the jingling of coins in the pocket, the peeling off of bank notes from a fat wad, the overtipping of waiters, or flying her to Acapulco. Flashing his money about is man's way of spreading his peacock's feathers; a girl who is being wooed expects to have money spent on her, and there is no doubt that an expensive dinner has more erotic value than a hamburger. It may be a poor reflection on human nature that it should be so, but if it were not, the restaurant business would be in a bad way, for it is noticeable that after marriage there is far less interest in going to expensive places. A man who runs a fashionable and very expensive restaurant says that 90 percent of his customers are entertaining for business, or are taking a girl out.

The peculiarly erotic effect of spending money on a girl is emphasized by its converse: meanness is sexual anathema. The man who argues about the bill, or for that matter checks it too carefully, is ruining his chances.

Why should a girl be stimulated by having money spent on her? It can't be simply that she's mercenary, because expensive dinners can't be stashed away in her bank account—nor does the generous tip he gives waiters or doormen do *her* any good. Is it that her greed is excited by the evidence of his wealth? This cannot be the entire answer, because women are affected by having money spent on them even if they know the man cannot afford to be doing it.

To shower someone with gifts is a traditional seduction ploy, and it is amazing that for all its obviousness it often still works. One married woman, with a small child, recalls how she was pursued by a man she had never met.[2] "It was a sort of bombardment," she says. "Flowers would arrive continuously, huge great baskets of them. I was intrigued by this extraordinary barrage of foliage that kept arriving. We all got terribly nervous about it. Then there were the bottles of champagne and cans of orange juice—because he'd found out I liked drinking champagne and orange juice. I was being literally bombarded with the stuff. There was his Rolls Royce outside the door at all times of day. And then came the pots of caviar, to be eaten by the spoonful. Well, it was money being used in a very *fascinating* way; he had to have a lot of money—unless you have a lot of money you can't send ten dozen red roses a day. Then came the mink coat, which I sent back. This went on for three days before he turned up himself at the door—he said he was the delivery man, but I could see from the beautiful cashmere sweater he was wearing and the beautifully cut blazer that he wasn't a delivery man." She found him very intriguing, very interesting, but at the same time, "I had contempt for his money, which was all he had to offer me. As the presents became bigger, I sent them back. I suppose what I enjoyed was having this power over him, being able to say—clean my shoes!"

But, for all her contempt, she did not send him packing, and eventually she went to bed with him. She can't imagine why—he was, in fact, a vulgar semi-crook, whereas her husband, whom she loved, was a man of substance. The element of physical attraction was not very strong either. She says in some perplexity, "I somehow got myself into it, and then I couldn't get out of it." There can be little doubt that this woman—attractive, mixing in circles where she was likely to receive sexual overtures all the time—succumbed to this particular pursuer because she was mesmerized by his lavish spending. Although she had no need of his money—she earned enough herself—and was quite able to buy her own caviar and champagne, she nonetheless was bowled over by his approach. One must postulate that as in the case of Danaë and countless other ladies, her head was turned by the shower of gold.

The sexual symbolism of spending, giving, showering, smothering in furs is, of course, fairly obvious, and from the social acceptance of such blandishments it is clear that their symbolic meaning is well understood; it is only when the gifts become too expensive that they are presumed to be a form of buying—the mink coat was sent back because accepting it was too committing.

Since ten dozen red roses a day are just too many red roses for anyone, it is clear that the purpose of such a floral barrage is not to please the receiver but to show off the buying power of the sender. The recipient concluded, as she was meant to, that only a very rich man would send flowers on such a scale, although of course you don't *really* need to be rich to do it. It is possible to see that extravagance can have a meaning of great sexual potency, that the man who throws his money about with élan creates a giving image of himself that women find peculiarly suggestive. This double entendre is acknowledged in the song "Big Spender."

There must also be in such behavior a direct appeal to the little girl's wish to be looked after by Daddy, the aptly named "sugar-daddy" being the recognized exponent of this technique. Whether she, in fact, needs being looked after is beside the point, for in this state what has been reactivated in her is the seducible child-woman, who is wholly dependent on Daddy's largesse. Hence the sort of dazed condition in which the surrender often takes place, with the girl not knowing afterwards why she "gave in" and explaining it by saying she was swept off her feet. In effect, she was seduced by the shower of gold, the advance publicity of Big Daddy, i.e., the big penis.

The sexualization of money can occur also where the spending is being done by a woman, though the circumstances in which this tends to happen are of a different sort. The most common way in which women sexualize their spending is in the sudden irrational spending spree. In its classic form this is usually the outcome of a simmering emotional tension, which explodes in a bout of heedless extravagance, in which things are bought that are later found to be useless or unneeded. During the spending spree there is a feeling of reckless elation, a throwing off of financial restraints, and an I-don't-give-a-damn indulgence of momentary impulse. Women will usually account for their behavior by saying that it gets them out of a low mood, relieves a feeling of depression, gives them greater self-confidence. The typical case is the woman who goes out to buy herself another hat *to cheer herself up.* But such an explanation is not adequate. For the characteristic of the spending spree is that it is followed by self-recrimination and regrets.

The psychoanalyst Karl Abraham came across this form of behavior in a number of his patients, and he found that, typically, the desire to spend came upon these women in a sort of attack as they left the house. In the case of one woman he found that "if she went out of the house and was overtaken by anxiety she used as a defence against it to spend money on all sides in a quite needless way." Karl Abraham connected this with the common female state of "street anxiety," which he found arose out of unconscious, and at times conscious, fantasies of prostitution. "Their unconscious wants to yield without restraint to every person they meet; but their conscious anxiety restricts the transference of their libido within the narrowest bounds." Abraham concluded: "A compromise between instinct and repression is made by which the patient, in a spirit of defiance, does expend—not sexual libido, but an anal currency."[3]

Thus the spending spree becomes the substitute for the desired, but forbidden, sexual rampage, the heedless, reckless giving of herself—to spend also means to come, to have an orgasm—to any and every man, as a prostitute does, which is acted out in the spending on useless objects, and passing quickly from one to the next.

For the duration of the spree they have an exhilarating sense of freedom which is wholly disproportionate to what they are actually doing, but is understandable in terms of its underlying meaning. They are, briefly, cheered up, for in their moment of uncontrolled spending they have a sense of having defied the strict limitations imposed upon their sexual freedom. It is most frequently middle-class women who have recourse to this form of substitutive behavior, because it is their sexual freedom that is usually most severely restricted. The state of transport in which the spending spree is conducted is a further indication of its sexual meaning; often, afterwards, the woman is hardly aware of what she has done. The state of mind of certain kinds of female shoplifters who go on shoplifting sprees is very similar. "I don't know what came over me," they say.

The reason why the spending of money is chosen as the substitutive act is because the kind of sexuality that is being acted out has very strong sadomasochistic elements; and money, because of its unconscious equation with feces, in this particular context, can be "evacuated" in what psychoanalysis terms an anal-sadistic way. The spree is conducted as a kind of sortie. The woman is aggressive, demanding, bossy, she orders people around, picks quarrels, sweeps in and sweeps out, often is rude, deliberately using her spending power as a means of making store clerks feel subservient and small— she makes them her servants, her menials, makes them fetch and carry for her, run for taxis, search for unavailable goods. If they oppose her peremptoriness, she explodes, calls the manager, threatens to have them fired. The sadism is evident. The masochistic element comes in the self-punishment of having to admit to the unjustified spending to a husband or to herself, and perhaps in having to appeal to the clerks to whom she was previously rude to let her return her foolish purchases.

This capacity of money to serve as an instrument of sexual sadism is brought out in the following passage from the novel *The Empty Canvas* (Italian title: *La Noia*) by Alberto Moravia:

> I pulled Cecilia violently towards me; and at the same time, as she turned her face away from me and my kiss landed on her neck, I slipped the two notes into her hand . . . I felt her body abandon its resistance, and I saw that she had lowered her eyelids as if ready to fall asleep— which was her way of showing me that she accepted my love and was prepared to enjoy it. And so I took her, without her undressing; with a fury and a violence greater than usual, for it seemed to me that her body had become a kind of arena where I had to compete with the actor in vigour and tenacity. I took her in silence; but at the moment of orgasm I blew the word "Bitch!" right into her face. I may have been wrong, but it seemed to me that a very faint smile hovered on her lips; I could not tell, however, if she smiled for the pleasure she was feeling or at my insult.

During the love-making, she had put her hand with the money to her forehead, so that the notes were before his eyes all the time. In this description one can see the use of money as a weapon of anal-sadism, with the attendant fantasy that the bitch, in her female masochism, enjoys her demeanment.

Money as an instrument of sadism is a key factor in prostitution. There might be occasions when paying a prostitute has no more than a practical significance, when there is a desire for a sexual experience, and paying for it is the only means of obtaining it. But I would suggest that the real erotic significance of prostitution lies in the physical handling and passing of money (or in the awareness of this having occurred). The money, with its power of compulsion, introduces the sadomasochistic element that characterizes the relationship. This is shown when middle-class housewives with no economic need of the money become afternoon prostitutes, as depicted in the Luis Buñuel film *Belle de Jour*. That this happens has been corroborated by a former Madam.[4]

Even more common is the situation of men with the pick of women available to them gratis going to a brothel—and not even in a state of arousal, but in a state of wishing to be aroused. As in the passage from Moravia, the money pressed into the woman's hand excites sadistic fantasies: the vagina becomes an arena in which the longstanding conflict with another is fought out to the death. The "blowing" of the word bitch into her face, on which the money is lying, is highly suggestive of a farting-fecal assault.

On the face of it, it is highly puzzling why the tactile sensation afforded by money in the hand, and the sight of it, should be productive of sexual fury on the man's part, and pleasure at the insult on the woman's. What is the erotic excitement derived from the notion of being compelled by money? Often it takes the form of imagining being compelled to perform acts that she may consider disgusting; fellatio or anal intercourse. She submits in response to the money compulsion. She is bought and therefore not free to choose. In this way responsibility for the disgusting act is denied—and there is the thrill of being a bought object, a slave. But she has *chosen* to imagine herself—or indeed put herself—in the position of being subject to such money-compulsions.

Women used to conceal their money in their bosoms or garters, or even vaginas, so that it would be safe, though in practice, secreting it in this way was quite likely to incite a robber to rape. In such ways unconscious sexual motives are disguised. The afternoon prostitute, of imagination or reality, compelled by an economic arrangement to submit to hideous humiliations, can be seen to have made her own bed *in order* to lie in it. In her private theater of cruelty she gives to money the role of a sexual compeller, and then submits to it, as to a rapist; which is not to deny the existence of an economic motive as well. The prostitute's money greed is clearly a factor in her choice of profession, but it is not the whole story by any means.

The following is an account of how a doctor's daughter, the proverbial "nice Jewish girl," became a prostitute and eventually the top Madam in New York. The speaker is Xaviera Hollander, a vivacious young woman, who talks rapidly and continuously, with the sort of nervous intensity often found in intelligent young actresses with problems. Telling of her initiation into prostitution, she might be describing her theatrical debut. I give her account as she told it to me,[5] because it does reveal graphically the way in which the economic money motive intertwines with, and acts as a cover for, the sexualized money motive.

"I was used to living well," said Miss Hollander. "My father was a wealthy doctor at one time, until he got a stroke, nine years ago. Because of illness and hospitalization we lost everything. He wasn't properly insured, and we knew what it was to be poor again, not poor that we have to go begging in the street, but we lived in a humble little one bedroom flat. And I thought to hell with it . . . The first time I got $100 from a man, that was in America. I was engaged to an American, who was pretty wealthy, but very stingy, which I didn't care because I loved him, and I was working full-time, but I lived for free with him, so I sent my money home to my parents, to support my father and mother. I respect my parents, you know, a nice Jewish family. I was working for the consulate and I didn't really have financial worries, but I liked to dress up nice, I liked to wear the type of clothes that I used to wear when I was wealthy—when my parents were wealthy—but he was so stingy, and I couldn't make it with my $150 a week, supporting my parents at the same time. And he said, 'You're crazy, why do you send your money home?' I said, 'Because I don't want my mother to go out working, she's in her fifties. If my father died, she's got nothing.' I always knew what it was to be poor, I mean on the verge of being poor. I have three big phobias in life; one is to be old and lonely, not to have any friends—not to be married, or not to have a close friend. Two: to be crippled, I mean I'd hate to be hit by a car and lose a leg, in other words to be dependent on other people. I hate to be crippled and dependent. And *three* is to be poor. I always have had a fear of being poor. If I walk through New York and see the bums on the Bowery, it's like a knife under my heart . . .

"I go through suicidal depressions. I've tried to commit suicide. The second time it was because of my boyfriend; he lived on the nineteenth floor, and I took a heavy load of sleeping pills, but obviously not enough, and I wanted to jump off the roof, and he said, 'Oh, I don't want a scandal,' and drugged as I was—I was sitting already on the veranda, and the lights were very inviting—and he said, 'Don't do it, don't jump, I don't want a scandal,' and I thought: You bastard, you're not worth committing suicide for in a thousand years, and so then I thought if there is only one person who loves you, which is my mother, I realized what it'll mean if you're, you know, dead, so I jumped the right side instead, and then I said, No man is worth knocking yourself off for, and I have *joie de vivre*. I can be happy in a minute again. Basically I'm happy, but I hate loneliness. I cannot concentrate on reading a book, I get nervous. Anyway, so the first time I got my first $100 I spent a week with this man in the Hilton Hotel, just because I liked him, not as a hooker. I was a secretary, I never thought of it. Then he gave me $100, and I said, 'What is this? I'm not a whore. It's an insult.' My parents told me take chocolates, take cookies but don't ever take money . . . So I said: 'This is an insult, I don't want it.' And then this friend said, 'Here's an envelope, put the money in it, send it to your parents in Holland, give it as a present to your parents.' That to me was—great, because I wasn't a whore. The next day he took me shopping. He bought for me $500 to $700 worth clothes, and I felt treated like a lady. However, meanwhile he said, 'Look, you're crazy. You're a good-looking, young, charming woman, you're giving it away for free. Any man would lick his five fingers to give you a present or to pay you something.' He more or less indicated to me to become a mistress, or to find a sugar-daddy. Now, I've got something against the idea of sugar-daddies because it means you're tied up with one fellow; he says 'It's my pad, I'm paying for it, I don't want you to see anybody else.' So then I got in touch, a few months later, with a Madam, who paid me $150 for not even performing sex because he was impotent. He just wanted to please me. And then I started saying, 'Hey, you know, this is not too bad. I had to work a whole week for that, and now it's easy money.' And that's how I got into it, and I got in touch with this Madam, and I said I wouldn't mind making some more money like this.

"I started on a $25 scale, and I had to pay 10 percent to the Madam, so I ended up with a lousy $10 by the time I paid my cab fare. And so I said, Xaviera, this is worth more than $10, so I raised the fee. I said I only want the *crème de la crème,* and so I made $50 connections. And then I became involved in the slave scene and the masochistic and sadistic scene, which is far better-paying, and also which stimulated me psychologically more, because that was really the field of prostitution that was my side of it. Because I like to know what makes people click, what turns them on, what makes them sexual deviates. It's great to have power, I like to have power, I enjoy power in general . . . It's in my family. My father was an extremely good doctor, and he was a good writer too, my aunt was a very good actress in America, and we always wanted to be Number One. When they had a discussion going on, they wanted to win the conversation. And this is something in our family that has made us pretty powerful as personalities. And when I was a secretary, in 1964, I was working for Manpower. They were begging me for jobs— girls, boys, typists, secretaries. Then I had on the other side the bankers, the lawyers, the company. So then it was the banker calling for a secretary, and later he was calling me for a blonde or a brunette.

"Women's Lib says you're oppressed sisters, you're forced into it. It's not true. If a man goes to a prostitute, remember he's the one who's got the hard-on, he's the one who wants to get relieved, so if the girl is greedy she can say: 'Yes, I want your money.' But she can very well turn him down, and say, 'I don't like you. I don't want your money. You stink. You're dirty,' or whatever. But once they go to bed, it's basically the woman who makes out the patter. It's the man who will say, 'I want you to do around the world.' So you say, 'I want another $50. I'm not going to kiss your ass unless you pay me $100.' Basically, a man knows when he goes to a prostitute he gets a fairly quick treatment, and if he pays more he gets a better treatment.

"I liked the running of a house. I liked the power over people. It excited me. I did not want a sugar-daddy because I want my freedom . . . I want to be able to have a young boy that I want to screw. Also, the whole slave scene turns me on. A man would come to me and say, 'I want a tall redhead with big boobs.' Well, maybe the girls I have are none of them tall redheads with big boobs. Maybe they're all skinny and short. It's me turning him on, and working him up, and rubbing against him, that makes him go to bed with the skinniest, shortest broad in the place. I would work his fantasy around, make him almost my slave, and make him do what I wanted him to do. That's power, that's nothing to do with money. Or if I saw a gorgeous man that I wanted for myself, I'd take him for myself, and I've never been rejected.

"When the stock market goes up, the cocks go up; when the stocks go down, the cocks go down. I never had so many cases of impotency, for instance, as when the stock market fell —not only stockbrokers, but jewelers, people just in general. When the market was down, and they were losing, they'd still go to a prostitute, but they'd just talk sometimes, and I wouldn't charge them, and they'd say 'What am I going to do now? I can't get it up. I don't know what to do.' So I had to build up their egos again. A prostitute in certain fields—and particularly me, because I was interested in the psychological aspect of it—can be considered a lay analyst . . .

"The more wealthy or genius the people were, the more freaky—I mean, the more deviate they were. Because with them, with their fantasies, they'd had everything—they'd had man, they'd had woman. So what had they come for to me? For something new—money can't buy you everything, I found out. Those men have bought boys, they've bought girls, they've bought masochism, they've bought sadism, tried it the Greek way, and they just end up completely blasé, and they don't give a damn about sex any more. They say, 'I've tried it all ways.' And quite a lot of them—the more wealthy they are—ended up as heavy, heavy slaves, as masochists. And I could virtually take $1000 off them in one night, and impotent too, because the more impotent a man is the more he'll pay, because he wants to get his ego boosted up. He wants to please the woman orally, or with his hands, or with vibrators, no matter for what price, just to hear her say, 'You're the greatest.' Because his wife never tells him he's the greatest. She tell him, 'You're a lousy fuck, you can't get it up.' So with their money they want to buy a built-up ego again.

"These people want to be in the slave position . . . The more powerful they are in their daily life, the more they want to be your slave. I myself am a masochist. If you ask me what are you, I'd say I'm a bit of everything—I'm a masochist, I'm a sadist, I'm a voyeur, I'm an exhibitionist, I'm a lesbian, and I'm a heterosexual. It depends on where you are standing in life. If I've had an active day, domineering—in other words, ordering people around—that night I've got to balance my life out, and I don't want to be aggressive again in bed. This happened—this is the story of my boyfriend, who is a nice forty-three-year old Jewish *shnook,* your nice guy. If you ask him to pick up the shit of the dog, he picks it up, throws it in the garbage, makes a princess of me. And this drove me mad. I could not get it up—if I was a man I couldn't get it up, couldn't come. 'Larry,' I said, 'pick up that rope'—the night before I'd had a slave scene—'pick up that rope there, tie me down, beat the shit out of me, rape me.' This is a sexual fantasy that a lot of women go through, they'll never confess it, but it's true, because every woman somehow likes to get slapped around. My boyfriend said, 'I can't hurt you, I love you.' 'Please,' I said—I had to beg him, and this is what turned me on more—'get the rope, tie me down, beat me.' So when finally he did it, the moment he touched me I

came. It was just fantastic. Because I had to balance myself
out. Now, what turns me on is the whole mental thing—have
you read *Histoire d'O*? I was so turned on by that book. It's
fantastic. I'd love to go to a castle and get the things, and get
humiliated, and . . . I don't know if I could take that much
pain, but just humiliation. I love to be humiliated."

To Miss Hollander, when we spoke, being offered money
for sex was still "a slap in the face," and she wouldn't take it
from anyone she loves, although she would take it in disguised
forms, as a present, or as a shopping treat. But actual money—
the man asking her "How much do I owe you?" immediately
afterwards—was experienced by her as humiliation, making a
cheap whore of her. And yet, of course, since she sought humiliation in certain moods, to get "balanced out," it is clear
that her profession served various of her needs, not only those
of her money greed.

In the charades of the bordello—the slave scenes, etc.—the
money changing hands plays a variety of roles.

The man whose money has failed him regains some sense
of its potency by seeing the humiliations it is still capable of
inflicting. The brothel will supply him with a partner who
will relish the humiliation of being bought, beaten, made
into a slave, insulted by the fecal gift, as the satisfaction of her
masochistic need to get herself "balanced out." The power of
money will thus be reasserted, and if that was what the man
originally sought to derive from it, to some degree his faith in
it is restored.

In another twist of the masque, he will seek slavery for
himself, wanting abuse, demeanment, humiliation, pain.
Then the prostitute, in her sadistic role, will revel in making
him pay, pay through the nose, pay till it hurts, and he, in
his avarice, will feel this money deprivation as the most
excruciating of tortures, the ultimate punishment that his

masochism craves. At his most extreme, such a man will ruin himself for a no-good woman, and her taking of his money will be the means of achieving this.

Money so readily lends itself to sexualization because of its power to compel, a power it shares with the rope, the gun, the knife, the whip, the chains, and as a result of this it can fulfill a similar role to these commonly recognized instruments of perversion. This is partially recognized in the setting of the brothel, where someone like Miss Hollander experiences the payment for her services "as a slap in the face" and at the same time is seeking this and other forms of humiliation as part of her addiction to "the slave scene."

This kind of usage of money is not confined to the night games of sex. It also occurs in broad daylight on the rialto, though in disguised forms. *The Merchant of Venice* can be seen as a comment on the sadomasochistic aspect of money transactions. The pound of flesh is not mere metaphor. It expresses the way in which money is commonly used to get a life-and-death hold over somebody else, and this must be regarded as a manifestation of the sadistic impulse. In contemporary terms the businessman will drive somebody to the wall, or hammer him into the ground, or wipe him out, or have his balls, or have his head, or hold the whip hand, and anyone who thinks that these are just expressions should bear in mind Sir George Harriman with blood spurting from his nose.

Business is business, but sometimes it is not *just* business, as Miss Hollander's bordello revealed: buying and selling is charged with all sorts of other meanings. Most people have known the sinister pleasure of holding the whip hand, in a money sense. Likewise, pretty well everybody has at some time known what it means to be at the mercy of somebody else's money power; and, in certain cases, they will admit to the masochistic thrill of that—the moment of submission to money, the ecstasy of selling out. The theater of buying and selling is rich in double entendres. Being on top or underneath, in our society, is an interchangeably sexual, financial, social or political condition; and the dominance (or subservience) that cannot be achieved in one sphere is often sought in substitutive form in another. Hence Lady Chatterley's lover, and the peculiar erotic excitement of a superior/subordinate relationship in one area being reversed in another. The desire to be "on top" or "underneath" varies from person to person and from time to time, to which such pairings as the boss and the secretary, the lady and the chauffeur, the daughter of the house and the master's valet, testify.

There are even more bizarre ways in which money is sexualized. There is the miser's passionate love of his gold, in which it is the actual sensuous handling of it that delights and inflames. Volpone wants to kiss his gold. Most people love the *feel* of crisp new bank notes, or, for that matter, of dirty old bank notes. They are excited by the *sight* of money. Think of the packed bundles in the robber's suitcase—the sight of them gives cinema audiences a *frisson* of money love. Most people, too, would testify to the peculiarly erotic ambience of the casino; prostitutes and "women of easy virtue" are well aware of this, and make it their beat. It may seem a rational explanation that a man who has gambled and won will be in the market for a woman, simply because he is flush. But the sort of people who gamble at casinos do not need to win in order to be able to afford to buy a woman, and, for that matter, the prostitutes are equally in demand among the ones who have lost. There does seem to be something sexually arousing about playing with money, and Freud was in no doubt about the masturbatory significance of such playing. The way those piles of chips are handled, caressed, stacked, spread, splurged, received—the white thighs of money.

How does money, or its various symbols, come to have this encoded sexual significance? It must come about in the way that any other fetish arises. In his analysis of a case of shoe fetishism,[6] Abraham traced the way in which an original fixation of a "disgusting" nature was converted into a passion for dainty shoes, which became the patient's sole object of erotic interest. Something very similar must take place where money is concerned. Considering that in certain cases the passionate interest in money is an offshoot of the infantile interest in feces, it can be seen how that "disgusting" fixation can advantageously be transferred to beautiful money. Instead of loving the anus, as a certain kind of homosexual does, the money lover—in a later phase of sublimation—concentrates his passion on a glamorized version of the anal product. Money, for him, stands in the same relation to the original fixation as the dainty shoe does to the coprophilic pleasure in a disgusting smell.

In other words, a certain part-meaning of money, in these circumstances, comes to predominate, and because of its secret connection with a deeply repressed impulse comes to exercise a wholly disproportionate hold over the person's sexuality. In such an individual money love can become the whole of his sexual life, as the love of shoes is the whole of the shoe fetishist's sexual life. This may only be discovered in its negative aspect—in the form of marital impotence. Such a person is a ready customer for a bordello such as Miss Hollander describes; there he can thrust his money, the true vehicle of his potency, into the whore's hand, and in this ersatz intercourse hear her cry out that he's the greatest, while his penis hangs limply dispossessed.

There is yet another way in which money is sexualized, and that is seen in the case of the prostitute with the heart of gold. Here a very different fantasy is operating; money greed and masochism are no doubt present too, but the overriding impression is of manic sexual bountifulness: I can feed the whole world out of my sex.

The heart of gold is another version of the inexhaustible breast, with which, in this instance, the prostitute is identified. It is said that such women do not exist except in fiction, where they have certainly flourished. But they can be found outside fiction, too, if not as whole people, then as aspects of whole people—the prostitute with the heart of gold is part of the prostitute. Miss Hollander also described herself in these terms, called herself "the happy hooker," and said she regarded her work as a form of therapy, a cure for the sexual misery of the world. Her heart could be touched, she could give herself to beautiful young men, whom she supported. The other side of O, whose history of humiliation so excited Miss Hollander, is Camille, the prostitute who is idealized.

And this other side of the story is that the money given to the prostitute can redeem her, save her, elevate her—"take her away from all this." This is the romanticism of the rich young man falling in love with the prostitute. *His* money is sexualized as a magical kind of potency that will restore and heal. The story of the man who heaps money on a "bad woman" is an illustration of the impulse to restore—by means of manic forms of generosity—what previously had been sadistically destroyed. The beaten, demeaned and humiliated woman is by natural progression next taken shopping. The money first used as an instrument of sexual compulsion becomes the next day reparation payment.

In both instances money has usurped the role of sexuality. It has been given functions that rightly belong to *human* relationships, and the result of such a transference is the atrophy of feeling. One of the imagined delights of money is, indeed, that it enables us "to buy our way out" of almost anything. The no-longer-wanted girl friend is given the kiss-off with a gift. The unsuitable girl that the son of the house gets pregnant is paid off. The abandoned wife is paid alimony. In each case, money produces a lessening of *caring* and personal responsibility; what would otherwise have to be felt in the form of guilt or misgiving or regret or pain is made all right by money. The resultant reduction of feeling is at first experienced as a delightful sense of being carefree. Painful scenes are avoided. A woman generously taken care of, monetarily, may consider herself well off and not make trouble; a man who makes handsome provisions for the loved ones he abandons considers he has behaved decently. In using money in this way to achieve states of painlessness, the power of human feeling is abnegated. In the end, so much of one's potency has been made over to money that as a person one is impotent.

And the trouble is that heaping somebody with gifts does not really restore—it is only a token restoration. A woman who has been demeaned by prostitution can only be restored by the *real* sexual potency of her lover: her sense of inner dirtiness cannot be alleviated by jewels and dresses and cosmetics, only by his lovemaking. If he fails in that, the shopping expeditions will not suffice to make her feel good, except momentarily. Miss Hollander told me that she three times tried to commit suicide, suffered from acute depressions, could not be alone long enough to read a book. "The price of my life," she said, "is loneliness. There is nothing more lonely than short-term relationships. When he puts on his clothes and leaves, that's a low, low point. I always sleep with pillows all around me, my behind, my front, my head—I need to feel surrounded by warmth and softness to be able to feel safe enough to be able to sleep."

The heart-of-gold fallacy is the same as the inexhaustible breast fallacy: it postulates a kind of limitless giving, an unaging, untarnishable source of goodness. Inevitably, reality intervenes. The romantic prostitute dies of consumption, or—another form of dying—becomes hardened. Miss Hollander said: "When a bunch of drunken Irish stockbrokers come in on Saint Patrick's Day you have to just get their money and get them out." And to her girls, who might have felt dismayed by certain clients, she said that they should shut their eyes and imagine they were sucking that famous ice cream cone. "After ten, twenty years," she said, "you couldn't have much of that heart of gold left. Once you've been at the top, you can only go down. There's a hooker hierarchy, and you fall down it. You end up with silicone operations, and going to darker and darker bars, because you cannot compete with time. After I was making it six times a day as a hooker, at the beginning, I was just numb. When you go into it, you always say you are going to get out, but you get greedy. You can make five hundred dollars a night. I became greedy too, I took chances. I was arrested. I got addicted to sleeping pills one time . . . I get bored with boyfriends . . . I get bored with everything." The final, ironical *cri de coeur* was, "I want to be respected not as a lady of the night, but as a lady."

The life of the prostitute shows the use of money in sexual relationships at its starkest. The compelling force is openly exercised, and no bones are made about the woman's being bought, and the man's being made to pay till it hurts. Outside this specific area, the role of money is kept more ambiguous. Giving and receiving—usually in the form of jewelry, furs, cars, houses, rarely *cash*—is conventionalized to the point where the purpose of such gifts does not need to be acknowledged by either party. It becomes part of the whirl—the money dance. Only when things go wrong, and one or other person has not got what was expected, is the tacit understanding put into recriminatory words. Then underlying meanings and intentions are bitterly questioned.

A few years ago, a beautiful society girl, whom we shall call Amelia, who was at that time married to a very wealthy man, went to the South of France, where her parents had a house. She accepted an invitation to dine on the yacht of a millionaire, whom we shall call Alexander. Amelia told him of the breakdown of her marriage; Alexander was sympathetic. The next day, also on the yacht, he told her of the breakdown of *his* marriage. They grew closer.

The next month, the society girl and her mother arrived at the millionaire's house in California. Within a few hours of her arrival, Alexander gave Amelia jewelry worth £14,000. She thanked him very much; she thought it was a most generous present. A few years later, Alexander went to court to obtain the return of these and other gifts, valued in all at some £250,000.

At the time of the first present in Palm Springs, Amelia's mother had suggested to Alexander that he should think of some independent security for her daughter once marriage had taken place. Alexander had not liked that conversation because, as he put it, he was not "buying" Amelia. But he was very much in love with her and felt that talk of security was not completely out of place. So a little later he gave Amelia a £68,000 "engagement ring," which she wore only on the day that he bought it, because they thought it was in bad taste to wear it while they were both still married to other partners. Other gifts followed. There was the gift of a flat in London, worth £44,000. A birthday present of a £25,000 diamond clip. Love was in the air, and nothing was spelled out too clearly. But when things went wrong, Alexander didn't mince words: "I want all the jewelry back—it's finished." And Amelia, unlike the girl in the song, didn't tell him to take it all back. She was keeping it. At the high court trial, Alexander claimed the gifts were conditional—they were given to the woman he was going to marry. Amelia said no, the gifts had been made outright.

After six days of acrimonious disputation, involving legal costs of around £60,000, the case was settled by the two parties, without the judge's decision being required. Amelia agreed to give back most of the gifts and the flat, keeping only about £50,000 worth of jewelry.

It was a case that revealed what usually does not become publicly known about that sort of life—the money it costs. Tokens of love were subjected to harsh legal scrutiny, and the intentions of giver and recipient became the subject of tough cross-examinations:

"Her birthday fell on that date?"

"I was told it was her birthday."

"What do you mean by that?"

"She *told* me it was her birthday."

"Is there any element of doubt about it?"

And later:

"It was a birthday present that I gave to a girl I meant to marry."

"A conditional birthday present?"

"Not said as such, but in my mind it was that she was going to marry me."

Later:

"You intended for her to have it as her property?"

"As a wedding gift."

"It was your property at the time?"

"Absolutely."

On this level money works entirely on the basis of tacit understanding, and this, of course, leaves room for doubt as to what was understood.

The mistress, in general, is not so directly or immediately compelled as the prostitute, but in the end she, too, is controlled by money, and when she does something that displeases, the love gifts are taken back. Their unspoken purpose, therefore, is to make her do the giver's bidding. It may not look like that at the time—Amelia got some of her fabulous jewelry gift-wrapped on a Christmas tree—but in the course of time it emerges that the presents *were* conditional. Conditional on what? On marriage, was the answer given in court in Alexander's case. But in other cases they are conditional on whatever the giver chooses to make them conditional.

In *The Empty Canvas* Moravia describes the narrator's attempt to possess his girl friend by arousing her venality. Every time he makes love to her, he gives her money, and so makes her come to expect it. Then he stops giving her the money to see if this will produce any change in her, or cause her to say anything. It does not seem to affect her one way or the other, and he is furious because if she is not venal he cannot hold her with money. This is money that he himself has to get from his rich mother, and she gives it to him because, as he realizes, "My mother, too, was seeking to get control over me by means of money . . ." Meanwhile, Cecilia, the mistress, was giving money obtained from a previous lover to her other boyfriend. In each case, control of the loved person is sought, consciously or unconsciously, through the medium of money. "I preferred to know that Cecilia was mercenary, rather than mysterious," says the narrator, "for the knowledge that she was mercenary would give me a sense of possession that mystery denied me."

Money ties replace emotional and sexual ties that it is feared might be inadequate. Thus the essential role of money in the lover-mistress relationship is that of binding and controlling someone who is otherwise felt to be too free. This implies, of course, a basic lack of faith in the other ties, and in due course, by shifting the emphasis to money ties, these other ties are bound to be weakened.

In these circumstances, venality on the woman's part and wealth on the man's are useful complementary conditions, since they contain the basis of a workable pact. An arrangement can be arrived at whereby the interests of both parties are protected by their mutual need. If the girl is not venal, does not care sufficiently about money, the relationship breaks down, because the man is denied the hold over her that he needs for his security. The girl's need of money is considered a more reliable basis for a relationship than her need of her lover's love.

The cause of such faith in money rather than love must go back to the very earliest need to control, which is so characteristic of the anal character. Such people are incapable of allowing others freedom of action; typically, they want to determine the tiniest details of the lives of those close to them. They are therefore very suited to keeping mistresses. By paying the rent of the apartment, and the maid, and the bills, they can maintain continuous control and scrutiny of the other person's activities. And they have the right—since they are paying.

This kind of controlling character will tend to be a numbers man, a collector, a money gnome—someone whose lifestyle is to have everything neatly arranged, planned, divided, "all worked out." He will have set nights of the week for spending with his mistress, and other nights devoted to his family; he will have people to whom his mistress can be introduced and those to whom he would not dream of introducing her. His life will be meticulously divided up into self-contained compartments in each of which there are people who fulfill his needs—and he manages to make it all work by the exercise of monetary control: wife, mistress, prostitutes; each is paid in accordance with her services.

The way in which this very practical system breaks down is shown in the typical Feydeau farce: the kind of person likely to be willing to submit to this kind of anal control is almost certainly a trickster, who will naturally deceive her rich protector with her young lover. It is only the trickster character who would pretend to submit to such controls and conditional gifts. Anyone else would openly rebel. Hence the controller becomes ever more controlling (since he has cause), and his mistresses ever trickier.

It often happens that people involved in such relationships end up talking about nothing except money. Everything between them is expressed in terms of it. Emotional questions are reduced to it. And freedom from the relationship too becomes a money matter. The recurring themes are purchases, marriage settlements, divorce settlements, trust funds, the community property law of California, tax arrangements, lawsuits for possession, lawsuits for recovery, lawsuits to establish ownership, payments for this, payments for that—nonpayment. Significantly, in the Amelia/Alexander saga a $150,000 piece of jewelry bought in Rome in 1966/7 as a love gift for Amelia was not actually paid for until January 1971— that is, long after the love affair was over—when the jewelry was already the subject of legal action. Meanwhile, the jeweler was making trips to Amelia and Alexander to try to get his money or his jewels back, but being at the fulcrum of the lovers' quarrel, wasn't having much success.

Evidently the problem about marrying Amelia was that Alexander's wife had not agreed to the financial terms of their divorce. On Amelia's side, she claimed that in order to be able to marry Alexander, she had obtained a quick divorce from her husband, thereby sacrificing the vast fortune she might have got.

Where money is used to obtain possession or control of another person, then the resistance, and the countermoves,

will be money moves too. If A tries to control B by means of a
conditional gift, that is, a gift that can be taken back if certain
conditions are not fulfilled, then B, for her part, will seek to
exercise all her charm and sexual prowess to make the gift
unconditional and thus remove the curb on her freedom that
A is seeking to impose. To anyone practiced in such love/
money games, all the moves are as well known as the moves
in a chess game, and are made more or less automatically.
They can become extremely sophisticated. Distaste of being
financially manipulated causes some rich men to adopt very
strict rules for their spending on women. *Playboy*'s Victor
Lownes on principle will never give girls large presents. He
says, "Hefner and I have discussed the fact that, being rich
men, he being very rich, one frequently realizes that one
could use one's wealth to bribe a girl into bed, say, but it
would take away from the pleasure of getting her into bed for
your own self. Now your own self being a rich man is part
of it, and you're not going to eliminate that, and I don't
spend a lot of my time torturing myself with concern over
that aspect of my appeal. But it isn't because she's going to
get a car or a watch or some lavish gift. I am consciously
reluctant to give gifts of great value—I'm consciously reluctant. Yes, I will give a gift, a small gift, not something that a
poor man couldn't afford too. A bottle of perfume, something
like that."[7]

And so the game-playing becomes more intricate, with
every opening gambit having its appropriate defense.

"There is a gold digger type," says Lownes, "and I think I
sense it immediately. How? You just get the feeling. I mean
you can tell if a girl is calculating. I mean, you just feel there
is an effort to manipulate you—and, you know, if people are
trying to manipulate you, you can feel it. And I shy away
from it. Girls have asked me for money—not a lot—perhaps a
few hundred dollars. There are people who travel in the

circle of ladies who ask for $10,000 but in my case if it ever happened it was so immediately turned down I don't even remember it. In the cases of people asking for small sums of money that are meant to stave off some real disaster, I agree to loan them the money, and I make them execute a note. I don't press for payment of the note, but the note itself is sufficient to keep them from asking for more. It's for her dignity too, I don't just give the money: she has a debt."[8]

Faced with this kind of stone-walling defense, a counter-move has to be developed. The prostitute waits till the man is in bed with her, and when he is highly excited she puts up her price. ("If you want me to do around-the-world, that's an extra fifty dollars.") The mistress uses less obvious methods. If the man is stingy, she finds reasons why she can't see him on this night or that night—she has to see somebody about work, about a job. Or she has to see somebody who has promised to put money into a venture of hers—a little boutique, a restaurant. Or he is a photographer for whom she is doing modeling work to earn money. Or she is working evenings as a waitress. "I don't want you to do it," says the man, seeing his hold loosened, and others having power over her. "But I need the money for my sick mother," she says. And so he says, "All right, I'll give you the money to send to your sick mother."

The sick mother's needs of course become progressively greater. Once giving her money has become established, stopping giving it means "You don't love me any more," and so he can't stop, because if he doesn't love her any more (if he did, he couldn't be so mean), why shouldn't she see Freddie? "I'm not *married* to you, am I? I have my future to think of too."

These are the common clichés of such relationships; baffled, bemused, sick at heart, the man says, "We're always quarreling about money." And she says, "That's because you're so stingy." And he says, "It's always money, money, money." And she says, "It's all right for you—I'm the one who has got nothing, who has sacrificed her chances and her security for you . . ." And so it goes on. Eventually, a financial accommodation has to be reached, or it all ends.

This situation, of course, does not arise where people are equally rich or equally poor, or totally indifferent to money. But in that eventuality one person does not have a *hold* over the other, which is precisely what a certain kind of person needs to have. Lownes, who staunchly asserts his refusal to bribe girls into bed, admits that it might be different when the natural process of aging has rendered it more difficult to get them any other way: he just hopes that as his attractiveness is reduced, his desires will be reduced correspondingly. Failing that, he can see that money might be the means of providing oneself with sexual security in old age.

Once money has entered a relationship, by whatever roundabout means, it becomes impossible to ignore it. Xaviera Hollander calls a certain kind of marriage negative prostitution. Men came to her and said: "What do I get for the $10,000 a year I give my wife—six lousy screws! I'm better off paying you $100 a time."[9] As soon as people operate a money value system, they are bound to evaluate everything in those terms. What am I getting? Am I getting my money's worth? And then the conclusion is arrived at that she's no bargain, or "I can get something better." On the other hand, the "freebie" suddenly says, "Hey, I'm giving it away." She sees other girls "getting something out of it" and feels foolish not to be doing so herself. They show their diamonds and furs, and she thinks, "All he ever buys me is a lousy hamburger." So money comes into it in a negative way; the girl feels disgruntled about making herself available so cheaply.

Soon she doesn't feel like it when he wants to, and the pressure is put on for him to give some tangible indication of his love.

It is far less common for a man to be kept as a love object by a woman, although it does happen, and the fact that it happens, sometimes, shows that there is nothing specifically masculine about the desire to have a lover who can be controlled by means of money. Usually when this happens the man will be a struggling artist, and the woman will assume the role of his patron or sponsor; even if he has no talent, even if he hardly ever paints, or composes or writes, the pretense of his artist status is maintained.

There is no reason to suppose that the money issues are fundamentally different when the relationship is turned around this way. The only difference is the evident need of most women to find some reason other than an emotional or sexual one for keeping a man. Most women, no matter how liberated, shrink from keeping a man simply as someone to make love to them—they need some other relationship as well. If the man doesn't have artistic talent, he will be made the woman's business manager, or her secretary, or an associate in her company, or her chauffeur—but he will usually be given some kind of other role, as a concession to bourgeois mores. Only on the level of society where these do not apply is the pretext dropped. Miss Hollander said, "Oh yes, I have kept men. If I see a gorgeous young boy and want him for myself I wouldn't hesitate to pay him."

She told the following cautionary tale:[10] "I was in New York. I fell in love with a young boy, nineteen years old. I like innocence, strange as it may seem. Maybe not strange, because I've seen so many cocks and cunts, to put it bluntly, seen so many men that are cheating on their wives, going to a prostitute, that what turns me on is innocence. So I met this young kid from Tennessee. He had a hillbilly accent, square looking, beautiful cock, fantastic. But I met him at a Madam who basically has male prostitutes, gay lords. I didn't think he was a prostitute—he'd just recently got out of the army—so I fell in love with him. And the kid hadn't got a stitch of clothes to wear. He had his army jacket, nothing, worn-out shoes—so I bought him boots, I bought him clothes, I bought him winter clothes, I had his car fixed. I spent about $1,000 on him in one month. He'd sleep over at my place. He'd sneak out when my boyfriend came home—it was a whole hidden thing, you know—and at night he would take off. I'd say to him, I'm running this place as a brothel, this is no place for a kid like you to hang around, why don't you go out? He said, 'Okay, I'll get a job, as a bartender.' I never asked where. I asked very few questions. He worked from eight to twelve, so I said great, I'll see you at twelve, then my business is closing down. So we would make love, and he was fantastic, but it would take him a long time, and orally he couldn't come, never, which sometimes turns me off, but he was a great, great lover. This went on for a month. For a month this went fine, and then by accident I found out, after I'd spent all the money, that this kid was one of the most sought-after male studs in New York City, and that he had made a lot of money, and that between eight and twelve he wasn't working as a bartender but was fucking five guys a night, and this turned me off emotionally, the idea that he had been up the rear end of five men and I'm sucking him, even though he took a bath or shower—the hustler being hustled. I mean here I was hustled for $1000 and this kid was playing the game . . ."

There is a type of man who does not mind what he does for money. The criminal D—— says, "I go with prostitutes sometimes, and they give me money. I never pay a penny. No, I would never pay a prostitute. When the time comes for that, you can forget it. But if they give *me* money, I don't mind. When a girl's had any aggravation with customers, I've told them to leave her alone, and then she doesn't have any more aggravation. I never refused money in my life. Sometimes I go down to Oscar's discotheque where these old birds go that are looking for somebody, and they say to you: 'All on your own, then?' They'll buy you suits or shirts, or give you money. They get a kick out of doing it with a real villain, somebody who's been had up for attempted murder. Gives them a kinky thrill. They're any age, I'm not fussy. Fifty or sixty, some of them. In their thirties too. Not really young ones. A lot of them are kinky. They like very young boys, sixteen or seventeen years old. Old women just want young boys, that's how it goes. I'd never say 'no' to anything, I shouldn't think. I'm not kinky or nothing like that, but I don't mind what the old birds want to get up to . . . if they pay."[11]

Different categories of gigolos, or male prostitutes, can be found in most of the pleasure spots of the world, some operating on a pickup basis, others in the older, more elegant style of the traditional gigolo. In Hamburg an all-male brothel for women customers is in the course of being launched, and 1,500 German men have offered their services there in return for a payment of approximately thirty-five dollars a time, and have declared their willingness to satisfy women of seventy.

From the woman's point of view, the desire for a paid lover is related to the same desire to control that motivates men who keep mistresses. The desire to have somebody to do your bidding is part of infantile fantasy, and because of one's dependence on love, the lover is the person one most wishes to control. Children try to order their parents about. They make all sorts of peremptory demands upon them, using a variety of expedients, from pleas and threats, and subtle forms of blackmail, to tantrum fits. Unless they lived in previous centuries and were heirs to the throne, they usually found that it didn't work, or didn't work all the time. But with the discovery of money and its power, the infantile desire to exercise control over another person is reactivated. Suddenly it becomes possible, because of other people's willingness to sell themselves.

From the gigolo's point of view, submission to this kind of control is something that appeals to his trickster mentality. She thinks she is having me, but really I'm having her. By whatever tortuous internal contrivance this is arrived at, it is the basis on which he sells himself. Such men are always scheming in their relationships, which is seen particularly in the case of homosexuals. Because the kept man constantly has to offset his monetary dependence on the other, he must strive to increase the other's sexual or emotional dependence on him.

There can be advantages, at times, in having sexual relationships on a monetary basis. Arthur Koestler, in his autobiography, *Arrow in the Blue,* has a nostalgic chapter about Paris brothels, and he sets out their advantages with characteristic rationality:

"The Paris Houses, while they were legal, were neither Sodom nor the idyllic places described in some novels; they were orderly, commercial establishments where sex, deprived of its mystery, was traded as a commodity. The sale of any human faculty as a commodity is obviously a degrading process; but it is equally obvious that the difference between trading one's embraces and other forms of prostitution—political, literary, artistic—is merely one of degree, not in kind. If we are more repelled by the former, it is a sign that we take the body more seriously than the spirit. It is absurd to expect that in a mercantile society the most potent human urge should escape the process of commercialisation."

There is another point to be made as to why sexual relationships can hardly ever be totally exempt from monetary considerations, and that is that it is clearly impossible to isolate one powerful human urge from another, and insofar as money is such an important part of our lives, to exclude it from one specific area is a kind of artificiality. Realistic appraisal of what goes on shows that it never is excluded entirely, except where romantic gestures are being made.

If we avoid moralizing—that is, do not concern ourselves with what ought to be but rather deal with what *is*—then we become aware of this fact: The consequence of introducing money into the sexual relationship is that some part of the sexual drive is "monetized" and some part of the money drive is sexualized. In certain circumstances, such interior devices may be the only way of dealing with otherwise untenable feelings. It may be more acceptable that the middle-class housewife with prostitution fantasies should go on spending sprees rather than give herself to every man she sees in the street, or that the businessman should satisfy his needs for enslavement or mastery in the stylized masque of the bordello rather than act them out on the world stage.

Total instinctual freedom being an impossibility in society, money functions as a transformer reducing the load. The loss of feeling involved has been noted, and it is clear that some of the heat is taken out of sex (sometimes to the point of impotence) where the dynamic becomes monetary rather than genital; but it also has to be said that some people may actually prefer this cooler kind of relationship.

The positive side of money is the hardness of hard cash; it has a certain satisfying exactness; it reduces the confusion and complexity of things to *how much?* It facilitates emotional abdication. Instead of everything's having to be referred to the higher court of feeling, matters can be settled routinely, matter-of-factly; the sheer automatism of this can be a relief.

People cannot live on Mount Olympus all the time; the money cipher can fulfill everyday human needs by reducing relationships to their minimal aspects. This may not be one of the highest functions of life, but it has its uses.

14

Money and the Family

The desire to keep money *in the family* is a powerful and primitive urge, often overriding familial feuds and hatreds. On some level below consciousness, blood ties and money ties interweave to form the binding that holds families together. In this way great financial dynasties arise, such as the Du Ponts, the Krupps, the Rockefellers, the Kennedys, the Guinnesses, the Dukes of Westminster, the Rothschilds, the Mellons. The way it happens is well illustrated by the story of the Du Ponts. They began rather modestly in 1803 as makers of gunpowder, with a capital of $36,000. E. I. du Pont de Nemours and Company did very well in the war of 1812 and marvelously in the Civil War. In 1872, with the market glutted by postwar surplus gunpowder, the company was not doing so well, and was thinking of selling out. But Alfred I, thereafter known as "Savior of the Du Ponts," brought in two cousins from another branch. They brought in two brothers. This sort of accelerative nepotism served them well, for today there are four Du Ponts estimated by *Fortune* to be worth between $600 million and $1.2 billion, as well as 246 other extremely wealthy Du Ponts who constitute the money elite in the family. There are apparently many more little Du Ponts, a bit less elite, but doing all right. Between them they are in E. I. du Pont de Nemours, in General Motors, in the U. S. Rubber Co., in the American Sugar Refining Company, in the Mid-Continent Petroleum Corporation and the United Fruit Company, just to mention a few. They also run about eighteen foundations, and have provided $122,559,001 for the upkeep of former Du Pont mansions, parks, estates as public museums and botanical gardens.[1]

Some of the greatest wealth has simply grown by virtue of time and circumstance. When Sir Thomas Grosvenor married a certain Mary Davies in 1677, she had a modest dowry of a few meadows. In 1972 a young man reaching his twenty-first birthday, Earl Grosvenor, son and heir of the 5th Duke of Westminster, inherited his share of the family fortune, valued at around £11 million. This inheritance came to him because Mary Davies' meadows happened to be situated in what was later to be Mayfair and Belgravia.

The Grosvenor fortune, said to be one of the largest in private hands in England, is a perfect example of the principle of keeping the money in the family. The present Duke of Westminster received five-twentieths of the residuary wealth under his cousin's will. Lord Grosvenor, the son of the present Duke, was left a three-twentieth share. But when his uncle, the 4th Duke, died in 1967, he did not leave an heir, and so Lord Grosvenor inherited a further six-twentieth, giving him nine-twentieths in all.

This might be called the upper-class English way of acquiring wealth by osmosis. The Greeks are less passive about it. The wealthy shipowner Stavros Livanos had two daughters, Tina and Eugenie. Twenty-five years ago a rising shipowner, Stavros Niarchos, fell in love with Tina. But he was turned down. Tina married another shipowner, Aristotle Onassis. Then Niarchos married Tina's older sister, Eugenie. The years went by, and eventually Onassis' interest in the opera singer Maria Callas led Tina to divorce him. Her sister, Eugenie, died. And Niarchos, now free to marry again, married Tina. And so whatever else happens, the money stays in the family.

"One man may amass the fortune," says Ferdinand Lundberg in *The Rich and the Super Rich,* "but if the fortune is to remain intact it must have heirs. Where the fortune-builder is a bachelor or fails to establish a family, the fortune simply disappears in a foundation or institutional grants. Heirs, then, are as important to a fortune as to a title of nobility. Most American fortunes, easily by a majority of 70 per cent, are in the hands today of heirs." A *Fortune* list of inherited wealth in 1957 showed some forty-two individuals with fortunes of between $75,000,000 and $1,000,000,000.

The urge to keep money in the family and perpetuate it is abundantly documented by any study of the genealogy of great wealth, or for that matter lesser wealth. Even where the acquisitions of a lifetime are small, there is an urge to pass them on to one's own. There are old ladies who worry about leaving something to their rich sons. And most people feel in buying a house or any other kind of property that it has, in addition to its immediate function of providing a home, or an income, that of being something to leave to one's children, or after them, one's relatives. Nearly all wills are in favor of the testator's family. Often a distant relative, whom the testator may never have seen, is chosen as a beneficiary in preference to, say, a very close personal friend or colleague. People cannot explain this, except to say that it feels more natural to leave money to your own family, even if you can't stand the sight of them.

In many cases, instead of this somewhat half-hearted loyalty to the family, there is a positive plan that family money shall serve the family interest, as in the case of the Kennedys. Where this sort of attitude prevails, complex trusts are set up, with interlocking fail-safe devices to ensure that no outsider shall be able to get control of the family fortune. Estate duty, which was meant to stop the cumulative piling up of wealth from generation to generation, is in practice so easily flouted that it has been called the voluntary tax. Most rich men nowadays spread their money around inside their own families as soon as they have made it, retaining control of it during their own lifetimes as the trustees of the foundations and trust funds whose rules they have themselves written. The heirs and beneficiaries are required to enact similar deeds and covenants, which spread the money among *their* children and their children's children. Families in which this has happened become powerful unified entities within the state—forces permanently to be reckoned with. A President holds office and power for a maximum of eight years, but the Fords, the Du Ponts, the Kennedys, the Rockefellers, the Mellons can continue to exercise the power and influence of their wealth throughout their lifetimes, and in effect (unless something goes wrong) through their heirs in perpetuity. The awareness that they will still be around and a force in the world when a particular politician is gone is what gives them their great standing and influence.

Like any other totemic object, money is a means of organizing people's relationships to each other in terms of their relationship to it. In primitive tribes the totem object was, for instance, a means of imposing the prohibition against incest—those "descended" from the same totem (a particular sacred animal, or bird, or plant) were not permitted to have sexual relations with each other. In this way, the tribes found a formal way of dealing with what they felt to be a danger. Of course, the danger did not lie in descent from a common totem, but this was an effective way of expressing it. Insofar as money is a totem object, it also imposes certain formal taboos. Those descended from the money totem shall not intermarry with those descended from the no-money totem, because in this way the money totem becomes degraded and weakened. The underlying fear is that such a marriage would be a drain on the family fortune, instead of consolidating it.

It is easy to see the practical advantages of keeping money in the family. But there is more to it than that. Where people hand down comparatively small sums, or some property such as a house, no question of power or influence is involved—and yet the desire that one's own family shall inherit what one has made remains very strong. This is not necessarily an expression of beneficence, because some men believe firmly that it is harmful to be left large sums of money, and yet leave money to their children.

Some aristocrats see the stately homes they inherit as prisons, of which they are not the masters but the victims. Lord Montagu, though he does not take this line, regards himself more as the caretaker of Beaulieu, the ancestral home in Buckinghamshire that he inherited, than its owner. He is, in any case, technically not its owner; as soon as he came into his inheritance, he was obliged to hand it over to a trust in favor of his children. Many of the family portraits which hang in the great house do not particularly please him as paintings, and on occasions when he entertains romantic notions of living more simply, he has also imagined banishing those ancestors from his sight. But not for long. They soon reassert their rights. Anyone who inherits a great house, or a family fortune, is dictated to by ghosts. "You feel," says Montagu, "a compelling sense of sacred duty to the people who built and developed your inheritance . . ."[2] This is precisely what the fortune-maker counts on creating in his descendants. With what he hands on, he binds the inheritors to a certain life. Few people are capable of rejecting an inheritance, or the strings attached to it.

In this way money asserts its immortality. It becomes the means whereby an individual can impose his influence or taste or style upon the future. It is the only present-day way of begetting a line of kings. But, as Freud has said in *Totem and Taboo,* kings are also chosen to be victims, and the show of honoring them tends to conceal this aspect of their role.

This is seen in the case of the Kennedys. Successive brothers have felt themselves to be the inheritors of the family's political ambitions, and have felt compelled to pursue a political career, despite the risks. The family money which finances, also binds. As kings were, in effect, bound by their "divine right to rule," the inheritors of great wealth are likewise impelled to exercise the "rights" that their money gives them, and they in turn impose these rights upon their sons. Some abdicate, but most do what is expected—money, like royal descent, carrying with it powerful coercive elements.

The present Lord Rothschild rebelled against family tradition by becoming a scientist, but his son, Jacob, has returned to the financial fold, and now runs the family bank in London. Even if a business is not on this scale, a founder imposes upon his heirs very powerful obligations. To be entrusted with the family fortune and not increase it or at least preserve it offends against basic instinct. Few people placed in that position can be indifferent to what is evidently expected of them; and more often than not, what is expected of them will come to have priority over what they might wish to have done, left to choose for themselves.

Their sense of obligation *to the money,* as if it were living stuff, must arise because of the association of money with the notion of viability. This suggests the equation of the capacity for survival with money. Therefore: the first duty is not to let go of it. It is endowed with a life of its own. People talk of

Krupp money, or Ford money, or Guinness money, as if the family genes are somehow incorporated in it. To preserve it, and multiply it, is to transmit the strain, keep the stock *viable*. Blood may be thicker than water, but money is thicker than both. When Gustav von Bohlen und Halbach married a certain Bertha in 1906, he reversed the normal custom and took her name, which happened to be Krupp. He became the living proof of the transmission of family characteristics through the agency of money by becoming the most infamous of all the Krupps—one of the main financiers of Hitler. He may have had von Bohlen und Halbach blood, but his money was Krupp money, and he acted in accordance with his monetary heritage.

How can we account for this intense urge to keep money in the family? If, as Freud has postulated, the primal crime was the murder of the father by his sons, for the possession of his property, his women and his powers, then we may conclude that one of the earliest forms of realpolitik was that of inheritance. The father, realizing that he would be attacked and superseded as his strength failed, must have devised a system whereby, while he was still strong enough to impose his own law, he divided his property among his sons. This division would serve several purposes. It would mitigate the envy of the young, who as yet had nothing. Secondly, by promising them their inheritance upon his death, he would have acquired a powerful hold over them, since he would now be able to disinherit a disobedient or otherwise displeasing son. And thirdly, by establishing that the inheritance belongs proportionally to different members of the family, he bought himself protection, since each brother now had a stake in the family fortune and was therefore interested in protecting it against the thievery of any other.

In the system before inheritance, the feared and envied

primal father was slain, "and in the act of devouring him [the sons] accomplished their identification with him, and each one acquired a portion of his strength. The totem meal, which is perhaps mankind's earliest festival, would thus be a repetition of this memorable and criminal deed . . ."[3] There must have been some politically inspired forefather of the race who saw that if he turned his property into portions and allocated them to his sons, he might avoid being apportioned in person before his time.

Our urge to keep the money in the family, then, would appear to have one origin in the primordial act of appeasing the younger generation knocking at the door. In the light of this explanation, our motive in leaving our wealth to our offspring can be seen to be, in part, a means of defending ourselves against their actual or imagined crimes of covetousness.

Support for this idea is provided by the novel *The Brothers Karamazov*. In this, the crime of parricide, in its various aspects, is intimately bound up with questions of money. The main suspect, Dmitry, is thought to have murdered his father for a few thousand rubles. He is a young man with a grievance. He had believed that he had an inheritance, but having drawn on it extensively before coming of age, he suddenly finds there is nothing left. "The young man was stunned, suspected his father of lying and deceiving him, was almost beside himself and really seemed to have gone out of his mind. It was this circumstance that led to the catastrophe . . ."[4] says the narrator in the novel.

At first the idea that a son might murder his father for money seems to trivialize so terrible a crime. But in the course of the novel, as the shadow of guilt moves from brother to brother, this particular crime begins to reverberate with echoes of the primal crime. It becomes clear that the book is portraying something very fundamental in human nature.

Given the murderous rage of the dispossessed towards the

possessors, it can be seen why the system of family inheritance should have become so strongly established. The fact that children are for so long dependent on their parents means that they may build up a tremendous store of resentment. The convention of keeping the money in the family reduces this to some extent by promising them their turn. The unbearable envy of the father's richness (in every sense) is reduced by the promise "It will all be yours some day." For this reason, to let the money go out of the family seems a contravention of natural law.

What are the advantages and disadvantages of inheritance?

In *The Republic* Plato puts forward the view that there are considerable advantages to inheriting money rather than making it. Those who have inherited it are not over-fond of it, whereas he makes Socrates say, "moneymakers become devoted to money, not only because, like other people, they find it useful, but because it is their own creation. So they are tiresome company, because they have no standard but cash value."

The anonymous captain of industry referred to in an earlier chapter has likewise taken the view that it is good for children to have money, and so has already given his their inheritance in the form of trust funds, over which he retains control as trustee. Many other rich men have done the same.

"The great advantage for them of having money," he says, "is that it gives them freedom of choice—they can do anything they wish with their lives. Their behavior can be totally unsullied by financial considerations. To the extent that making money corrupts, they would be incorruptible. They would be able to behave in accordance with their consciences independent of commercial pressures." Had he had the same freedom of choice, he might have become a concert pianist or a pure mathematician instead of a businessman.[5]

There are some undeniable advantages to inheriting money. But there are also formidable disadvantages; the most obvious being the element of disincentive, resulting in dissipation, playboy tendencies, unwillingness to work, and the arrogance that can come of the illusion of being totally independent. The son of a very rich man faces a massive obstacle to the successful working through of his normal Oedipal complex, in that it may appear *impossible* to do better than *his* father. Paul Getty says that one of his main motives for making a great deal of money was to show his father that he could do it; since his father had made millions, he had to make a billion. But some sons just give up, and spend their father's money, which results in a failure to fully establish their own adult selves. They can never throw off the feeling of living off Daddy, which is disastrous to their development.

This can be overcome if sons take up a different line and obtain their sense of identity from accomplishments in spheres outside moneymaking. But it does not dispose of another kind of danger that befalls those brought up in a high degree of affluence. In such homes there is an inevitable tendency to deal with the problems, burdens and anxieties of family life with money. The rich who find it too trying to raise their own children, hire servants to do it for them. This happened to such an extent among the upper classes in England that Winston Churchill felt closer to his nanny than to his mother.

Where women have dealt with the anxieties of child-rearing in this way, a crisis finds them without the human resources to cope. It may not be unconnected with the generation gap, which seems to have become so apparent in the past few years, that the mothers and fathers of youngsters now in their teens and early twenties, were the first of the affluent parents of the postwar period. Part of the resentment of the young has been of the money values to which their parents supposedly subscribe, but the grudge may be a more personal one. It may be that, as a generation, they were weaned on bribery; that in the first heady experience of having money, many parents discovered the secret of "shutting them up" with presents, treats, goodies, and the bought services of others. If this was so to any degree, the resultant alienation of a whole generation of children from their parents would become more understandable. The common cry of: "But we always gave them the best," meaning the most expensive, would seem to bear out this theory that paying out money can easily be made to serve as a substitute for human responsibility.

The connections between marriage and money are long established. The bride-price and the dowry have been features of the marriage rites among Semites, Babylonians, Chinese, Japanese, Africans, Polynesians, Eskimos, aborigine Australians. These customary payments have their modern equivalent in the form of wedding presents, or wedding payments. Among primitive peoples the trading aspect of marriage is quite open. In Kenya, among the Mkamba of the Kitui district, wives were bought and sold as goods. "Many men invest all their capital in wives, considering them more profitable even than cattle, so a wealthy man may have 6 to 10, and chiefs 20 to 40. The average 'price' is 3 or 4 cows and a bull, but naturally a father will get as much as he can . . ."[6]

Thorstein Veblen believed that the whole institution of ownership probably began with the ownership of women. They were in the first place captives, the prize of victory in battle. Their possession, then, was a durable sign of a man's prowess and bravery. By extension, the products of the women's labor also came to have this meaning; a man who possessed many goods must have taken many female captives and therefore must be a great warrior. In this way, the concept of status through possession of goods and women first began.[7]

It is, therefore, by no means contradictory for a wife to be both status symbol and captive—it is the fact of her being his captive that confers status upon her possessor. And the more desirable the captive a man possesses, the greater his status. At one time desirability was measured in terms of the woman's industry, or perhaps her skills in serving her owner-husband and lord, but nowadays such capacities are not so highly rated (since we have machines to do a lot of women's work) and what we value most highly in women is their beauty and the sexual skills that are imagined to go with it. Thus, it is the possession of beautiful and voluptuous wife-slaves that most enhances the warrior-husband's prestige.

Even when it was no longer a matter of capturing her in battle (at any rate not in physical combat), the possession by a man of a desirable wife retained its ancient symbolic significance and raised his standing in the eyes of others. By this circuitous route it became customary for men to buy themselves desirable wives (politely called offering them security) for reasons of prestige. In this way women became a kind of currency (you could always cash in one of your forty wives for a few head of beef) and symbols of wealth. Today, too, since the most desirable women, unlike "cheap sluts," are known to be expensive, possessing one of them is a sign of success. From which it follows that anyone who wants to give the impression of being a warrior-chief has to have one. In this respect, the role of women has changed very little from the time when they were dragged off by the hair by a man with a club. They may now be dragged off in a Rolls Royce or Cadillac, or yacht, but they are still to some extent booty, and their purpose is to reflect glory upon their possessors.

Such a state of affairs naturally leads to a thriving trade in nubile prestige symbols, in the form of the marriage market.

It is a market in which those that are most bed-worthy *looking* go to the highest bidder; the fact that these often turn out to be unbedable, and sometimes even when bedded very poor lays, is neither here nor there. Their main purpose is to be living proofs of the fact that their husbands can afford them (and therefore by sophistic deduction are great men) ; and so these symbols of success are hung with jewels and furs, and sent off to the hairdressers so that they may reflect credit on their husbands.

It should be said that quite a lot of women wish they would be so lucky. And for a really desirable specimen the bride-price nowadays can be truly colossal.

When the former Jackie Kennedy married Aristotle Onassis, a marriage contract[8] was drawn up that gave her: 1) in the event of his leaving her, a sum of nearly £4 million for every year she has been married to him; 2) in the event of her leaving him, she would get around £7½ million. During her marriage all her taxes, rents, personal staff wages, telephone and electricity bills were to be paid direct by the Onassis secretariat in New York—about £4,000 a month. As pocket money she was to receive another £4,000 a month, and for beauty care, cosmetics, massage, chiropody, etc., a further £3,000 a month.

After all that, the contract specified that they were always to have separate bedrooms.

In the upper reaches of this kind of society, money, power, prestige and prestigious women are so readily interchangeable that marrying for money is the conventional thing to do; to rephrase Dr. Johnson, only a fool would think of marrying for anything else.

The principal drawback of this system is that prestige symbols are for show, not for use; though it is true that comparatively cheap sluts will probably do for the latter, it makes for complicated arrangements. The prestigious wife has her lovers; the warrior-chief has his women; and marriage is split up into its various component parts—the sexual, the social, the financial, the parental, with each one the province of a different person, the best in his or her line. What tends to happen when you can afford the best is that then only the best will do. And if no one person embodies all the desired qualities, you get a team.

Basically, this is exactly the system of the infant in the first months of life, when instead of apprehending whole people, with their good and bad aspects, their satisfying and frustrating characteristics, he splits them up into bits, dispensing with whatever does not serve his needs. Of what remains he constructs his perfect unreal world. He is said to be capable of relating only to part objects, and not to whole people. After the first three months of life, this begins to change. Under the pressure of the reality principle, development takes place; people who are both satisfying and unsatisfying are admitted into the schizoid paradise, and there comes the infinite sadness of the loss of perfection. What is desired is seen to be at variance with what is. Loss is experienced in all its bitterness. The satisfying nipple is not forever and ever. Frustration occurs, and is borne—to some extent. What Melanie Klein calls "the depressive position" is entered. Insofar as the very rich feel they can defy the reality principle, and receive perfect service from the world, they make their marriages on the basis of each doing what he or she is best at. They revert to "part-object relationships," not accepting whole people but only those bits of them that are of immediate use. Americans will speak of a girl as "a gorgeous piece of ass," and many men call their wives "Mother," and many wives see the man to whom they are married as "the provider," while other men are thought of as lovers. This is the system of reducing people to the role in which they are considered best, denying their other aspects. While everybody has a tendency to do this, "ordinary people" are usually obliged to put up with the fact that the great lover is a poor provider, or vice versa. But the rich do not have to put up with this, and often don't. They get the best—the best lay, the best mother, the best hostess, the best connection, the best-looking . . . Out of deference to the busyness and single-mindedness of people living in this kind of money society, those chosen to serve them instinctively reduce themselves to those parts that are wanted—they become the "gorgeous piece of ass" or "mother earth." But, of course, their other parts are not eliminated, just banished from sight, and like Banquo's ghost tend to return unbidden to spoil the celebrations.

Marrying for money is, in effect, the marriage of "part objects"—of the prestige symbol and the prize winner, for instance. Each is expecting to get something specific from the other, and tends to resent the unwanted stuff that goes with it. It's a bore if the gorgeous piece of ass gets suicidal depressions or if the mother earth has a taste for sailors. That wasn't the deal. On the other hand, such marriages can work out, insofar as the partners make limited demands upon each other. If people do not seek to relate on all levels, but only on one or two, then there is that much less chance of differences arising. Each goes his own way, except in those specific areas where they have agreed at specified times to go the same way. It may not be a union in the sight of God, or a total commitment, or even a love-match, but it is in keeping with the spirit of our time that the respective rights of such a marriage should be clearly spelled out, as in any other contract. When Jackie Kennedy married Onassis their marriage agreement embodied not only the details of the financial arrangements, but also specified, for instance, the amount of time she had to spend with him every year, and altogether 170 clauses of fine print covered all foreseeable contingencies.[9]

The contractual marriage, in black and white, may be exceptional, but in all money marriages there is, if not a written deal, a tacit one. One partner agrees to provide one thing, and the other partner reciprocates in kind.

It is clear that in a money society not to be paid for what you do, not to have your merit attested to by the amount you get, is felt to be humiliating. The Women's Lib writer Germaine Greer asserts that wives are unpaid workers in their husbands' houses, and it is a point of view that many women today share. Miss Greer says that women should bargain openly for better terms, and get some kind of business contract with safeguards and indemnities written into it.[10] This is in accordance with the Zeitgeist. If money is the universal measure of excellence in our society, then to be unpaid is an insult. Top women want top pay for what they do. They want the tribute of money, not to be treasured, cherished, looked after and given dress allowances. Jackie Onassis gets monetary proof of her worth as a wife, and so do a few others. The majority don't, and probably regard it as "prostitution" to equate marital worth with money. But such moralistic concepts are becoming outdated, as doing things for money loses the pejorative connotation it once had. If it means being valued in terms of cows, or yachts, this is not nearly so bad as being undervalued. The ghastliness of the market is not of being sold, but of being sold cheap. "There is nothing so exciting," says Xaviera Hollander, "as being the subject of an auction, having people bidding for you, and raising the bidding." And nowadays many perfectly respectable women in their hearts would agree.

Perhaps because it is so much easier for men to obtain a sense of their value in other spheres, it is not usually in the marriage market that they seek to have a price put on them, although, of course, fortune hunters do exist, and finding a rich wife has long been regarded a way out of one's financial difficulties. But, on the whole, men are not competitive in this area: a rich woman is enough; she doesn't have to be richer than the other fellow's in order to make me feel worth more than him. Perhaps this is an acknowledgment of the fact that the market for men marriage partners is not yet sufficiently established to be a really accurate indicator of individual worth.

Whereas there is definite status for a woman in marrying a rich man (just as there is for him in having an expensive wife), it is still in the area of the raffish to marry a woman for her money, and anyone who does this will usually deny it (unlike Zsa Zsa Gabor, who says cheerfully that she married Conrad Hilton for his money). While many poor young girls marry old rich men, what the fortune hunter is traditionally looking for is the beautiful young heiress. It says something about money that women can marry it regardless, whereas men usually need the excuse that it is also young and beautiful, or at least young. The implication is that money has the meaning of maleness and that to put oneself at its disposal is to make oneself subservient in a feminine way. Significantly, in homosexual relationships, there is no kind of stigma about a young man being kept by an older man with money. This is commonplace, and thought of as a natural arrangement, and one must assume that it is because the young man, far from feeling uneasy about submitting to the maleness of money, actually relishes it. But in marrying an older woman with money, the young man probably feels to some extent emasculated, and unless he has a strong passive homosexual streak he will not find this agreeable.

With the young heiress it is different, because her money is her dowry, a prize that goes to the winning suitor. Coming from the older woman the money is not so much a prize as a reward. There is an essential difference between the two—a prize reflects greater distinction upon the person who wins it than on the person who bestows it, whereas a reward is like a tip, it reflects credit on the giver, and the receiver is in a subservient position. A prize is what the winner's merit entitles him to, whereas a reward is what the giver's generosity makes him give. The older woman *rewards* her young husband with money, and rewards are always conditional on services; whereas a prize is something one walks off with.

There is bound to be a large element of parasitism when a man marries a rich older woman and lives off her. The underlying fantasy is of getting inside the source of wealth, and controlling it from within. The money*maker* seeks to get hold of wealth, the parasite to get inside it. Basically, he wants to get back inside Mummy and live in her luxury pad as a kept man, and to run her whole show from his privileged inside position. Such a man can be ingratiating, insinuating, inveigling, and often charming; that is, he has the capacity of putting a spell on the person he proposes to invade. The typical parasitic desire to *run* the person being exploited finds expression in a bossy attitude towards the meal ticket. Under the pretext of looking after her, and having her best interests at heart, the parasitic husband says, "Now, you shouldn't do that," and "You know that isn't good for you," and "Leave those questions to me because you know you've got no head for money," and "If I weren't here to look after your interests you'd be cheated left and right, you're so trusting."

The parasite's nemesis is claustrophobia. He is caught by the balls. He fears and is in the grip of the *vagina dentata*—the toothed cunt. Having taken over the source of wealth from inside, he can't get out. He is trapped. He smothers in luxury.

In its external manifestations, the feeling that such a man has is of being hemmed in, unable to move. He has got to get out. But because the woman is his meal ticket he is tied to her, and she in satisfaction of her complementary needs is not beyond emphasizing this point.

Living in becomes less and less congenial; the atmosphere deteriorates; there is simmering violence, because in a trapped situation a man feels that he can only get out by violent means. It can go as far as the murder of the host by the parasite. In some instances, the woman deviously invites this. She takes in an avenging angel to devour her from within, by way of satisfying her masochistic needs. Short of homicide, such a relationship sooner or later develops to the point where the man breaks out—usually running off with her money or jewels. The wife will tend to be mysteriously philosophical about this, and one might suspect that on some level she knew it was part of the scenario.

When a man has married an heiress there is another pattern. Parasitism requires that the chosen host be something of a victim figure, someone with a need that can be exploited. The woman with a passion for a much younger man is in this position. But the young heiress is not. It is true she may be pursued and courted and married for her money, but she is not exploitable in the same way as the older woman; she is not so desperate for love, and therefore it is not the parasite who will be drawn to her, but the fortune hunter. Although in practice he may also end up being kept by her, his is a different case. Unlike the parasite who worms his way in and then controls by virtue of his inside position, the fortune hunter regards the heiress as his prize. Feeling himself lucky and a winner, he does not make her his base (as the parasite does), but will go out to conquer other worlds, be they financial or female.

Being a prizewinner and a romantic, he will rely on his lucky star rather than on rigidly controlling his source of wealth—such men tend to be gamblers, adventurers. Having once won, he is forever looking for another lucky win; and because he believes in his special destiny he is impervious to the lessons of reality. Sometimes the fortune hunter does get lucky twice—it may be a second heiress, when the first has had just about enough; or it may be that one of his many gambles comes off. He has in his favor an innate confidence (that comes from his faith in the inexhaustible breast that will support him forever in the style to which he fully expects to become accustomed), and moving confidently in the milieu of money, once he has married his heiress, the chances of golden opportunities coming his way are certainly better than average. He is seen at his most successful when the romantic and the hustler in him get together.

One such man, having risen from humble beginnings and carried off one of the world's most beautiful heiresses, spent years trying to establish himself in his chosen line. The money helped, of course, but still he did not get very far. Being a gambler, he continued to try his luck. Meanwhile he lived on the millionaire level with the élan of one who believes it is the only level to live on. In time his marriage ended. But our fortune hunter was lucky. Most of his projects had not turned out, but in the course of wheeling and dealing he had acquired certain rights and interests, not particularly valuable at the time, which later events turned into a gold mine. He had to go through lengthy legal proceedings to establish his rights, but he fought and fought and in the end won, and it made him a millionaire.

This is the fortune hunter revealing his most striking trait —his unwillingness to settle for less. It arises out of a firm conviction that he is entitled to the utmost. It may take the form of a secret belief that he is really the bastard son of a duke or a prince—he *feels* royal or aristocratic and that he was meant to live on a certain scale. However delusionary, such inner conviction often conveys itself to others. One of nature's aristocrats, they say, or that he has glamor, star quality, charisma, style . . . In other cases, the notion of being meant for better things is related to an overriding sense of his own lovability. Such a person is in love with himself, and cannot imagine that anybody else might not be similarly infatuated. He believes that ultimately people will give him what he wants, because, after all, *he* cannot refuse himself anything.

There is no such thing as a need that somebody somewhere does not have a need to satisfy, and so the fortune hunter gets his heiress, and she the sense of being a great prize, a king's daughter. There is a common belief that heiresses are neurotically sensitive about men only being after their money; but they can also use the money as a come-on, and enjoy the feeling of being fought over and competed for. To be the object of somebody else's ambitions, even if they are monetary, can be exhilarating, and few heiresses have such a low opinion of money that their suitor's desire for it offends them. They identify with their money, and therefore experience their suitor's inordinate avidity for it as a bodily—if perverse—desire for them. That heiresses often are attracted to fortune hunters is borne out by the fact that they frequently run off with them; it is the parents, who do not experience the thrill of being prized and sought after, who tend to look unfavorably on having their daughters carried off in this manner. This is a view the heiress may come to share after marriage; once won, she cannot go on feeling herself to be a precious prize, especially since after the event the fortune hunter takes the view that he only got what he was entitled to. This later attitude is considerably less flattering than the one which treats her as someone uniquely unattainable.

The curious denouement to such marriages is that once the money is *his,* the fortune hunter and the heiress find that their financial polarity having been resolved, a good deal of the excitement has gone too.

There is also a form of marrying for money that consists of only marrying somebody as rich as oneself. This is the social norm among the rich. From the money point of view, there is little to be said about such marriages, for their purpose, in part, is that money shall not be a factor. Where both partners are equally used to having money, have had it on the same scale, and are not financially dependent on each other, there will be little chance for them to act out emotional problems in financial disguise. Emotion needs disparities to spark; the equally wealthy tend to have their money problems with their children, their lovers or their mistresses, where such disparities do exist.

Even if the vast majority of people do not marry for money, there are many who *stay* married for money. After years of marriage they have arrived at a deep financial intimacy; they have accommodated each other's money quirks; they have worked out what their priorities are, in what areas they will be extravagant or mean. They are buying a house, paying for children's education, supporting a mother or mother-in-law, buying goods on credit. The husband is probably paying large insurance premiums on his life, written in his wife's name. Their private health insurance schemes cover them as a family unit. Possibly they have joint bank accounts. The marital home belongs to both. They have entered into a union of moneys, and in this respect are virtually inseparable.

Where a couple has just enough money for their life together, a separation, involving the setting up of two establishments in place of one, entails such *financial* upheaval that many unhappily married people put up with their situation rather than face the alternative. The choice before them is usually between continuing as they are, or separating and both accepting a drastic reduction in their standard of living. In these circumstances, unless there is a more compelling factor, such as one or other partner falling in love with somebody else, the usual decision is to make do. There may be no conscious awareness that any such decision has been taken. It is simply accepted that they can't afford to part. They may even arrive at the sort of mutual accommodation that produces reasonable contentment.

Such marriages are shaken, and often broken up, by sudden money. As soon as it becomes *possible* to set up separate households, living together in a way that is less than ideal seems intolerable. The author John Pearson says that it was partly as a result of making around quarter of a million dollars for his biography of Ian Fleming that his marriage broke up. "There is nothing that keeps two people together so much as having to," he says.[11]

Once the financial constraints have gone, people become very aware of *"their happiness."* As with their health, they subject it to constant checkups. Am I really happy? they ask themselves, the way the hypochondriac asks "Am I really well?" And, of course, the inevitable discovery is that one is not *really* happy, which is hardly surprising if happiness is by definition an episodic phenomenon, arising out of the sudden satisfaction of some long dammed-up instinctual need (Freud).[12]

The rich are in a position to pursue such episodic phenomena by *looking for happiness,* as if this were an attainable permanent condition. Those without wealth take the view that their finances don't allow such idle luxury. In both cases, money pressure has determined the course of action. The rich, feeling that their money opens up for them vistas of attainable happiness, feel bound to go in pursuit of it again and again; the moneyless decide that as happiness is something they can't afford to pursue, they must put up with things as they are. What they put up with for lack of money can be as unreasonable as what the rich go after in vain.

It can be seen that the role of money is not limited to implementing existing desires, but is also to produce desires. They arise from the availability of the means of satisfying them. Money, by creating other possibilities, puts all existing structures and arrangements in question. Paul Getty, five times married, asked whether it was possible to be rich and happily married, conceded that there was difficulty in combining the two.

The other side of this is that if money is what makes things possible, then the lack of it can be used as an excuse for non-action and acceptance of the status quo.

The way in which money affects the most basic behavior patterns and even modifies the deepest instincts can be seen in the case of a mother's relationship to her child. Seeing simple Italian women with their babies, one might take the view that nothing is so strong as the maternal instinct, that a mother's closeness to her child is one of the inviolable laws of nature. But, in fact, with the possession of money, this instinct undergoes drastic modifications and even suppression.

Britt Ekland, ex-wife of Peter Sellers, says, "I maintain my apartment in Mayfair all the year round, and I have a permanent nanny for Victoria [her nine-year-old daughter by Peter Sellers] which means I can come and go as I please. The one thing a failed marriage has taught me is the value of independence."[13]

The rich can pay somebody else to assume responsibilities that the poor must assume of necessity.

Money does alter the most basic life urges. The more money that is available to her, the less does a woman feel the need to feed and look after her own children. This is an astonishing modification of instinct; it is unlikely that the preponderance of nannies among the English upper classes was due to the fact that the women of those classes were all constitutionally less maternal than, say, the mothers of southern Italy who went through life clutching babies to their bosoms. The explanation must be that when money opens up possibilities of other ways of doing things, even the most fundamental instincts undergo curtailment and change. Anna Karenina, abandoning husband *and child* to run off with her soldier lover, is indulging a romantic passion born of wealth, or at any rate rendered possible by it. Women who have to personally look after their children do not usually leave them to run off with their lovers. Their lovers, like themselves, have to stay put, since freedom of movement, too, is a prerogative of wealth. This was illustrated in the film *Elvira Madigan,* in which the runaway lovers literally starve, and in the end kill themselves because they do not have the means to keep going together. It is one of the rare love stories to acknowledge the omnipresent money factor, and the way it affects even the deepest relationships. For every nobleman who runs off with a tightrope walker and starves, there are a thousand who think better of it and stay with their wives. Love affairs also need to be financed.

In all marriages there is a money relationship between husband and wife, which can be good or bad, neurotically determined or basically sound; but, on the whole, it is not discussed. Sexual and emotional incompatibilities receive widespread attention and remedial services; but money quarrels tend to be hushed up. There is felt to be something curiously shameful about them. At their most virulent, and irreconcilable, they are due to the opposition of two basic character traits—parsimony and extravagance. There are many permutations of this fundamental antagonism of instincts, but the nature of the conflict is best seen in the example of The Mean Husband and The Spendthrift Wife.

The husband finds it profoundly irritating that his wife boils an entire kettle of water to make two cups of tea. It drives him mad. Whenever he can, he pours out the surplus water. This drives her mad. They are locked into their respective positions: she goes on overfilling the kettle as a matter of principle and he, as a matter of principle, goes on emptying it. No accommodation is possible. To him, she is thoughtlessly wasteful, frittering away the money he has worked so hard to make. To her, he is disgustingly mean, saving on the cost of boiling a bit of water. You don't have to pay the gas bills, he throws back.

It isn't just the water in the kettle. It is everything, as they are quick to point out to each other, with venomous relish. He has the horrible habit of putting unused mustard from his plate back in the pot. In response to her taunts, he lectures her, "It's not the mustard you use, but the mustard you leave on the plate that makes Mr. Colman rich." He saves pieces of string, coiling them and putting them away in drawers. String costs money, he points out. When he gets a parcel, he folds up the wrapping paper to be reused when needed. The psychoanalyst Karl Abraham had a patient who bitterly resented spending money on things like journeys, concerts, exhibitions, which gave him nothing permanent in return. He avoided going to the opera for this reason, but he bought the scores of the operas he had not heard, because in this way he got something lasting.

The wife of such a man, if she has the opposing character trait, will find this sort of behavior an incitement to extravagant spending. For his compulsive saving, which he wishes also to impose on her as part of *his* neurotic need, is also a repression of hers to spend, spend, spend. Each considers the other's attitude to money appalling and *shameful*.

In one contemporary marriage,[14] the husband, who admitted to being stingy, would take his wife on vacation to the South of France, sit on the beach, and order one Coca-Cola for the two of them. The opposing character traits became clearly defined. Before their marriage, the woman, who was highly paid, followed her own inclinations in money matters. Other people she knew drove Mercedes cars, and so she bought herself a Mercedes for $6,875, which a dealer brought around to her one lunchtime, without haggling over the price—just making out the check there and then. This was her way of doing things. She let the gardener use her old car, a Triumph. Her housekeeper did all the shopping for her and was given whatever money she said she needed. She trusted people implicitly, and was sure she was never cheated.

When she married the "one Coca-Cola man" the conflict between their money attitudes became apparent. He could see no point in their having two cars, and letting the gardener use one. (He did not drive himself.) And the Mercedes was costing huge sums in maintenance and repair bills, and using twice as much gasoline as the smaller car. So he got her to sell the Mercedes and keep the other. The housekeeper was simply being given money whenever she asked for it. She was totally trustworthy, but nonetheless the husband found such a situation unacceptable. In future, she would only buy specific items that she had been instructed to purchase by one or the other of them, and would have to produce bills. In the matter of the household expenses, since both husband and wife were high earners, he worked out a system whereby each had a separate bank account, and each put $62.50 a week into the household kitty, out of which the routine expenses would be met.

The system broke down in the first week. The wife said, "There is nothing in the kitty—the girl didn't have enough

money to do the shopping. That's where I think you are
mean, in leaving us without money." He said, "If there was
nothing in the kitty it's because you've spent it all." To the
wife this was irrelevant. If it had been spent, it had been
spent. But he wanted to know why so much had been spent,
and what on.

Ultimately, he agreed that his wife was someone who
trusted others in money matters, never checked, and was
hardly ever cheated; whereas he did not trust people, always
checked and double-checked, and was cheated. There was
the element of self-fulfilling prophecy in their respective patterns. People were trustworthy with her *because* she trusted
them. They were untrustworthy with him *because* he did not
trust them. Hence she was confirmed in her money behavior,
and he in his.

In another contemporary marriage, the husband, an industrialist and millionaire, took the view that his wife's expenditure on clothes was excessive. It was not that they couldn't
afford it—she was herself an heiress and her father was giving
vast sums of money to charities—but the husband considered
her expenditure unnecessary and therefore irresponsible, and
it offended him. Her retort was why couldn't she have her
own allowance so that she would not have to ask him for
money? "You won't have to ask me what I've spent it on." He
replied, "I will never not ask you—it is not in my nature."
He explained his position: "I have taken the view that extravagance is a bad thing, and should be nipped in the bud.
In my wife's case spending in that sort of way was largely a
compensating thing. In her youth she was overshadowed by
an older sister, and my wife's education was neglected. As a
result, now that her children are grown up, she finds herself
asking: 'What am I doing?' She feels that if she had her own
allowance she could be independent. It's that odd flash of

wanting to break out—first she wanted to be independent of her father's allowance, and now she wishes to be independent of me."[15]

The industrialist conceded that his wife had not spent one third of the amount on clothes that other women in a much lower income bracket spend, but he felt the need to control her spending to be a moral imperative. "I think that women are more open to decadent influences than men," he said. "If my wife were allowed to buy expensive clothes, or whatever, it would affect our daughter. I do know what women spend on their clothes, and it is absolutely appalling, unbelievable. There are women with an insatiable need for money. It is a form of weakness. It has to be stopped because a woman's standards of morality are more critical, since men behave in a way to seek the approval of women, and so if women become decadent the whole of moral standards go."

This is an eminent man, a leader of industry, who has earned his high position and the esteem of government for his inflexible dedication to efficiency and the elimination of extravagance. Companies now under his control saved much money by his efficiency methods. To him waste was wicked, an activity of the Devil, and to be stopped for a combination of practical and moral reasons. He was the man who in the process of cutting down extravagance among the 200,000 people in his employ queried why one company director received two copies of *The Financial Times;* then, coming to think about it, decided that there was no reason why even one copy should be paid for by the company.

This type of man, in marriage, finds himself opposing on principle the extravagances of his household. "These men," writes Karl Abraham, "delight in keeping their wives permanently dependent on them financially. Assigning money in portions which they themselves determine is a source of pleasure to them."[16] This sort of attitude is not affected by the possession of vast wealth. When members of John D. Rockefeller's family asked him to pay for something that he considered extravagant, he'd reply, "What do you think we are—Vanderbilts?"

In this kind of situation the wife will find herself impelled to extract what her husband finds is so painful to give. His parsimoniousness inflames the spendthrift in her. The climax of their irresolvable struggle is that she goes on a spending spree. We have already seen that this can have a specifically sexual meaning for her in the sense of being an acting out of prostitution fantasies. But there is another strand of meaning that derives from the awareness of *whose* money she is spending in this wild way. Insofar as it is her husband's money, she is taking his means away from him in the act of throwing his money away, and in this she expresses her hostility towards him and makes a sadistic, *wasting* attack upon his sexual capacities. It is a way of ruining him, and many women doing this are acting out a primitive desire to castrate.

Such unconscious hostility is always present to some degree; the parsimonious man senses it, magnifies it, and makes it the justification of his controlling attitude. "If I didn't control my wife's spending, she'd ruin me," he says lightly (or not so lightly) ; he has settled into the husband's role, which by ancient tradition is that of controlling his wife's spending, and she consequently must find ingenious ways of getting the money out of him. In this way, respective positions become perpetuated in an eternal charade.

It happens on the lowest money levels too. One woman used to be given port money by her husband. When they went to the pub they each had a fixed sum to spend. She was an attractive woman, and men she knew would often buy her drinks. When this happened, the husband would afterwards demand the return of the port money she had saved. She insisted that *she* had been bought the drinks, and so she was entitled to keep her port money. He furiously maintained she was not. So bitter and constant were these quarrels that their daughter remembered them vividly thirty years later.

Whether it is the industrialist limiting his wife's expenditure on clothes or a working man not seeing why he shouldn't benefit from his wife's being bought drinks by other men, the conflict arises because husband and wife are different money types.

The sphincter action is the first bodily function over which the infant learns conscious control. Since it carries with it the injunctions of parental authority, control, when it is achieved, embodies not only a physical but also a moral satisfaction. The later equivalent of this can be seen in the way such controlling characters take moral pride in their handling of waste, and regard their controlling of their wives' spending as a duty.

Such characteristics are well known to drive wives mad. When she says, "But it's only boiling a bit of extra water," he says, "Assuming that the extra amount of water means an extra two minutes of heating time, and assuming that one gas ring burning for X minutes uses one therm of heat, and assuming that you put the kettle on an average of eight and a half times a day, do you realize that in one year you waste X dollars, which amount, if invested at six and a half percent, would over the period of a lifetime that you are boiling water in kettles amount to . . ." By this time she has probably thrown the kettle at him, or run out of the house to really waste his money.

But, of course, such men have their uses, even if these are not most conspicuous in the home. Freud found that they showed reliability, dependability. They could be trusted not to neglect their duties, or to leave things half done. In business they proved themselves very persevering, to the point of being able to overcome obstacles that would have had others beaten, and they showed themselves to be highly ingenious in such matters as putting waste products to some use, in the form of sewage farms, or in recycling processes. The collecting instinct has obvious beneficial aspects in librarians, archivists, statisticians, curators of museums. Ernest Jones pointed out the way in which their love of possessions could extend to showing the most exquisite tenderness to children. He refers to the fact that a miser like Shylock had also a passionate fondness for his daughter. There was a clear equivalence in the plot between Jessica and the ducats, both of which he is in the end deprived of.[17]

With the exception of a passionate fondness for children, most of these qualities are sources of irritation in family life. They produce, at worst, the tyrannical father, intolerant of any signs of independence on the part of any members of his family, over whom he rules by virtue of paying the bills. Even his fondness for children tends to become overprotectiveness or overpossessiveness. Insofar as his children are his most valuable possessions, his treasures, he can no more let them go than he can let his money go. The outcome is bitter strife and the rebellion of the young, and perhaps, earlier, of the wife. Karenin was such a man, and there is no doubt that it is partly his behavior that drives Anna to break out and run off with Vronsky.

There are of course many permutations of this extreme pattern. There are weak men who allow their wives to waste their "means" and do not put a stop to it, and it must be presumed that *they* are "losers" conspiring in their own downfall. There are women who because of their spendthrift natures have chosen to marry very controlling men, in the unconscious wish that they will be controlled. It must not be assumed that every controlled woman is controlled against her wishes, but it can be assumed that in every such situation somebody's freedom has been taken away, whether by mutual consent or by imposition.

There is also the reverse situation, which is The Squanderer Husband and The Avaricious Wife. In this instance it is the wife who goes around turning off the electric lights, emptying the kettle, making pies out of leftovers, all of which, up to a point, is a part of normal household management, but can clearly be carried too far. In this sort of family structure the husband is usually a feckless individual, a gambler perhaps, usually of the "loser" type. He pawns his wife's jewelry. He doesn't pay bills, and so the telephone and electricity are cut off. He gets behind in his credit payments, and so the family car is repossessed. The wife scrapes and saves and hides the money under the floorboards.

On the higher money levels, he is probably the sort of man who has made his way in the world, and as part of this wants to indulge in display, wants to exhibit a degree of largesse appropriate to the position that he has attained, or hopes to attain. He goes to a charity auction and bids three times the price of an air ticket to Rome, and then redonates it to the charity. It makes him feel big and powerful and shows that he has arrived. To his wife, if he is going to buy an air ticket for charity, he might at least keep the ticket. Does he have to indulge in ego games with other fools to bid the price of a $200 ticket up to $625—*and then give it back?* What for? To show off. And she knows that business is not so good. He told her so himself. That, he explains, is exactly why it is necessary to make a bit of a splash. To her this is all wicked nonsense, just as it is to run an expensive car, live in the best part of town, employ a maid to wait at table. Is it necessary? She is happy to serve the food. What is the point of having a powerful car that in city traffic can never go much over twenty miles an hour? She sits at home washing and pressing his shirts, mending his trousers. Send them to the laundry, he says; throw them away, he says. We can afford it. She can't bring herself to do it. He tells her she should have a fur coat, she owes it to her position to have one—she owes it to him. She doesn't want a fur coat. The idea of spending all that money offends her. She would not feel happy wearing it. Jewelry— she does not need jewelry. It would just make her nervous. She would be frightened all the time that it was going to be stolen. Secretly, she saves from the housekeeping money, putting it away, hiding it, investing it in government bonds— for at heart she is convinced that the fall will come, and so is accumulating her nest egg.

This type of woman is usually someone who has been left behind by her husband's progress and success, and cannot really believe in it. Since she has not achieved it herself, has not grown with him, the money he makes does not seem real to her. It is all winnings, and winnings can stop tomorrow. At the same time, she fears the envy that her new-found affluence might arouse, and since she does not have the additional self-confidence that comes of moneymaking, she has no extra resources for dealing with other people's resentment. Her sole tactic, then, is appeasement; by being very careful with her money, she denies that she has that much of it, and also limits her husband's success—either by implying that it is less great than he thinks, or by suggesting that she doesn't believe it is going to last. Both are ways of undermining him and expressing her hostility towards him. She castrates him with snide innuendos that the way he is going he will soon exhaust his means, he will not be able to last.

He feels her attempts to belittle his achievements by refusing to spend his money are expressions of her inability to keep up with him—she can't stand the pace. He naturally turns to somebody who can, and will spend his money as vaingloriously as him, and thereby confirm him in his picture of himself as a big spender and a big shot. When he comes home, his wife gives him the sort of look that says, One day you'll come unstuck, and then picks up the loose change he sprinkles about. Her melancholic pessimism is so deflating to his manic optimism that he comes home less and less, and probably in the end leaves her.

Of course, if the fall does come, as it often does in such cases, the wife comes into her own. It is her caution and carefulness that have saved the day. When he thought they were ruined, she reveals, no, no, secretly, all this time, she has been saving here and there; she has put her money into investments, into houses, into gold bars, or Swiss francs, and, with a few economies, by selling this and selling that, and rearranging the other, they will manage. This is the triumph of the penurious wife, and in a way her fantasy, so that she partly conspires to bring about the downfall and ruin of her husband.

15

Money and Society

By and large, we live in money groups, the cohesiveness of which depends on everybody in them remaining roughly on the same financial level. The young chairman of a publishing company says, "I don't sit down and work out what I can afford. I presume that I can afford what other people in my position have got." This works as long as nobody in the group drastically increases or diminishes his means; if that happens, strains arise.

One man who made a great deal of money over a short period of time gives this account of his difficulties. He is a scientist and author, and his friends are also scientists and authors. In the past they were all more or less equally hard up; now he is rich, having made about a million dollars from a remarkable best seller. When he now invites his old friends to dinner, he is faced with the following excruciating problem. "In the old days," he says, "we all used to drink plonk. Now if they come to dinner and I serve them plonk, they will consider me a cheapskate. On the other hand, if I serve them the kind of wines I now drink, when I go to them they will feel uncomfortable about giving me the plonk, since I evidently now drink the better stuff."

He has found, too, that many of his friends and colleagues have been affected by the fact that he has made so much money; they are envious. He believes that some of the unfavorable reviews he received for his latest book are due to this. Of course, he says, he has kept his close friends, but some of the others seem to resent that he has made so much money, since they feel they could just as well have written the best seller that he wrote. "Is it really true," people say to him at parties, "that you are very rich now?" and "What's it like to have all that money?" and "Of course, *you* don't have to think about economizing nowadays, do you?" He finds this boring, and disturbing, since he wishes to be known for his ideas, not his money. So now he tells everybody evasively, "Money isn't important to me." He admits that this isn't true, but it's the only way he can get people to shut up about it.[1]

This is the fairly typical experience of anyone who has made a great deal of money suddenly. Either friends try to ignore the fact, as if it hasn't happened, or they treat it with fake flippancy—"Now that you're rolling in the stuff, how about buying us all another drink?" Whatever attitude is taken, the group finds it difficult to behave naturally. It feels the awkwardness of the financial disparity between itself and the newly rich member. "It isn't," says one man who moved on, "that one doesn't have time for old friends any more. It is that *they* find it awkward to be with you. So it isn't that you drop them, it's that they can't keep up with you. They can't really accept the new circumstances."

The usual outcome of these tensions is that the man who has made a lot of money moves into a new group, where others are at the same money level as he, serve the same wines, go to the same restaurants, take the same sort of vacations—

with whom he does not have to feel apologetic about his new affluence. Of course, some of the old group will hang on to him, hoping they may be able to make the upward move on his shirttails. Others will maintain their friendship by assuming a kind of moral superiority based on not having made money, with the implication that by doing so he has sold out, has lowered himself, or destroyed his true talents. The fact that this is sometimes the case does not prevent such an attitude on the part of friends being the sanctimony of the untempted.

People getting to the top move into better neighborhoods not merely to live in a better house on a nicer street, but in order to escape from the anxieties that great disparities in money levels cause. Of course, there are some who, because of their particular psychological make-up, *want* to be a big fish in a small pond—and there are even some big fish who will go to great lengths to find themselves the smallest possible pond, but these are the exceptions.

In the course of this century, people have become increasingly uncomfortable about lording it over others in too direct a way. When Tolstoy experienced the torment of great wealth and became determined to give it all away, even if it meant impoverishing his wife, most people in his society thought this a strange way of behaving. But that was at a time when it was still possible to own serfs without feeling it to be the offense against humanity that it was to Tolstoy. *He* felt the need to reduce himself to their level, even if only in a token way, a compulsion that had some comical results. For instance, to show that he was no better than the humblest cobbler on his estate, Tolstoy decided that he would in the future mend his own shoes, and to this end the cobbler of the village was commanded to attend upon the Count, daily, to instruct him in cobbling.

The picture of the poor cobbler struggling with his last

and tools up to the great house to teach the master how to mend shoes does not inspire much faith in the rituals of humility through which the rich have sometimes sought to expiate their sense of guilt. But it does point to the anxieties that are aroused by having more than somebody else in one's immediate environment. The tension, of course, is also felt by those who have less, and this is a factor in the high crime rate of dense urban concentrations, i.e., areas where the haves and have-nots are in close proximity. The so-called flight from the cities is a kind of regrouping process, with the well-off seeking to isolate themselves from the less well-off and the poor.

The whole pressure is for people to live at their own money levels, in groups that will not make them feel either too guilty or too envious. It accounts for the way poor, middle-class or rich neighborhoods spring up and maintain their homogeneity. J. K. Galbraith has said it is not possible to accept the explanation that areas of poverty are produced solely by local conditions. He says, "Connecticut is very barren and stony and incomes are very high. Similarly Wyoming, West Virginia, is well watered with rich mines and forests and the people are very poor. The South is much favored in soil and climate and similarly poor and the very richest parts of the South, such as the Mississippi-Yazoo Delta, have long had a well-earned reputation for the greatest deprivation."[2] Social and economic factors—such as a woman's remaining as the head and breadwinner of a broken family—account for a good deal of poverty; but Galbraith recognizes that another factor in producing such islands of the deprived is "a shared sense of helplessness and rejection."

How does it come about that a particular geographical area not poor in soil or resources should happen to have in it a group of people characterized by a mental disposition towards poverty? It must be that anyone who didn't have such a disposition left long ago. In this way people choose the social setting that will validate their state of mind. For various reasons that we have already seen, some people need to be "winners" and others "losers," and the social aspect of this is that they will tend to seek out others with a similar make-up, and together with them will create a self-contained world in which what they need to believe will be confirmed by the others.

People whose inadequacies prevent them from getting on will get themselves into places where everybody else is as trapped as they are, and will thus corroborate the *impossibility* of getting ahead—in the existing system, or in this day and age, or if you are a woman, or if you are a black, or if you were born on the wrong side of town . . . That such factors may be truly limiting makes them all the more effective as rationalizations for those who are in the first place limited by their basic natures. Equally, those with the "winner" mentality will get into groups where others—be they blacks, women or outsiders—are winning, lucky, making it, pulling it off, and will thus be confirmed in *their* faith.

The basic function of every such money group is to create for its members a condition of not being indebted. Their equality of means ensures that vis-à-vis each other they can be quits. That there is a great desire for such a state is indicated by middle-class anxieties about *owing* invitations, and having to return dinners and buying the next round of drinks. Behind these social conventions lies the deep unease at being indebted to somebody else. Some people cannot ask a favor because they may be asked to return it some day, and this would hang over them. A good deal of present-giving serves the purpose of discharging indebtedness. A woman who had been sick had her shopping done by a neighbor. When she was well again, she felt a compelling obligation to "repay" the neighbor's kindness with some sort of gift. The neighbor genuinely didn't want anything, and was faintly embarrassed by the insistence that she *must* accept something; but it was evident that the woman who had received the good turn would not be easy in her heart until she had discharged her debt. There are people who are all the time giving small gifts because of their anxiety at being indebted to somebody.

Underlying this intolerance of indebtedness is an incapacity for gratitude. Gratitude involves recognition of having been given something for which one can never adequately repay the giver. You cannot give back life to those who gave you life, nor knowledge to those who gave you knowledge; nor is the inheritance of the world returnable. The appropriate emotion in these circumstances is gratitude, but it is an emotion we are often quite incapable of feeling because it involves the imagined humiliation of feeling small and inadequate in relation to somebody else's bigness and richness. The impulse is to be quits, to return the gift, and thus prove oneself equally big and potent. The role of money here is that it enables us to turn an undischargeable emotional indebtedness into something that can be repaid in cash, thereby alleviating that uncomfortable sense of owing. But to owe is the real condition of everybody's life; it is the *folie de grandeur* of the self-made man that he has done it all himself. This conceit is a way of denying his original debt, which in the end he must pay with his life.

One way to alleviate such a disturbing sense of fundamental indebtedness is to be a giver—a giver of parties, of money, of charity, of time, of energy. Such people give, give, give. They drug themselves with giving so as not to be too conscious of what they have been given and must eventually give up. This kind of character make-up manifests itself in such common social anomalies as the great host being a poor guest (shining at his own parties, where he is said to be in his element, but dull and critical at other people's) ; or the gen-

erous giver who cannot be given anything by others. One
such man confided that he did not like getting gifts because
"I have everything I need, and therefore I can only be given
something I don't want."

It is characteristic of the ingrate that he must always mini-
mize what he is given by others, so as to spare himself the
need to feel gratitude. He does this by always giving a bigger
party or a bigger present in return. German people, when
they insist on being allowed to return some hospitality they
have received, say, *"Du musst mir erlauben mich zu revan-
chieren"*—You must allow me to have my revenge. It is possible to perceive the thinly veiled violence in the way people
insist on paying for their round of drinks, or aggressively
demand their turn to fork out—this time the treat is on them,
they won't hear of the other person's paying, they absolutely
refuse. Put back your wallet, they say, or I'll take it as an
insult. In few other social circumstances do people on friendly
terms with each other allow themselves such open expressions
of their aggressiveness as in the matter of insisting on paying.
The meaning of such behavior is confirmed by the feelings of
awkwardness, and of having somehow been put down or out-
done, that the loser—in this context, the person who has not
been allowed to pay—usually feels. So charged is this relationship between the person who pays and the person who is
treated that by common consent a kind of balancing out is
necessary if friendships are to continue on an equal basis.

Self-respect is closely bound up with paying one's way. This
can produce some odd paradoxes. The criminal D——, who
will take money for anything—for beating up somebody, for
having sex with an elderly woman, for information—nonetheless scrupulously insisted on paying for every other round of
drinks while talking to me in a hotel bar. He might be a thug,
but he was no sponger.

The tensions that the question of "Who pays?" produces

are dealt with by a variety of social conventions. Between men and women, the rule is—still—that the man pays. It is true that the woman nowadays can be allowed to pay in certain circumstances; but there is unease if the woman repeatedly pays, whereas this is not the case where the man repeatedly pays. On the deepest emotional levels it is felt to be natural for the man to pay and for the woman to receive, and this must have to do with the basic physiological relationship of the sexes. In the case of an older and a younger man, it is the older man who pays. What makes this socially acceptable is the father-son model, which bestows naturalness on such a custom. The unspoken assumption is that the older man has already made his way, while the younger man is still making his, and that the father traditionally helps the son. Wherever a paternal or avuncular role can be legitimately adopted by one person towards another, there is no great difficulty about the one being the benefactor and the other the protégé, though such relationships are liable to have homosexual undertones. It depends on the genuineness of the paternalism on the one hand, and of the filial acceptance of it on the other, whether or not such relationships can be maintained without strain.

Outside these special categories, for which some justification exists in natural law, it is difficult for one person to be permanently in the position of giving and the other permanently in the position of receiving. We deal with this difficulty by living in the sort of money groups where we are able to adhere to the convention of returning such hospitality as we receive. If you can only return a cup of coffee there is strong pressure on you not to move in circles where you will be offered a whiskey and soda.

By and large, people choose to live in the group in which they can feel confident of being able to discharge such indebtedness as they may incur. If they feel very insecure about their capacity for repayment, they will live among people somewhat poorer than themselves. If they feel highly confident of their potential capacities, they will live in a group that is somewhat more affluent than they are, and will count on eventually discharging their debts. There is some latitude both ways. But the penniless upstart can only live among the wealthy as a sponger or fortune hunter.

It may not be agreeable to accept that we organize our lives in this way, but if we consider the social groupings in which most people do in fact live, the existence of such unconscious selectivity is borne out. This was always attributed to the class structure of society, and as long as the class divisions more or less corresponded to the money divisions, such an explanation held good. But now we see that the class structure theory is not really adequate. There are no impenetrable class barriers for a hairdresser like Vidal Sassoon or a footballer like George Best, or an entertainer like Sammy Davis, Jr. In practice, there is no problem about a wealthy person from the working classes living in the same group as a wealthy aristocrat. Lord Montagu of Beaulieu points out that the English aristocracy never had much compunction about marrying into trade, as long as it was a paying proposition. The difference in manners is a matter of fashion. When there is a working-class fashion the sons of lords adopt working-class modes of dress, speech and behavior, and when there is an aristocratic fashion, the upstarts cultivate posh accents and elegant gestures. These are not fundamental differences, as long as people have enough money to live on the same level as others in the group, and are able to pay their debts. The way in which money practices determine a person's sense of class was indicated by a man who announced that he had left the working class and entered the bourgeoisie. Up until then he had been giving his wages to his wife and keeping pocket money for himself. Now he was giving his wife a housekeeping allowance and keeping the rest.

What defines the working *class* is that its members belong to money groups in which they enjoy no credit, or very limited credit. Because workers earn only just enough for their immediate needs, they have no surplus to engage in the trial-and-error type of activity. The working-class person is reluctant to move, because to move costs money, and so he only moves when he is sure; he tends to be xenophobic because he doesn't know what foreigners are like, and it costs money to find out, and so he sticks to what he knows.

The most fundamental social distinction is between those whose earnings only pay for a few days ahead, and who therefore must stick to their last, and those whose earnings are sufficiently great to enable them to undertake doubtful ventures. It is not necessarily thought out in this way. The working-class man simply feels a hatred of foreign things because they are strange and unfamiliar, but if that hatred is broken down, what he is expressing is his feeling that he may spend time and money on something he won't like. By contrast, in the top money groups, it is accepted that much money will have to be spent on things that are not liked before something that is liked is found. This is seen on all levels, whether it involves trying a new restaurant, or a new car or a new wife.

What holds each money group together in a state of dynamic equilibrium is the urge to be quits with the others in it; this is the underlying motive of keeping up with the Joneses. The importance of this keeping up is that it is a way of limiting envy, which to the envious person can be unbearable torment.

The backbiter, the spoiler, the carping critic, the knocker is an easily recognized figure. Chaucer described him as "the man who praises his neighbour but with wicked intent, for he always put 'but' at the end . . ." Such people are in a perpetual agony of not having something that somebody else has that they desire, and so must devalue it, debase it. The way of avoiding, or limiting, such painful feelings, which spoil everything good in order that it need not be envied, is to make one's life in a group in which one *can* keep up. If one has more or less what everybody else in the group has, envy is not too excessive, nor does one fall into a state of indebtedness that cannot be discharged.*

Of course, even within one's own money group, envy operates, but it is mutual rather than one-sided. Everybody has something that the other envies, and insofar as this enables one to politely take one's revenge the group maintains its cohesiveness. Among lower-paid workers, keeping up may be just a matter of being able to buy a friend a drink, or of having the money to put on a horse, or of being able to buy the wife a washing machine. Moving up the money scale, being quits with others in the group becomes more sophisticated. The house you live in, its size, its furnishings, its accouterments, the number of times you entertain, and how many people, and the kind of wine and food served, and by whom—such things become the counters in an elaborate game of mutual envy.

The desire of suburban hostesses to outdo each other in various seemingly trivial ways is often noted. The satisfaction of avenging oneself in this way is that by stirring up envy in others, one's own envy of them is momentarily alleviated. But such gains are short-lived, because people one has made

* Even if the group wished to "carry" one of its members who has fallen behind, if he cannot keep up by his own efforts he will feel humiliated, and his impulse will be to drop down into a lower group where he can be quits. People have an instinctive knowledge of their capacities and when they are out of their depth; the highest rat race casualties are known to occur as a result of people's being driven into a money group in which they can't keep up.

envious are felt to be very dangerous. This is why we allow them *their* revenge—to get even with us. And if they are no longer able to keep up, we drop them because we fear the malice of the overenvious.

This sort of thing happens on all levels. For instance, in the very highest money group the two great Greek shipowners Stavros Niarchos and Aristotle Onassis are said to be locked in a perpetual struggle to get even with each other. As in any suburban money group, the need is to be quits, which means to be relieved of envy of the other. When Onassis bought his first wife, Tina, a six-story house in New York, Niarchos responded by buying his wife, Eugenie (Tina's sister), two stories of a skyscraper. The tale is told that Tina sniffed at these two stories, whereupon her sister said she found the accommodation sufficient for the moment "and I can always have more if I want—my husband has bought the whole skyscraper." When Onassis wanted to buy a home in the Caribbean for his new wife, Jackie, Niarchos forestalled him by buying the most sumptuous property in Bermuda, Blue Horizons. And so it goes on.

On a less extreme scale, one sees it in the great importance that the Italians attach to what they call *una bella figura,* cutting a good figure. It means maintaining the style of affluence appropriate to your group. The great emphasis on show, on visible evidence of position, is related to the fact that envy is only effectively balanced out when those in the group not only keep up but are *seen* to be keeping up. Anyone who did not cut a good figure might be suspected of having fallen behind, and therefore of being a dangerously envious person. At the same time, by *seeing* the best that the others can do, the individual member of the group can match that best, and so can feel "I'm as good as they are," which means that he does not have to be excessively envious of his fellows. The essence of cutting a good figure is to have the good taste not to overdo it, that is to say, not to give bigger parties or bigger presents or live in a costlier style than others in the group. Anyone who does do that sort of thing has to move out.

To be able to live in a money group in which one cannot keep up calls for very special character traits. Such people do exist, and they range from the out-and-out sponger to a Beethoven being supported by his aristocratic patrons.

There is, for instance, the permanent guest. Lord Montagu of Beaulieu describes the type as follows: "They are usually very good company. They're good conversationalists. Often single men who make up a dinner party, or sometimes even a single woman. They're in demand because one says, 'Oh, we've got one more man here—oh, let's get old so-and-so . . .' And they spend their life going from one country house to the other, and once having been accepted they start inviting themselves. They say: 'I'm coming down to this particular place in August. Can I come and stay for a few days?' You just haven't got the nerve to say 'No.' Well, you know, they're all right, and after all, they know your friends now. I know several like that. When they go abroad, they pay their own fare and when they get there, wherever they are going, they rarely put their hand in their pocket. Occasionally they don't even pay their fare. Very smart party-givers charter planes to fly their people around. But mostly they have got just enough money to pay their own fare from A to B. But after that they don't pay at all. Almost they have a set pattern: they go to the South of France, they go to Venice, Paris, London. They make it their life work to get themselves invited . . ."[3]

The poet Rainer Maria Rilke had a genius for getting members of the European aristocracy to loan him their castles and palaces. On one occasion a somewhat oversolicitous host asked the poet if there was anything he lacked. To which

Rilke, never one to be bashful in his demands, said yes, he needed seclusion in order to commune with his Muse, whereupon the nobleman and his family promptly moved out to a nearby hotel. Whether it is a man of poetic genius, or merely a witty conversationalist, it is characteristic of the great guest that he regards his presence as sufficient recompense in itself. He does you the favor of eating your food, drinking your wine, using your house. Sometimes such an assessment of his own value may be perfectly accurate—it undoubtedly was in the case of Rilke; the princesses and noblemen who afforded him hospitality are largely remembered for that and nothing else. Those with the capacity to recognize talent may consider themselves privileged to be able to succor the artist who possesses it. But the number of geniuses among the self-invited is few—the majority are superior spongers and freeloaders, which is not to say that these activities do not require some talent.

The technique varies. There is the permanent guest, as described by Lord Montagu. There is also the kind of person who attaches himself to some great or wealthy figure and contrives to make himself indispensable. An example of this type was Stephen Ward, the key figure in the Profumo-Keeler scandal; he had been given a cottage free of charge on the Astors' estate at Cliveden, and through his friendship with the then Lord Astor obtained admission to the highest levels of English society and wealth. Stephen Ward was a skilled osteopath, and was able to afford relief from pain to many rich people, in a way that sometimes seemed to them almost miraculous. Having charm and intelligence and a gift for being a guest, he was invited by these people to their houses and their parties, where he met other famous and wealthy people, who invited him to their houses and parties. For his part, he knew pretty young girls of the sort who enliven any stately home, with the result that he was much in demand.

Many a permanent guest gets himself invited on this basis, though usually with less disastrous consequences. Indeed, it is because he has certain connections that the guest keeps himself on the invited list. Ward had developed this to a fine art. He was befriended by Cabinet Ministers because he was intimate with people like Lord Astor. The American millionaire Huntington Hartford would come to his cottage because, after all, it was on the Cliveden estate, and after dinner Ward often took his special guests up to the big house and introduced them to Lord Astor. For many years Ward lived on this sort of millionaire level on comparatively modest earnings. He did this by never paying for anything if he could possibly help it. If he met a girl he liked (and he met girls he liked all the time) he'd ask her to dinner, but instead of booking a table at a restaurant he'd ring up Lord Astor, or some other lord that he knew, and invite himself to dine at his house. If for some reason this didn't work out, he'd ask the girl to come to his cottage at Cliveden. There the other guests (it was open house, and there were always other guests) provided the drinks, and whoever got landed with driving into the village to buy the food ended up paying for it. Ward, in keeping with the type, was a supreme pocket fumbler at such moments. "Oh, let me," he'd say and then search in vain for the pound note that he was sure he had somewhere; meanwhile others sprang forward to chip in, making the pound note, when and if it was found, no longer required.

The permanent guest usually retains a measure of independence by getting invited to enough places. But there is a type who confines himself to one person or household. This is the hanger-on, who becomes by stages cohort, yes-man and ultimately stooge. Many a rich man feels the need of an entourage, a sort of traveling court that satisfies his various needs for sensual, mental or emotional stimulus, and the hanger-on can function in any of these categories. He can be a licensed intellectual, tolerated for the satisfaction it affords the rich man to make a lap dog of a person of greatly superior intelligence. He may be a procurer, someone who has the charm and the ease to approach attractive women and bring them into his host's orbit. Or he may be a joker, a spiritual adviser, an emotional counselor, a helpmate, a soothsayer, a palm reader. In the traveling circuses of very rich men with a taste for kingship, most of such types, if not all, will be found. Sometimes they are there on a permanent guest basis, having their bills paid; other times they succeed in actually getting on the payroll.

Yet another variant is the person who doesn't attach himself to any one source, and probably works for a living, but by calculated freeloading lives on a much higher scale than his income would allow him to. He moves in money groups not his own, by virtue of a position that he occupies and which can be exploited. Certain kinds of journalists practice this with great élan. There was one who had worked out a system whereby he could spend his year going from one film festival to the next, each time as the guest of the festival authorities. Other influential journalists—and this applies to influential people in general—allow themselves to be cultivated. They get free trips from foreign governments. They go on wine-tasting shindigs to Cyprus. They try out the state-rooms of ocean liners for their readers' benefit. They test new models of cars, at the makers' expense, in the Dolomites. They investigate new ski resorts in the French Alps at the invitation of the developers. They are the guests of film producers on film locations in Greece or Spain. By assiduous contrivance, they manage to live in money groups which they could never enter on the basis of their earnings.

What all these different types have in common is a belief in their unique qualifications for being kept, or paid for, by others. As one journalist put it: "I consider it due to

my position that the companies jolly well service me—I *expect*
the tickets and the books and the passes and the trips and the
invitations to come rolling in." And of course where publicity
is sought, newspapermen are serviced in this way. But it does
not automatically go with the job; it is something that the
person who has a taste for it has to elicit. This is apparent from
the fact that those with a distaste for buckshee entertainment
manage to avoid much of it, and probably work in areas
where it is not offered. Crime reporters are not much entertained by the police, nor are war correspondents subjected to
fleshly blandishments by the military. But the person with the
characteristics of the freeloader ensures that he is serviced by
his sources, and he is the one who is seen *everywhere* quaffing
champagne with his caviar with all the world-weary self-sacri-
fice of someone on perpetual night call.

   This type of person may be described in psychological
terms as being predominantly "oral." Karl Abraham has
written: ". . . the pleasure of the sucking period (in infancy) is to a great extent a pleasure in taking, in being given
something . . . some mothers indulge the craving for pleasure in their infants by granting them every wish. The result
is that it is extraordinarily difficult to wean the child . . ."[4]
The baby wishes to be the breast's permanent guest. A person's entire character can come under the sway of the oral
fantasy. Such people are perennial optimists—they always expect there will be somebody to feed them. They feel it is
their due. They are described in the phrase "the world owes
them a living." This being so, they naturally have no compunction about accepting the endless hospitality of others.
On the contrary, they believe they are so extraordinary—
aren't they asked everywhere?—that it is an honor for them to
turn up. It is true they may do a little procuring or fixing or
stooging too, but that is by the way; it is really for themselves
that they are cultivated. And it is they who are being culti-

vated, not the other way around, just as this kind of infant believes that the breast seeks his mouth in order to be eased of the burden of its milk, which he does it the honor of taking in.

Abraham has pointed out another characteristic that this type often has, which comes in very handy for someone who has to talk his way into beneficial situations. By a displacement of the oral wish, this type also has a need to give by the mouth, which means—the gift of gab.[5] "Persons of this kind," says Abraham, "have the impression that their fund of thought is inexhaustible, and they ascribe a special power or some unusual value to what they say." This fits in with Lord Montagu's and most other people's impression of the permanent guest as conversationalist and verbal charmer.

Money enforces what must be regarded as one of the most fundamental relationships between people—that of master and servant. On the personal level, the attempt to achieve the former position and avoid the latter constitutes much of the dynamic of endeavor within our present society. And on the national and world scale most of the problems with which men are confronted are in fact questions of who shall dominate.

The proclaimed issue may be justice, liberty, equality; but at heart, the desire is to achieve mastery over others. In its most brutally obvious form, this objective is proclaimed by a Hitler, who declared the Germans to be the Master Race and consequently entitled to treat other nations as sources of slave labor. The desire for mastery runs through the whole system of society, and is often achieved in such sophisticated and conventionalized ways that its underlying motive is effectively disguised. Money is the most powerful and subtle (if need be) weapon of dominance available to us. We use it to achieve power over others, and also to avoid falling into others' power. Much of the violence that money produces—on the individual, the class, the national and the world-wide scale—is due to its role in these power struggles.

In primitive societies such struggles were mostly resolved by trials of strength. The stronger made the weaker his slave. Nowadays we do the same sort of thing by means of money. We become bosses and make others our wage slaves. Or we are the sort of people who *have* to work for ourselves, who find the idea of working for somebody else intolerable, which must be due to this underlying meaning of being the other's slave. Elliott Jaques says that, in certain circumstances, a person in a superior position will experience the exercise of his authority as "wielding destructive and sadistic power," while the person who is being ordered about will, on certain levels, experience this as "being subjected to persecuting omnipotence."[6] It can be seen why the relationship between superiors and subordinates, necessary for many social tasks, is such a fraught one.

Below the level of practical necessity, which is supposedly dictating decisions, people may be unconsciously motivated by the sheer love of aggression, on the one hand, and the desire to submit to it on the other. Wherever a social contract places one person exclusively at the disposal of another, limits his right of appeal to the person exercising power over him, and gives the subordinate no possibility of redress for unfair treatment, a situation is created that caters to the mutual desire to master and be mastered.

This was often seen in the old days of servants. Significantly, where there is no extremely poor class it becomes impossible to get servants. As one aggrieved rich Englishman put it, "It is amazing that with a million unemployed, people should be so unwilling to take on the comparatively easy and well-paid work of being house servants. But they just don't want to do it." In the United States more and more of the very rich are having to sell their large mansions and move into hotel suites, because of the impossibility of getting staff. It is going into domestic service that people object to; they are still prepared to go into hotel work. Lord Montagu says: "The old family retainers that a great many families relied on are now really dying out. And quite apart from the fact that they are expensive (that is not necessarily a bar), they are extremely difficult to find because there aren't many people going into 'service.' This hit America a long time before us, and one knows that in the States to find servants anywhere is quite a rarity. Therefore a whole way of life changes. . . . People are not prepared to carry out servant type jobs. The only draw at the moment which is keeping some servants is the opportunity of free accommodation in nice surroundings. If I weren't able to offer my butler a jolly nice cottage at Beaulieu, I obviously couldn't get servants."[7]

In any highly conventionalized relationship, there is powerful denial of underlying motives, and this is obviously so where masters and servants are concerned. An area where the relationship becomes explicit is the sexual. In the annals of erotica the servant girl has always occupied a very special place: countless frisky chambermaids have cavorted through farces and lewd tales and adolescents' reveries, taking their knickers down with the alacrity of those trained to serve. If one is to define the peculiar erotic appeal of the type, it is that, traditionally, she may be taken advantage of at will. This is how the narrator in *The Empty Canvas* treats the new maid who is serving him lunch in his mother's house: "Rita obediently turned back and held out the dish to me once again. Again I used one hand . . . Meanwhile I ran my other hand, which I had left dangling beside my chair, up Rita's leg, right up to her thigh. Through her ample dress I could feel the muscles of her leg quiver beneath my hand, like those of a horse when its master strokes it."

There is no mention of money, nor is money offered. But it is the unspoken dominance asserted by it that permits a line of behavior which would be unthinkable in relationships between monetary equals. Some coffee spilled on the man's trousers provides an excuse for him to take them off and for the girl to clean them, whereupon without further ado the master takes the girl's hand and places it on his penis. It's the sort of thing he would only think of doing in that way with a servant. The housemaid's special erotic appeal lies in the fact that she is in theory obliged to permit everything. She is not in a position to take offense. If the master wanted to feel her up under her dress, or to come in her mouth, or in her anus, the convention insisted upon her compliance. As a tendency to submissiveness was probably a factor in her choice of going into service, the ingredients of a compact are there. In this, money may play no more than a symbolic role. Its importance is that it is known to exist, and that therefore submission to it can be ritualistically required as a matter of course. The excitement lies in the element of *compulsion,* even if it's only a sort of pretense of compulsion, as the whip is in the charades of the bordello.

As soon as the compulsion no longer applies, as when there is a considerable degree of independence for anyone wanting domestic work, the sadomasochistic bond is broken. Then such relationships are preserved only in the bordello, where the prostitute (for a fee) will pretend to be a compliant chambermaid, obliged to submit to the master's peremptory lusts. Thus in the brothel we see how things were once, and what it meant; and it suggests that these master-servant relationships must have found new disguises in contemporary society.

The young girl who *had* to submit to the master in the domestic setting may long ago have become an anachronism, but her equivalent in the film studios of Hollywood was a reality until quite recently. Observation and popular myth testify to this, but interestingly most of the casting-couch tycoons deny the element of duress. One was refreshingly frank in not subscribing to the usual line. "Why do they go to bed with me? Look at me. It can't be for my looks. It's not categorically for the money—I don't give them money. It's to get into the milieu of money. It's to move around with money, to partake of it in some way."

To observe such powerful men in action, there can be no doubt that they use their money in a half-serious, half-kidding way as a bait and means of coercion. "Honey, I'm so rich, I could even afford you." "Baby, I never believe in offering women money, but for you I'll make an exception. *How much?*" This sort of vulgar kidding approach is both an actual offer of money (if the girl chooses to take it up) and a way of creating a certain kind of erotic excitement. Norman Mailer conveys this in a scene in *An American Dream:* ". . . it was a smell that could be mellowed only by the gift of fur and gems, she was money this girl, she cost money, she would make money, something as corrupt as a banquet plate of caviar laid on hundred-dollar bills would be required to enrich that odor all the way up to the smell of foie gras in Deborah's world. I had a desire suddenly to skip the sea and mine the earth, a pure prong of desire to bugger . . ."

We see in this description the way in which ideas of money, of paying, of buying, of enriching, of corrupting, serve to stimulate a certain kind of sexual violence; and this kind of using of money as an instrument of sadistic pleasure is often a key factor in the master-servant relationship without necessarily being admitted. Mailer is giving his writer's insight into the sort of feelings going on under the surface. The girl is a servant girl.

Once outside the sexual sphere the sadistic element in seeking mastery over others is more hidden. It was obvious in the ship's captain who flogged a press-ganged crew into submission; it is far less obvious when the submission is extorted by means of the subtle exercise of money, as in the case of the boss who never has to raise his voice to make his staff run around for him. Elliott Jaques, in his paper "The Human Consequences of Industrialization," says that one of the fundamental needs—and hence rights—of a person working in an industrial society is "independence from control by any individual without recourse to public process of review of that control by others." But he points out that almost nowhere do such individual appeal systems exist. The result, he says, is a strengthening of psychopathological processes and eruption of violence.

While money is such an important factor in our lives, and has such a variety of unconscious meanings, anyone who controls its supply, who can arbitrarily increase or diminish the amounts we shall have, who can cut off the flow entirely if he so wishes, and on the other hand can "make us rich" if he chooses to do so, is inevitably cast in the role of a master, and those dependent on him are to some extent bound to serve him. To avoid this, requires a conscious decision not to exercise the power of money, and this calls for a degree of maturity and balance that is by no means general among the rich. In order to free themselves from a domination that is felt to be, and probably is, oppressive, people strive to make themselves financially independent of others. This usually involves making others financially dependent on them, and so the vicious circle is perpetuated.

Where enough people collectively experience the oppression of money, there are the makings of revolution. For this to happen, the monied elite has to use its money with sufficient brutality to incite those without it to act. But we tend nowadays to be much more devious in the exercise of money power, and modern capitalism does not make the mistake of too crudely demonstrating the disparities between the haves and have-nots. The former Duke of Bedford who had *two* houses in Grosvenor Square is not likely to be emulated today. The prevalent attitude is to disclaim great personal wealth. Getty insists that he does not have the money in realizable form *to use*. In effect, what is being denied is the sort of brute master-servant power possessed by anyone who can deploy his money, and dispose of it, in any way that he wishes. As Herbert Marcuse put it succinctly: "Domination is transfigured into administration." Marcuse's argument in *One Dimensional Man* is that by the calculated blurring of superficial differences between classes, their fundamental antagonism is softened, and "the class struggle" deprived of its primitive force. He writes: "If the worker and his boss enjoy the same television programs and visit the same resort places, if the typist is as attractively made up as the daughter of her employer, if the Negro owns a Cadillac, if they all read the same newspaper, then this assimilation indicates not the disappearance of classes, but the extent to which the needs and satisfaction that serve the preservation of the Establishment are shared by the underlying population."[8]

Marcuse is arguing from the point of view of someone who subscribes to the belief that what limits human freedom and perpetuates antagonisms is the *forms* of our social structures. According to this argument, a more equitable distribution of money and property would produce the kind of just society in which men could live as equals and as brothers. It is the argument of the Marxist utopian. Freud dealt with this in *Civilization and Its Discontents:*

> The communists believe they have found the path to deliverance from our evils. According to them, man is wholly good and is well-disposed to his neighbours; but

the institution of private property has corrupted his nature. The ownership of private property gives the individual power, and with it the temptation to ill-treat his neighbour; while the man who is excluded from possession is bound to rebel in hostility against his oppressor. If private property were abolished, all wealth held in common, and everyone allowed to share in the enjoyment of it, ill-will and hostility would disappear among men. Since everyone's needs would be satisfied, no one would have any reason to regard another as his enemy . . . I am able to recognize that the psychological premises on which the system is based are an untenable illusion. In abolishing private property we deprive the human love of aggression of one of its instruments, certainly a strong one, though certainly not the strongest; but we have in no way altered the differences in power and influence which are misused by aggressiveness, nor have we altered anything in its nature. Aggressiveness was not created by property. It reigned almost without limit in primitive times, when property was still very scanty, and it already shows itself in the nursery almost before property has given up its primal, anal form; it forms the basis of every relation of affection and love among people (with the single exception, perhaps, of the mother's relation to her male child). If we do away with personal rights over material wealth, there still remains prerogative in the field of sexual relationships, which is bound to become the source of the strongest dislike and the most violent hostility among men who in other respects are on an equal footing.[9]

Essentially the conflict between the Marxist and the Freudian view of life (which Marcuse has attempted to reconcile) may be stated as follows: The Freudian view insists on the primacy of psychic reality and says that our social structures are expressions of psychic conditions. The Marxist view is that social conditions determine psychic structures. Clearly there is interaction and interdependence between social and psychological forces. The child comes into a world in which financial inequality exists as a social fact; his psychological development is bound to take heed of such realities and to adapt (or fail to adapt) to them. But this inequality would not be of such fundamental significance to him if it did not correspond to the *feeling* of inequality in him that is a condition of coming into the world and being dependent on the "richness" of the parents for survival. And so from the beginning an outer inequality that is, theoretically, capable of being remedied, takes on the aspects of a more basic and oppressive inequality that is not capable of being remedied. Insofar as the drive to remedy that external inequality is actually motivated by the desire to be equal with the parents, it is doomed to failure. Revolution cannot make the child the equal of the father. Even when the child grows up and becomes a man, there is a part of him that continues to relate as child to father figures. Much revolutionary fervor is wasted on the attempt to change this unchangeable state of affairs.

It is partly as a means of compensating themselves for this inescapable inequality that men seek to dominate others in the external world, thereby seeking to disprove their inner feeling of not being half the man that Daddy was. The point is that this feeling of inferiority is inevitable and natural in the child part of the man, and is the dynamic of all striving for betterment; but it is also uncomfortable to a degree that some people cannot bear; for such people all situations that seem to impose a subservient or subordinate role on them are intolerable. They cannot work for others, only for themselves. They cannot take orders. They usually cannot learn, because it involves the humiliation of admitting their ignorance in relation to somebody else's knowledge. Such people are driven to become revolutionaries or bosses. As a measure of self-survival they have to achieve financial or political power over others. These others, in turn, have their apprehensions of being at somebody else's mercy (with good cause), and struggle against being dominated in this way. And so money becomes both the means of enslavement and the means whereby the slaves believe they can free themselves.

The dynamics of our society encourage everyone to believe that he too can be the master. This is what a Marxist critic like Marcuse considers the great fraud. The democratic process, he says, channels the revolutionary impulse into safe areas, and by making everyone a bit of a capitalist, a bit of an exploiter of others, gives him enough vested interest in a system of exploitation to preserve it. In fact, we contrive to face both ways at the same time. Towards those financially dependent on us, we are the masters, while being the servants of those on whom we, in turn, depend. By maintaining this double role, we contrive to be quits with ourselves.

Our money relationships in society need to be seen in the light of this dual need for mastery and subservience. For this reason it is a mere makeshift to isolate the oppressors as a class, and to seek solutions in terms of its overthrow. The capitalistic instinct is not a class phenomenon—as we have traced it, it arises out of a variety of primitive motives, some anal, some oral, in their origins, but all of them universal.

The problem of organizing a more just society becomes, then, a matter of dealing with the "capitalist neurosis" as an endemic condition of our time and place. And this means that it cannot be defined solely in terms of the possession of money, which is merely its most striking expression. Basically, we are confronted with the question of the true nature of human nature. Is it economizing? Or is it squandering? The fact that a man must expend millions of spermatozoa in order for one to fertilize the ovum and make a new human being is a good argument for the spendthrift theory of nature. On the other hand, the woman is more economical, with her one ovum every month.

The spendthrift spirit is passionately promulgated by Norman O. Brown in his book *Life Against Death*. He says that it is not merely the hoarding of money that is anal in origin, but all forms of economy, and goes so far as to quote Sándor Ferenczi's notion that even thinking, insofar as it is a means of preventing a squandering through action, is "a special expression of the tendency to economize" and as such "has its origin in anal eroticism."

The substitution of the word "ruminating" for "thinking" makes this idea more acceptable: the obsessive ruminator who cannot make up his mind on a course of action for fear it may be the wrong one and wasteful of his efforts could be described as hoarding his energy in an anal way.

Brown concludes that ". . . possessive mastery over nature and rigorously economical thinking are partial impulses in the human being (the human body) which in modern civilization have become tyrant organizers of the whole of human life; abstraction from the reality of the whole body and substitution of the abstracted impulse for the whole reality are inherent in *Homo economicus*. In contrast, what would a nonmorbid science look like? It would presumably be erotic rather than [anal] sadistic in aim. Its aim would not be mastery over but union with nature. And its means would not be economizing but erotic exuberance."[10]

There is something obviously appealing about the espousal of erotic exuberance and a perpetual giving forth in place of saving. And the possibility that human affairs could be organized on such a basis certainly deserves consideration. If "a carefree letting go of one-self," in Rilke's phrase, were a feasible way of living, it would perhaps be more splendid

MONEY AND SOCIETY   309

than a policy of self-conservation. But where would such a letting-go lead? What would people do in Brown's un-economizing world? The answer is they would play. As a solution of the human predicament, it has charm. "The life instinct, or sexual instinct, demands activity of a kind that, in contrast to our current mode of activity, can only be called play," writes Brown.

The program implicit in all this was immediately promulgated by the counterculture. To the dropouts and the flower children, Brown seemed to be saying that they were right to reject work and the competitive system, and right to make their lives into a celebration of their sensuous inheritance. Was not the unsublimated ("polymorphous perverse") body of childhood the natural expression of the life force? Therefore the money motive, involving the repression of primary instincts, was to be deplored.

The reason that Brown's thesis at first sounds convincing is because it is half true and, in a money-mad world, a salutary corrective to the prevailing obsession. As such it is welcome. The sacrifice of human for money values has also been one of the main themes of this book. In this context, I would cite Marx's illuminating idea that insofar as money acts as an intermediary of exchange between people, it usurps the mediating activity of human social action; and so when man endows money with the role of intermediary between himself and others, he himself is active only as an exiled and dehumanized being. Man, says Marx, should be the intermediary between men, and by giving this function to money, he makes himself its slave. The intermediary becomes the real god, since the intermediary has the real power over that which he mediates.[11]

But true as this is, it is only half the story. Every symbolic act involves a sacrifice of a physical activity: every love letter is a loss of a love act. If we could act out everything that we feel, we would have no need of symbolic modes of expression. But all of human culture is based on the partial sublimation of primary instinctual drives in symbolic activities: rituals, masques, competitions, games, art forms, systems. In the rituals of moneymaking, many human instincts find expression. When a symbolic activity becomes too remote from the drive that produced it, what happens is a degeneration into obsession, superstition, magic. To a large extent this has happened with money, and it has been one of the objects of this book to retrace the links between money behavior and the elemental impulses out of which it arises. I have sought to bring such connections to consciousness.

And so, in opposition to Brown's ideal of a play paradise, it has to be said that people have need of symbolic as well as bodily activity, and that the world of childhood is by no means the paradise he suggests. On the contrary, it is the fact that the child's playing is his *work* that makes it gratifying to him, and it is by no means simply an indulgence in sensuous gratification. The pleasure of playing, for children, lies in dealing in symbolic form with the dangerous demands of instinct. Destructiveness is made tangible, in a controllable way; and it becomes possible to make good again what had been destroyed. Such symbolic modes of dealing with instinct become progressively more complicated and are variously expressed in the institutions and systems of society. Money is one of these systems. It is undoubtedly a system that has gone wrong, but that is because it has been made to carry and express far too much of human instinct. But to blame *money* for the acquisitiveness of human beings is an absurd inversion. And it is naïve to suppose, as Brown does, that liberated from what he calls "the unnatural perversion of money-making," natural man could function on a basis of endless giving out. This is a magical notion that denies the basis on which giving out must function: namely, a prior taking in.

It denies the economic problem of the psyche by positing a limitless well. This is once more the illusion of the inexhaustible breast.

By equating capitalism with anality, Brown confines the origin of the money motive to a single bodily source. It has been the argument of this book that no such single source is capable of accounting for the extraordinary variety of forms in which the money motive has been shown to manifest itself. It is not only man's anal economizing nature that finds expression in money. His manic eroticism may express itself in the form of the spending spree. His aspirations to omnipotence may seek implementation by means of money, and so on. The discoveries of psychoanalysis which linked money to excrement were only part of the story. In analyzing the anal character Freud found that one of his symptoms was the hoarding of money. But it does not follow that greed for money is invariably anal in origin. It is the popular acceptance of the non sequitur that has led to the false equation: money = excrement. *Sometimes* it does, for some people, in certain circumstances. But it can also mean something entirely different. In another aspect, it can be seen as the most potent opium of the people.

Even insofar as money is anal in character, one would have to say that the function of the anus is not to be despised. The displacement of *all* eroticism to it may be a misfortune, and the overestimation of its products may be delusion, but the anus does serve the body, and its capacity for retention is also vital to the preservation of life.

Money behavior is related not to any one bodily function, but to the sum total, to the whole body economy. This being so, it becomes apparent that Brown's advocacy of a policy of nothing but spending is as untenable physiologically and psychologically as it is in terms of classic money economics. The human psyche has to introject loving objects in order for it to be able to give out love. It is this introjection of the good which so readily deteriorates into greedy acquisitiveness, and desire for possession, and control over what is possessed, and in its external manifestations to the worst excesses of capitalism. But, again, there is no giving out without taking in. The psyche is bound by economic laws. Erotic exuberance can only work in alternation with erotic greed. The cornucopia has to be refilled. The person who spends himself extravagantly, or spends his money extravagantly, must eventually exhaust his reserves.

A theory of money that isolates the anal-retentive aspects of capitalism for condemnation is incomplete; modern psychology also contains the concept of "manic generosity." The miser/collector/hoarder is a certain kind of money neurotic; but the other side of his nature is the big spender.

It is the contention of this book that our ambivalence about money expresses the modus operandi of the unconscious: the union of opposites. Put another way, the part of us that wishes to retain, keep, hold on to, hoard, permanently possess, is in conflict with another part that wants to expend, spend, spread around, give, bestow. John D. Rockefeller's adviser, who urged him to keep his benefactions in pace with his enormous earnings, clearly had an intuitive understanding of the psychological need to keep these conflicting elements of the personality in a state of balance.

Of course, if money were not so closely bound up with the deepest psychological processes, it could be made much more rational. But anything in such common use, that serves such broad and general human aspirations, is bound to be invaded by motives derived from other sources. The only way of making money rational would be to eliminate it. In a moneyless society the neuroses that now find expression in money dealings would require other outlets. Another system of calibrating human endeavor would have to be devised. It is possible that another system might work better, might be fairer to everyone, and less capable of being adapted to the neurotic needs of individuals to exploit and be exploited. But what is certain is that another system would not remove those needs, and they would find satisfaction elsewhere. Also, in a moneyless society there would still be in all of us a desire for possession, since this preceded the institution of property and has its origins in the human constitution. Similarly, the desires to make good again, to repair, restore, repay, compensate, be quits with, and not be indebted, would also persist, since they, too, are inherent in the psyche's way of functioning. Thus the abolition of money could not abolish the money motive, but only the particular manifestation of it that we now see.

One final aspect of money needs to be considered in the context of its uses in society, and that is its relationship to time. The saying is that time is money, but it is actually the other way around: *money is time*. First, money is time in the sense that, for example, *the cost* of the American space program, expressed in tens of millions of dollars, is really time— the time put into it by all those engaged on the project. The real cost of anything is the man-hours of time put in. And this is *a cost* because it is so many hours of life-time used up.*
A millionaire's houses, cars, clothes, airplanes, yachts have cost the time that it took to make them—that is, thousands upon thousands of hours of other people's life-time. By comparison, a moneyless man—say, Robinson Crusoe—possesses only what he can make in his own time. Ultimately, being rich is a way of possessing part of other people's life-time, in solid form. This would explain some of the passionate attachment to money, if it is, in fact, an attachment to life-time.

---

* Of course, limited resources are also being used up, but what this means is that future generations may be deprived of some, or all, of their life-time.

The main characteristic of time is that it is passing and cannot be saved up; there is no way of hoarding it, or collecting it, it can only be spent; and since everybody has the same amount of it, more or less, as far as anyone can know, no one person can be richer in time than another. But by means of money it is possible to buy time; that is, if it is not possible to have more of one's own, one can have some of other people's; if one cannot actually obtain more life-time one can obtain the things that it would require a thousand Robinson Crusoe lifetimes to make oneself. In this way, one obtains the illusion of extending one's own life-time.

Significantly, it has been found that most money misers are also time misers—they conduct their lives on time and motion principles, always trying to save time in various ways.

Life-time is what the death instinct ultimately brings to an end, and it is surely—in part—our wish for more life than we are allowed, or can get, that makes us so greedy for the stuff that, if it cannot extend our own life-time, will buy us large amounts of other people's, in this way giving us an illusion of a richer, fuller, longer life. In this sense, money is the distorted image of time, multiplied as in a hall of mirrors, illusory, but also beguiling and seductive, with its many faces.

Notes

PART ONE THE FORTUNE

CHAPTER 1 The Dream

1   J. M. Keynes, *Essays in Persuasion* (Macmillan): "The love of money as a possession—as distinguished from the love of money as a means to the enjoyment of the realities of life—will be recognised for what it is, a somewhat disgusting morbidity, one of those semi-criminal, semi-pathological propensities which one hands over with a shudder to the specialists in mental disease."

2   Karl Marx, Economic and Philosophical Manuscripts (1844), Marx Engels Gesamtausgabe. Excerpt from *Karl Marx, Selected Writings,* editors Bottomore and Rubel, p. 181. (Pelican Books)

3   Name withheld at request of interviewee.

4   J. Paul Getty, *How To Be Rich,* p. 9. (Playboy Press Book)

5   Lionel Bart, interview, *Sunday Express,* Dec. 17, 1972.

6   A. Hingston Quiggin, *Primitive Money,* p. 152. (Methuen)

7   Donald Zec, *Some Enchanted Egos,* p. 20. (Allison & Busby)

8   André Maurois, *Prometheus: The Life of Balzac,* p. 306. Translated by Norman Denny. (Pelican) "His [Balzac's] 'unassailable retreat' in the Rue des Batailles included a

specially decorated boudoir with a white cashmere divan fifty feet in circumference" say Maurois, who also tells of Balzac's invitation to Henriette de Castries to "come at the time when I get up, to perch like a bird on the divan, just for an hour? Who in the world would know?" (Maurois, p. 308)

9   Robert Muller, interview with the author, 1971.
10   Alvaro, interview with the author, 1971.
11   Sigmund Freud, *Collected Papers,* Vol. V, *Dostoievsky and Parricide* (1928), pp. 240–1. (Hogarth Press and Institute of Psychoanalysis)
12   Ernest Jones, *Papers on Psychoanalysis,* chapter XXIII, *The Phantasy of the Reversal of Generations,* p. 407. (Baillière, Tindall & Cox, 1948)

CHAPTER 2   The Quest

1   Ferdinand Lundberg, *The Rich and the Super Rich,* p. 24. (Nelson)
2   "Slater's Next Ten Years" by John Davis, *The Observer,* May 7, 1972.
3   Allan Nevins, *Rockefeller, Study in Power,* Vol. 2, p. 110. (New York, London: Scribner's)
4   'Adam Smith,' *The Money Game,* p. 101. (Pan Books)
5   Christopher Marley, the London *Times,* March 15, 1972.
6   J. K. Galbraith, *The Affluent Society,* particularly chapters 10 and 11. (Pelican Books)
7   C. G. Jung, *Collected Works,* Vol. 13, *Alchemical Studies.*
8   Geoffrey Crowther, *An Outline of Money,* p. 32. (Nelson, 1947)
9   Christopher Marley, the London *Times,* March 15, 1972.
10   Rainer Maria Rilke, *The Sonnets to Orpheus,* second part, in *Selected Poems by Rilke,* translated by J. B. Leishman. (Penguin, 1964)
11   Jung, *Alchemical Studies,* p. 217.
12   Jung, *Alchemical Studies,* p. 217.
13   Nevins, *Rockefeller,* Vol. 2, *Study in Power,* Appendix III, p. 478.
14   Nevins, *Rockefeller,* Vol. 2, pp. 130–131.

15   Nevins, *Rockefeller,* Vol. 2, p. 129. William Warden to Rockefeller.

16   Nevins, *Rockefeller,* Vol. 2, p. 217.

17   Michael Merritt, *New Scientist,* April 6, 1972.

18   Nevins, *Rockefeller,* Vol. 2, Appendix IV, p. 479.

19   Charles Reich, *The Greening of America.* (Penguin Books)

20   Nevins, *Rockefeller,* Vol. 2, pp. 246–252.

21   C. Raw, B. Page, G. Hodgson, *Do You Sincerely Want to be Rich?* p. 67. (André Deutsch)

22   *Do You Sincerely Want to be Rich?*

23   Max Rayne, interviews with the author, 1971 and 1973. Rayne provides these additional technical details about the Eastbourne Terrace development: "The equity of the development company (in which the Church Commissioners shared equally) was small, but the scale of the project (some 400,000 square feet gross) and the total sums involved were large, so that any small margin of profit or loss on the enterprise inevitably represented a high percentage of the original investment. Initially, the surplus generated by the venture was modest, but with the cost financed at a fixed rate of interest, the effect of inflation was to increase dramatically the value of the equity and, years later, this represented a substantial sum. The original rents were fixed for a term of fourteen years at an average of about 75p per square foot. At the end of that period, both the rental value and the building costs must have increased five-fold. In material terms I was fortunate in finding myself in a field where the measure of success was financial and the amounts involved were large; but this was almost incidental to the satisfaction of vindicating a highly personal view of the potential of a seedy and generally despised area; of commissioning and being intimately involved in the creation of a group of buildings which was both commercially successful and universally acclaimed as an outstanding example of the best in postwar office design; and, perhaps above all, of pioneering an approach entirely new to the Church Commissioners."

24   Interview with the author.

25   Victor Lownes, interview with the author, 1971.
26   Walter Gruber, interview with the author, 1972.
27   Michael Merritt, *New Scientist,* April 6, 1972.

CHAPTER 3   Origins and Consequences

1   Melanie Klein, *Contributions to Psycho-Analysis, 1921–1945, Early Development of Conscience in the Child,* p. 268. (Hogarth Press and Institute of Psychoanalysis)
2   Melanie Klein, *Envy and Gratitude,* p. 5. (Tavistock Publications)
3   Klein, *Envy and Gratitude,* p. 3 (Tavistock Publications)
4   Prof. Norman Morris, conversation with the author.
5   Freud, *The Origins of Psycho-Analysis, Letters to Wilhelm Fliess 1887–1902.* (IMAGO Publishing Company, London). Freud wrote to Fliess on January 16, 1898: "I send herewith the definition of happiness . . . Happiness is the deferred fulfilment of a pre-historic wish. That is why wealth bring so little happiness; money is not an infantile wish."
6   Victor Lownes, interview with the author, 1971.
7   John Pearson, interview with the author, 1971.
8   Victor Lownes, interview with the author, 1971.
9   Freud, *Civilization and its Discontents,* p. 13. (Hogarth Press and Institute of Psychoanalysis)
10   Freud, *Civilization and its Discontents,* p. 13. (Hogarth Press and Institute of Psychoanalysis)
11   Interview with the author, 1961.
12   Nevins, *Rockefeller,* Appendix IV, p. 479.
13   Interview with the author.
14   Interview, *Sunday Express,* Dec. 17, 1972.
15   Interview with the author, 1971.
16   *Playboy* magazine, "The High Cost of Fame," Jan., 1971.
17   Conversation with the author, 1971.
18   Elliott Jaques, *Work, Creativity, Social Justice,* p. 203. (Heinemann Educational)
19   Jaques, *Work, Creativity, Social Justice,* p. 109. (Heinemann Educational)
20   Aristotle, *The Politics,* Book 1, chapters 8, 9, 10, and 11. (Penguin)

21   *The Politics*, Book 1, chapter 11, p. 48. (Penguin)
22   *Fear and Trembling, The Sickness Unto Death*, p. 51.
      (Doubleday Anchor Books)

CHAPTER 4   Uses

1   Richard J. Whalen, *The Founding Father*. (Hutchinson)
2   Interview with the author, 1971.
3   Helen Lawrenson, London *Sunday Times* Colour Supplement, March 19, 1972.
4   Interview with the author, 1971.
5   Interview with the author, 1971.
6   Lundberg, *The Rich and the Super Rich*, p. 261.
7   Interview with the author, 1972.
8   Interview with the author, 1972.
9   Theodore Sorensen, *Kennedy*, p. 20. (Hodder)
10   Norman Mailer, *Advertisements for Myself*, p. 222. (André Deutsch)

PART TWO   MONEY TYPES

CHAPTER 5   The Romantic

1   Jonson, *Volpone*, I, i, 11–21 (*Works of Ben Jonson*, ed. C. H. Herford, P & E Simpson. Oxford: Clarendon Press, 1925–52)
2   William Manchester, *The Arms of Krupp*, p. 79–82. (Bantam Books)
3   Lord Beaverbrook, *Men and Power*. (Hutchinson)
4   Interview with the author, 1972.
5   Interview with the author, 1972.
6   Graham Turner, *The Leyland Papers*, p. 174. (Eyre & Spottiswoode)
7   *Do You Sincerely Want to Be Rich?*, p. 145.
8   Manchester, *The Arms of Krupp*, p. 83.
9   J. J. O'Neill, *Prodigal Genius*. (Spearman)

CHAPTER 6   The Company Man

1   Theodore H. Whyte, *The Organization Man*, p. 69. (Pelican Books)

2   Conversation with the author, 1972.
3   Interview with the author, 1962.
4   Conversation with the author, 1973.
5   Interview with the author, 1972.
6   John Davis, *The Observer*, May 7, 1972.
7   Interview with the author, 1971.
8   Vincent Hanna, "The Company As God," the London *Sunday Times,* Oct. 19, 1971.
9   Lundberg, *The Rich and the Super Rich,* p. 92.
10   Henning Sjöström and Robert Nilsson, *Thalidomide and the Power of the Drug Companies,* p. 266. (Penguin Special, 1972)
11   Sjöström and Nilsson, *Thalidomide,* p. 267.
12   C. G. Jung, *Four Archetypes,* p. 59, referring to Le Bon's formulation in *The Crowd.* (Routledge & Kegan Paul)
13   Jaques, *Work, Creativity, Social Justice.*

CHAPTER 7   The Collector

1   Lundberg, *The Rich and the Super Rich,* p. 41.
2   Ernest Jones, *Papers on Psycho-Analysis (Anal-Erotic Character Traits)* , p. 413.
3   Freud, *Collected Papers,* Vol. II *(Character and Anal Erotism)* , p. 50.
4   Freud, *Collected Papers,* Vol. II, p. 49.
5   Freud, *Collected Papers,* Vol. II, pp. 49–50, footnote.
6   Jones, *Papers on Psycho-Analysis (Anal-Erotic Character Traits)* , pp. 413–414.
7   Sándor Ferenczi, *First Contributions to Psycho-analysis (On the Ontogenesis of the Interest in Money).* (Hogarth)
8   Jones, *Papers on Psycho-Analysis (Anal-Erotic Character Traits)* , pp. 413–414.
9   Karl Abraham, *Selected Papers on Psycho-Analysis (The Anal Character).* (Hogarth)

CHAPTER 8   The Hustler

1   Ferdinand Lundberg, *The Rich and the Super Rich,* pp. 77–78.
2   Interview with the author, 1971.
3   Manchester, *The Arms of Krupp,* pp. 26–27. (Bantam)

4   Oliver Marriott, *The Property Boom*, p. 60. (Pan Books)
5   Marriott, *The Property Boom*, p. 200. (Pan Books)
6   John Bainbridge, *The Super-Americans*, pp. 84–85. (Gollancz)
7   Peter Black, *The Mirror in the Corner*, pp. 80–81. (Hutchinson)
8   Willi Frischauer, *David Frost*, pp. 153–154. (Michael Joseph)
9   Jan Wenner, *Lennon Remembers*, p. 87.
10   Told by the businessman to the author, 1971.
11   Wenner, *Lennon Remembers*, p. 87.
12   Freud, *Collected Papers*, Vol. 4 (*Instincts and their Vicissitudes*), p. 78.
13   Mailer, *Advertisements for Myself*, p. 21. (Deutsch)
14   Mailer, *Advertisements for Myself*, pp. 233–235. (Deutsch)
15   Interview with the author, 1972.

CHAPTER 9   The Double-Dealer

1   Alvaro, interview with the author, 1971.
2   Alvaro, interview with the author, 1971.
3   William Davis, *The Guardian*.
4   Christopher Marley, the London *Times*, March 15, 1972.
5   Interview with the author, 1971.
6   Marvin Kitman, *George Washington's Expense Account*. (New York: Simon and Schuster)
7   Alan Osborn, *Sunday Telegraph*.
8   The London *Sunday Times*.
9   Sjöström & Nilsson, *Thalidomide and the Power of the Drug Companies*, chapter 12, particularly pp. 264–269. (Penguin Special)
10   Told to the author by "David" in 1971.
11   Interview with the author, 1972.
12   *Do You Sincerely Want to be Rich?* p. 174.
13   The *Listener*, May 31, 1973.
14   Interview with the author, 1972.

CHAPTER 10   The Criminal

1   All material on the criminal D—— was supplied by him in an interview with the author. His name has been withheld for obvious reasons.

2   Melanie Klein, *Contributions to Psycho-Analysis 1921–1945 (Criminal Tendencies in Normal Children)*, pp. 185–201. And also in the same work, *On Criminality*, pp. 278–281. (Hogarth Press and Institute of Psychoanalysis)
3   Interview with the author, 1972.
4   Gay Talese, *Honor Thy Father*, p. 77. (Souvenir Press)
5   Industrialist in an interview with the author, 1971.
6   Klein, *Contributions to Psycho-Analysis, 1921–1945*, pp. 185–201.
7   Interview with the author, 1972.
8   Interview with the author, 1972.

CHAPTER 11   The Gambler and the Loser

1   Lauterbach, *Man, Motives and Money*, p. 44.
2   Name withheld at art collector's request.
3   Pauline Kael, *The Citizen Kane Book*.
4   Kael, *The Citizen Kane Book*.
5   Freud, *Collected Papers*, Vol. 5 *(Dostoievsky and Parricide)*, pp. 222–242.
6   Interview, *Sunday Express*, Dec. 17, 1972.
7   All the material comes from author's interview with Dee in 1972.
8   Beryl Sandford, *New Directions in Psycho-Analysis (An obsessional man's need to be kept)*, pp. 226–281. (Hogarth Press and Institute of Psychoanalysis)
9   Freud, *C.P.* Vol. 5 *(Dostoievsky and Parricide)*, p. 238.
10   Freud, *C.P.* Vol. 4 *(Mourning and Melancholia)*, p. 162.

CHAPTER 12   The Non-Player

1   Richard Neville, *Playpower*, p. 213. (Random House)
2   Ernest Hemingway, *A Moveable Feast*. (Jonathan Cape)
3   D. H. Lawrence, *Selected Letters*, p. 44. (Penguin)
4   Lundberg, *The Rich and the Super Rich*, pp. 293–294.

PART THREE   MONEY RELATIONSHIPS

CHAPTER 13   Money and Sex

1   Catherine Stott, *The Guardian*, April 13, 1972.
2   The story was told to the author by the woman in question in 1972.

3   Karl Abraham, *Collected Papers on Psycho-Analysis* (*The Spending of Money in Anxiety States*), pp. 299–302. (Hogarth Press and Institute of Psychoanalysis)
4   Xaviera Hollander to author, 1972.
5   The story was told by Miss Hollander in an interview with the author, 1972.
6   Abraham, *Selected Papers*, pp. 125–136.
7   Interview with the author, 1971.
8   Interview with the author, 1971.
9   Interview with the author, 1972.
10   Interview with the author, 1972.
11   Interview with the author, 1971.

CHAPTER 14   Money and the Family

1   Lundberg, *The Rich and the Super Rich*, pp. 108–114.
2   Interview with the author, 1971.
3   Freud, *Totem and Taboo*, pp. 141–142. (Routledge)
4   Feodor Dostoevsky, *The Brothers Karamazov*. (Penguin)
5   Interview with the author, 1971.
6   A. Hingston Quiggin, *Primitive Money*, pp. 8–9. Methuen, 1963.
7   Thorstein Veblen, *Theory of the Leisure Class*.
8   Christian Kafarakis, for ten years chief steward on the Onassis yacht, gave the details in *The People*, Oct. 31, 1971.
9   Kafarakis, *The People*.
10   *The Female Eunuch*, pp. 241–242. (Macgibbon & Kee)
11   Interview with the author, 1971.
12   *Civilization and its Discontents*, p. 13.
13   *Sunday Express*, Dec. 17, 1972.
14   Details provided in interview with the author, 1972.
15   Interview with the author, 1971.
16   Abraham, *Selected Papers* (*Contributions to the Theory of the Anal Character*), pp. 370–391.
17   Jones, *Papers on Psycho-Analysis* (*Anal-Erotic Character Traits*), pp. 413–437.

CHAPTER 15   Money and Society

1   Conversation with the author, 1971.
2   *The Affluent Society*, p. 261. (Penguin)

3   Interview with the author, 1971.
4   Abraham, *Selected Papers* (*The Influence of Oral Erotism on Character-Formation*), pp. 393–406.
5   Abraham, *Selected Papers*, pp. 393–406.
6   Jaques, *Work, Creativity, Social Justice* (*The Human Consequences of Industrialization*), pp. 1–17. (Heinemann Educational)
7   Interview with the author, 1971.
8   Herbert Marcuse, *One-Dimensional Man*, p. 24. (Sphere)
9   *Civilization and Its Discontents*, pp. 49–51.
10   *Life Against Death*, pp. 209–210. (Sphere)
11   *Karl Marx*, ed. Bottomore and Rubel, p. 180. (Pelican). Originally from Marx-Engels Gesamtausgabe I/3, p. 531.

Bibliography

The following books have been of importance to the author either as source material or for their ideas and theories:

Aristotle. *The Politics*, translated by T. A. Sinclair. London: Penguin, 1970.

Bainbridge, John. *The Super-Americans*. London: Gollancz, 1962.

Balzac, Honoré de. *A Harlot High and Low*, translated by Rayner Heppenstall. London: Penguin, 1970.

Beaverbrook, Lord. *Men and Power, 1917–18*. London: Hutchinson, 1956.

Brown, Norman O. *Life Against Death*. London: Routledge, 1959.

Caine, Mark. *The S Man*. London: Hutchinson, 1960.

Crowther, Geoffrey. *An Outline of Money*. London: Nelson, 1948.

Dietrich, Noah. *Howard, the Amazing Mister Hughes*. New York: Fawcett Publications, 1972.

Ferenczi, Sándor. *First Contributions to Psycho-analysis*. London: Hogarth, 1952.

Fitzgerald, F. Scott. *The Great Gatsby*. London: Penguin, 1969.

Freud, Sigmund. *The Origins of Psycho-analysis*. Letters to Wilhelm Fliess, Drafts and Notes: 1887–1902. London: Imago, 1954.

Collected Papers, Vols. II (1969), IV & V (1957). London: Hogarth.

Beyond the Pleasure Principle. London: Hogarth, 1971.

Totem and Taboo. London: Routledge, 1950.

The Ego and the Id. London: Hogarth, 1962.

Civilization and Its Discontents. London: Hogarth, 1969.

Frischauer, Willi. *David Frost.* London: Michael Joseph, 1972.

Galbraith, John Kenneth. *The Affluent Society.* London: Hamish Hamilton, 1958.

Getty, Paul. *How to Be Rich.* New York: Playboy Press, 1965.

Genêt, Jean. *The Thief's Journal.* London: Anthony Blond, 1965.

Golden Book of Fairy Tales, including stores by the brothers Grimm and tales from the Arabian Nights. London: Collins, 1966.

Gussow, Mel. *Darryl F. Zanuck—Don't Say Yes Until I Finish Talking.* London: W. H. Allen, 1971.

Jaques, Elliott. *Measurement of Responsibility.* London: Tavistock, 1956.

Equitable Payment. London: Heinemann, 1961.

Work, Creativity, Social Justice. London: Heinemann, 1970.

Jones, Ernest. *Papers on Psycho-analysis.* London: Bailliere, Tindall and Cox, 1948.

Jung, C. G. *Collected Works,* Vol. 13, *Alchemical Studies.* London: Routledge, 1968. *Four Archetypes.* London, Routledge, 1972.

Kael, P., Mankiewicz, H. J., Welles, O. *The Citizen Kane Book.* London: Secker & Warburg, 1971.

Keynes, J. M. *Essays in Persuasion.* London: Macmillan, 1931.

Klein, Melanie. *Contributions to Psycho-analysis, 1921–45.* London: Hogarth, 1965.

New Directions in Psycho-analysis (Klein with others). London: Tavistock, 1955.

The Psycho-analysis of Children. London: Hogarth, 1963.

Envy and Gratitude. London: Tavistock, 1957.

Developments in Psycho-analysis (Klein and others). London: Hogarth, 1952.

Koestler, Arthur. *Arrow in the Blue*. London: Collins and Hamish Hamilton, 1952.

Lauterbach, Albert. *Man, Motives and Money*. Oxford University Press, 1954.

Lawrence, D. H. *Selected Letters*. London: Penguin, 1950.

Lundberg, Ferdinand. *The Rich and the Super Rich*. London: Nelson, 1969.

Maas, Peter. *The Valachi Papers*. London: Panther, 1970.

Mailer, Norman. *Advertisements for Myself*. London: André Deutsch, 1959.
    An American Dream. London: Deutsch, 1965.

Marcuse, Herbert. *One Dimensional Man*. London: Routledge, 1964.

Marriott, Oliver. *The Property Boom*. London: Hamish Hamilton, 1967.

Marx, Karl. *Selected Writings in Sociology and Social Philosophy*. Editors: Bottomore and Rubel. London: Pelican, 1970.

Maurois, André. *Prometheus: The Life of Balzac*. Translated by Norman Denny. London: Pelican, 1971.

Moravia, Alberto. *The Empty Canvas*. Translated by Angus Davidson. London: Secker & Warburg, 1961.

Neville, Richard. *Playpower*. New York: Random House, 1970.

Nevins, Allan. *Study in Power, John D. Rockefeller* (Vols. I & II). New York: Charles Scribner's Sons, 1953.

Podhoretz, Norman. *Making It*. London: Cape, 1968.

Reich, Charles. *The Greening of America*. London: Allen Lane, 1971.

Manchester, William. *The Arms of Krupp*. New York: Little, Brown, 1968.

O'Neill, John J. *Prodigal Genius: The Life of Nikola Tesla*. London: Spearman, 1968.

Orwell, George. *Down and Out in Paris and London*. London: Penguin, 1971.

Packard, Vance. *The Hidden Persuaders*. London: Longmans, 1957.

Perrott, Roy. *The Aristocrats*. London: Weidenfeld and Nicolson, 1968.

Plato. *The Republic.* Translated by H. D. P. Lee. London: Penguin, 1955.

Quiggin, Hingston A. *Primitive Money.* London: Methuen, 1963.

Raw, C., Page, B., and Hodgson, G. *Do You Sincerely Want to Be Rich?* London: Deutsch, 1971.

Ross, David. *Aristotle.* London: Methuen, 1966.

Sampson, Anthony. *The New Anatomy of Britain.* London: Hodder and Stoughton, 1971.

Shaw, George Bernard. *The Intelligent Woman's Guide to Socialism, Capitalism, Sovietism and Fascism.* London: Constable, 1949.

Sjöström, H., and Nilsson, R. *Thalidomide and the Power of the Drug Companies.* London: Penguin, 1972.

"Smith, Adam." *The Money Game.* London: Michael Joseph, 1968.

Sobel, Robert. *Panic on Wall Street.* New York: The Macmillan Co., 1968.

Sorensen, T. *Kennedy.* London: Hodder, 1965.

Talese, Gay. *Honor Thy Father.* London: Souvenir Press, 1971.

Taylor, A. E. *Plato, the man and his works.* London: Methuen, 1969.

Troyat, H. *Tolstoy.* London: Pelican, 1970.

Turner, Graham. *Business in Britain.* London: Eyre & Spottiswoode, 1969.

   The Leyland Papers. London: Eyre & Spottiswoode, 1971.

Wenner, Jann. *Lennon Remembers.* London: Talmy, Franklin, 1972.

Whalen, Richard J. *The Founding Father: The Story of Joseph P. Kennedy.* London: Hutchinson, 1965.

Whyte, William H. *The Organization Man.* New York: Simon and Schuster, 1956.

Zec, Donald. *Some Enchanted Egos.* London: Allison & Busby, 1972.

Index

Abraham, Karl, 111, 113, 117, 118, 215–216, 228, 271, 274, 297, 298
Adam, Robert, 68
Adler Company, 104
Alexandria Quartet (Durrell), 55
Alvaro (restaurateur), 98, 147, 152
American Dream, An (Mailer), 302
American Jewish Committee, 134
American Sugar Refining Company, 247
American Telephone & Telegraph (ATT), 175
Anglo-American Oil Company Ltd., 26
APCOA Company, 102
Arab Boycott Office, 101
Aretusa Club, 146
Aristotle, 64–66
Arrow in the Blue (Koestler), 243
Astor, Lord, 294, 295
Astor family, 294
ATV Company, 131
Avis Company, 102

Backus case, 27
Balzac, Honoré de, 11, 12–13, 123, 134
Bank of America, 35
Barbary Shore, The (Mailer), 140
Bart, Lionel, 9, 58, 188
Beatles, 134, 135, 136
Beaverbrook, Lord, 83
Bedford, Duke of, 304
Beethoven, Ludwig van, 76, 167, 293
Behan, Brendan, 167
Belle de Jour (motion picture), 218
Belmondo, Jean-Paul, 173
Bentley, John, 37, 38
Best, George, 289
"Big Spender" (song), 214
Biwabik Mountain Iron Company, 29
Black, Peter, 167–168
Blitz (play), 188
Bluhdorn, Charles, 37
BMH Company, 87
Bohlen und Halbach, Gustav von, 252
Bonanno, Bill, 176

Bout de Souffle, A (motion picture), 173
Bowater Company, 131
BP Company, 52
Braine, John, 134
Brenman, Eric, xiii, 142, 164, 180, 181
British Motor Corporation, 87
Brody, Michael, 57
Brothers Karamazov, The (Dostoevsky), 200, 253
Brown, Norman O., 308, 309, 310, 311
Buñuel, Luis, 218

Callas, Maria, 248
Census Bureau, 122
Central Intelligence Agency, 75
Cézanne, Paul, 74
Chaban-Delmas, M., 154
Chaplin, Charlie, 15
Chase Manhattan Bank, 73
Chaucer, Geoffrey, 290-291
China, 5, 256
Chrysler Corporation, 175
Churchill, Winston, 255
Citizen Kane (motion picture), 186
Civil War, 246
Civilization and Its Discontents (Freud), 304-305
Collier's (magazine), 166
Commentary (magazine), 134
Connolly, Cyril, 141
Constable, John, 171, 173
Consumer Report, 118
Cornfeld, Bernie, 32, 33, 88, 113, 166
Cotten, Jack, 58
Courtaulds Company, 155
Crichton, Michael, 58
Crossley, David, 58
Crowther, Geoffrey, 22-23

Daily Mirror Group, 57
Dandolos, Nicholas "Nick the Greek," 184
Dante, xiii
Darvi, Bella, 185
Davies, Mary, 247
Davis, Sammy, Jr., 289

Davis, William, 147-148
"Death of Actaeon, The" (Titian), 67
Death of a Salesman (Miller), 13, 126
Dee, Simon, 58, 188-191, 193
Deer Park, The (Mailer), 76, 140
Dostoevsky, Feodor, 186-187, 199, 200
Douglas, Paul H., 129
Down and Out in Paris and London (Orwell), 198
Du Pont, Alfred, I, 246
Du Pont family, 19, 246-247, 249
Du Pont de Nemours and Company, (E. I.), 246, 247
Durrell, Lawrence, 55
Dürrenmatt, Friedrich, 8
Duryea Motor Wagon Company, 19

Edison, Thomas Alva, 129, 130
Einstein, Albert, 71, 207-208
Eisenhower, Dwight D., 39
Ekland, Britt, 269
Elvira Madigan (motion picture), 270
Empty Canvas, The (Moravia), 217, 234, 300

Federal Bureau of Investigation (FBI), 175
Federal Reserve Board, 122
Ferenczi, Sándor, 110, 111, 113, 308
Ferris, Paul, 57
Feydeau, Georges, 236
Financial Times, The, 274
Fischer, Bobby, 167
Fitzgerald, F. Scott, 70, 83-84, 201
Fleming, Ian, 52, 268
Food and Drug Administration, 89
Ford, Henry, 10, 84
Ford family, 19, 249, 252
Ford Foundation, 10, 74, 75
Ford Motor Company, 114, 175
Fortune (magazine), 18, 19, 95-96, 205, 246, 248
France (liner), 68
Freud, Sigmund, xii, xiii, 13, 45, 48, 54, 108, 109-110, 114, 117, 136-137,

Freud, Sigmund (*Cont.*)
172, 200, 227, 251, 252, 268, 276,
304–305, 311
Frost, David, 131, 189

Gabor, Zsa Zsa, 211–212, 262
Galbraith, J. K., 21, 284
Gates, Frederick T., 28
Geneen, Harold S., 102
General Electric Company, 131, 175
General Motors Corporation, 19, 175,
247
Genêt, Jean, 178
Getty, J. Paul, 6, 19, 52, 67–68, 117,
255, 269, 304
Gillespie, Dizzy, 11
Glacier Metal Company, The, 59
Godard, Jean-Luc, 173
Godfather, The (motion picture),
41, 146
Godfather, The (Puzo), 37, 51
Goethe, Johann Wolfgang von, 54, 93
Grade, Lew, 130, 131
Great Gatsby, The (Fitzgerald), 83–
84
Greene, Graham, 141
Greer, Germaine, 261
Grimm, Jacob and Wilhelm, 6
Grosvenor, Earl, 247
Grosvenor, Lord, 247
Grosvenor, Sir Thomas, 247
Gruber, Walter, 39–40
Guccione, Bob, 84–87
Guinness family, 246, 252
Gulf Oil Corporation, 52
Gulf & Western Industries, 37, 41

Hamlet (Shakespeare), 143
Harlot High and Low, A (Balzac),
123, 134
Harriman, Sir George, 87–88, 226
Hartford, Huntington, 295
Hartford Company, 102
Havemeyer, Henry O., 68
Hayward, Doug, 123–126
Hearst, William Randolph, 68–69
Hefner, Hugh, 10, 11, 52, 53, 72, 237

Hello, Dolly! (motion picture), 41
Hemingway, Ernest, 140, 201, 206
Hepburn Committee, 27
Hilton, Conrad, 211, 262
Histoire d'O, 225
Hitler, Adolf, 252, 298
Hollander, Xaviera, 219–225, 226, 228,
229, 230, 231, 239, 240–241, 261
Hope, Bob, 11
House of Northcliffe, The (Ferris),
57
House of Representatives Report
(1962), 74
Hughes, Howard, 19, 22, 49
Hughes Tool Company, 19
"Human Consequences of Industriali-
zation, The" (Jaques), 303
Hunt, H. L., 19
Hutton, Barbara, 8
Hyams, Harry, 34

Imperial Tobacco Pension Fund, 131
Internal Revenue Service, 129
International Business Machines
Corporation (IBM), 10, 40, 41, 103,
104, 157, 175
International Data Corporation, 41
International Telephone & Telegraph
(ITT), 102, 103
IOS Company, 88, 166
ITA, 131

Jagger, Mick, 4
Jaques, Elliott, xiii, 50, 59, 60, 61, 62,
63, 75, 106, 299, 303
Jesus Christ, 202
Johnson, Lyndon B., 39
Johnson, Dr. Samuel, 258
Jones, Ernest, 14, 108, 110, 116, 178,
277
"Juan de Pareja" (Velásquez), 68
Jung, C. G., 21, 24, 105, 132

Karp, Harvey, 34–37
Kazan, Elia, 11
Kefauver Committee of 1951, 184
Kennedy, Joseph, 68

Kennedy, John F., 76
Kennedy family, 246, 249, 251
Keynes, John Maynard, 3
Kierkegaard, Soren, 66
King, Cecil, 57
Kinsey Report, 4, 74
Klein, Melanie, xii–xiii, 45–47, 48, 50, 92, 172, 178, 259
Knapp Commission, 149–150
Koestler, Arthur, 243
Krupp, Alfred, 82–83, 91
Krupp, Arndt, 127
Krupp, Bertha, 252
Krupp, Gustav, see Bohlen und Halbach, Gustav von
Krupp family, 18, 82, 127, 246, 252

Lake Superior Consolidated, 30
Lampman, Robert J., 121–122
Land, Dr. Edwin, 37
Lansky, Meyer, 181
Lauterbach, Albert, 184
Lawrence, D. H., 206
Lawrence, Frieda, 206
Lee, Laurie, 206
Lennon, John, 134, 135, 136
Leyland Company, 87
Life Against Death (Brown), 308
Littler, Prince, 131
Livanos, Eugenie, see Niarchos, Eugenie
Livanos, Stavros, 247
Livanos, Tina, see Niarchos, Tina
Lombard Banking, 131
London Cooperative Society, 131
London Evening Standard, 206
London Merchant Securities, 33
London Times, 20, 57, 151
London Weekend Television, 131
Lownes, Victor, 52, 53–54, 72, 237–238, 239
Luce, Henry, 72
Lundberg, Ferdinand, 107, 248

McClure's Magazine, 27, 56
Mafia, 150, 174–176
Maggie May (play), 188

Mailer, Norman, 11, 76–77, 140–141, 302
Making It (Podhoretz), 134
Man and Superman (Shaw), 169
Mankiewicz, Herman, 186
Marcuse, Herbert, 22, 304, 305, 307
Marx, Karl, 3, 309
M*A*S*H (motion picture), 42
Mason, Albert, xiii, 169, 174
Mature, Victor, 85
Maurois, André, 12
Mayer, Louis B., 86, 186
Medici family, 76
Mellon family, 18, 246, 249
Meltzer, Donald, xiii
Merchant of Venice, The (Shakespeare), 226
Merritt, Michael, 41
Merritt brothers, 29–30
Metro-Goldwyn-Mayer, 186
Mid-Continent Petroleum Corporation, 247
Miller, Arthur, 13, 126
Mills, Ivor, 115, 201
Milton, John, 89
Mirror in the Corner, The (Black), 167
Montagu, Lord, 250, 289, 293, 294, 298, 300
Moore, Henry, 68
Moravia, Alberto, 141, 217, 218, 234
Morgenthau, Robert M., 175
Morris, Desmond, 59
Morris, Norman, 47
Morton Company, 102
Mourning and Melancholia (Freud), 200
Muller, Robert, 11

National Bureau of Economic Research, 121
National Health Service hospitals, 152
National Theatre (Britain), 166
Neville, Richard, 205
New Anatomy of Britain (Sampson), 58

New Scotland Yard, 128
Newman, Otto, 184
Newsweek (magazine) , 39
Niarchos, Eugenie, 247, 248, 292
Niarchos, Stavros, 8, 247, 248, 292
Niarchos, Tina, 247, 248, 292
Nobel, Alfred, 10, 93
Northcliffe, Lord, 57

Odescalchi, Principessa Marizina, 70–
71
Oh! Calcutta! (play), 166
Oliver (play) , 9, 58, 188
Onassis, Aristotle, 248, 258, 292
Onassis, Jackie, 258, 260, 261, 292
Onassis, Tina, *see* Niarchos, Tina
One Dimensional Man (Marcuse) ,
304
O'Neill, John J., 130
Orwell, George, 197–199
Oxford University, 131
Oz (newspaper) , 205

Paradise Lost (Milton), 89
Paramount Pictures, 37, 186
Parnell, Val, 131
Pearl Assurance Company, 131
Pearson, John, 52–53, 268
Penthouse (magazine) , 84, 85, 86
Plato, 254
Playboy (magazine) , 10, 84, 86, 237
Playpower (Neville) , 205
Podhoretz, Norman, 134–135
Poseidon share boom, 43
Preminger, Otto, 69, 93
Profumo-Keeler scandal, 294
Prudential Company, 117
Puzo, Mario, 51

Radio Caroline, 188
Radio Corporation of America
(RCA), 175
Raleigh, Lady, 91
Raleigh, Sir Walter, 17, 43, 89, 91,
157, 191–192
Rayne, Sir Max, 33–34, 69, 73–74

Republic, The (Plato) , 254
Revolutionary War, 153
Rich and the Super Rich, The
(Lundberg) , 107, 248
Richman, Stella, 191
Rilke, Rainer Maria, 23, 293–294, 308
Rio Tinto Zinc, 43
Robbins, Harold, 38
Rockefeller, David, 73
Rockefeller, John D., 18, 25–29, 38,
43, 44, 51, 56–57, 63, 113–114, 275,
312
Rockefeller family, 18, 246, 249
Rockefeller Foundation, 74
Rolls Royce, 41
Room at the Top (Braine) , 134
Roosevelt, Franklin Delano, 68, 76,
166
Roosevelt, James, 166
Rothschild, Lord, 251
Rothschild, Jacob, 251
Rothschild family, 246
RTZ Company, 103

Sabat, Henri, 67
Sahl, Mort, 11
St. Francis of Assisi, 202
Sampson, Anthony, 58
Sanders, George, 72
Sandford, Beryl, 196, 197, 200
Sartre, Jean-Paul, 202
Sassoon, Vidal, 289
Schell, Maximilian, 70
Schulberg, Budd, 11
Schweitzer, Albert, 202
Scott Company, 102
Scottish Life Association, 37
Sellers, Peter, 269
Sellers, Victoria, 269
Shaw, George Bernard, 169
Shell Oil Company, 52, 103
Sheraton Company, 102
Simon Dee Show, The (TV show) ,
191
Sinatra, Frank, 11
Slater, Jim, 18, 37, 99, 167

Slater, Walker Company, 18, 37
Socrates, 254
Solitron Company, 20
Sons and Lovers (Lawrence), 206
Spitz, Mark, 167
Standard Oil Company, 26, 28, 52, 56, 175
Standard Oil Trust, 28
Stokes, Donald, 87–88

Tarbell, Ida, 27, 56
Teresa of Calcutta, Mother, 194, 202
Tesla, Nikola, 93–94, 129, 130
Texaco Corporation, 52
Thales, 65, 66
Theory of the Leisure Class, The (Veblen), 43
Thief's Journal, The (Genêt), 178
Thomas, Dylan, 167
Time (magazine), 167
Tolstoy, Leo, 283
Totem and Taboo (Freud), 251
Turner, Glenn, 71
Twentieth-Century Fox, 42
Tynan, Kenneth, 166–167

United Fruit Company, 247
U.S. Bureau of the Census, 19
U.S. Congress, 153
U.S. Department of Justice, 103, 157
U.S. Department of the Treasury, 122
U.S. Industrial Commission, 68

United States Rubber Company, 247
United States Steel Corporation, 175

Van Gogh, Vincent, 68
Vanderbilt, George W., 67
Vanderbilt family, 275
Veblen, Thorstein, 43, 256
Velásquez, Diego, 68
Vidal, Gore, 97
Visit, The (Dürrenmatt), 8
Volvo Company, 115

Wall Street Journal, The, 175
Ward, Stephen, 156, 294, 295
Warner, Suzanne, 130–131
Washington, George, 153
Watson, Arthur, 157
Watson, Thomas J., 10
Weidenfeld and Nicolson, 131
Weinstock, Sir Arnold, 131
Western Union, 155
Westinghouse, George, 129, 130
Westminster, 4th Duke of, 247
Westminster, 5th Duke of, 247
Whicker, Alan, 97
Winchell, Walter, 136
Wonder Bread, 102
World War I, 13
World War II, 208

Xerox Corporation, 22

Zanuck, Darryl F., 185
Zeiss Ikon, 41

About the Author

THOMAS WISEMAN is an author whose work has ranged over a wide area, from the dream empires of Hollywood in his first novel *Czar* to Europe during World War II in *The Quick and the Dead*, which *Time* magazine described as "a brilliant tour de force of rare psychological depth and complexity." Besides his four novels, he has also written a play, *The Private Prosecutor*, and a history of the movies, *Cinema*.

Before embarking full time on the career of an author, Wiseman was for many years a leading journalist, working on the London *Evening Standard* and the *Sunday Express*. More recently, he has written a regular column on the arts in *The Guardian*.

The subject matter of Wiseman's books has arisen out of the events and experiences of his life. He was a child in Vienna at the time of the Anschluss and escaped to England with his mother just before the outbreak of war. His journalistic work involved him in Hollywood and the world of films. As for the present book, a long-standing interest in and involvement with different aspects of psychology and psychoanalysis led him to attempt to unravel the complexities of the money motive which bedevils so many aspects of human affairs. Mr. Wiseman is married; he lives with his Italian wife, Malou, and his son, Boris, in a house in Hampstead, England.